# Focused Issues in F

**Series Editor**

D. Russell Crane, Brigham Young University, Provo, UT, USA

More information about this series at http://www.springer.com/series/13372

Shruti Singh Poulsen • Robert Allan
Editors

# Cross-Cultural Responsiveness & Systemic Therapy

Personal & Clinical Narratives

Springer

*Editors*
Shruti Singh Poulsen
University of Colorado Denver
Denver, CO, USA

Robert Allan
University of Colorado Denver
Denver, CO, USA

ISSN 2520-1190              ISSN 2520-1204  (electronic)
Focused Issues in Family Therapy
ISBN 978-3-030-10050-6      ISBN 978-3-319-71395-3  (eBook)
https://doi.org/10.1007/978-3-319-71395-3

© Springer International Publishing AG, part of Springer Nature 2018
Softcover re-print of the Hardcover 1st edition 2018
This work is subject to copyright. All rights are reserved by the Publisher, whether the whole or part of the material is concerned, specifically the rights of translation, reprinting, reuse of illustrations, recitation, broadcasting, reproduction on microfilms or in any other physical way, and transmission or information storage and retrieval, electronic adaptation, computer software, or by similar or dissimilar methodology now known or hereafter developed.
The use of general descriptive names, registered names, trademarks, service marks, etc. in this publication does not imply, even in the absence of a specific statement, that such names are exempt from the relevant protective laws and regulations and therefore free for general use.
The publisher, the authors and the editors are safe to assume that the advice and information in this book are believed to be true and accurate at the date of publication. Neither the publisher nor the authors or the editors give a warranty, express or implied, with respect to the material contained herein or for any errors or omissions that may have been made. The publisher remains neutral with regard to jurisdictional claims in published maps and institutional affiliations.

This Springer imprint is published by the registered company Springer International Publishing AG part of Springer Nature.
The registered company address is: Gewerbestrasse 11, 6330 Cham, Switzerland

# Introduction

We are pleased to be co-editing a special topic volume on multiculturalism and systemic therapies. We would be remiss if we did not mention, at least briefly, that when we began this project a little over a year ago, the USA and much of the world was undergoing seismic and dramatic political, social, and cultural upheavals. As we wrap up this project and this volume at this time, it is clear that these upheavals are here to stay and that now more than ever, the need for cross-cultural responsiveness, social justice, and advocacy by systemic therapists, educators, and scholars is critical. Thus, we sincerely and genuinely hope that this volume will be reflective, provocative at times, and ultimately helpful for systemic clinicians in a variety of settings who are engaged in the important work of making accessible in culturally responsive ways the powerful healing potential of systemic therapies to diverse and often underserved client populations.

While the historical trajectory of the USA and the world was being impacted over these past couple of years, our own personal histories were also shifting and experiencing change. For the entirety of the 2016–2017 academic year and the duration of this book editing process, I (SSP) was living and working in Istanbul, Turkey. I was in Turkey on a Fulbright Core Senior Scholars Program, teaching and engaging in clinical supervision activities at a private university in Istanbul. This experience was undertaken as my first sabbatical leave after earning tenure at my home institution in 2015. During this time period, Robert was in the USA at our home institution working toward his 4-year, pre-tenure review process. We collaborated in this co-editing venture separated geographically, yet connected by our commitment to, and common interests in, cross-cultural responsiveness and social justice and their impact on systemic therapies. We also were able to collaborate and connect due to our common yet unique lived experiences of being immigrants to the USA, me as an Asian Indian female and Robert as a White male Canadian of European descent. These personal and historical contexts gave our collaboration with each other and the authors contributing to this volume a unique perspective and isomorphism with the topic of this volume. We "lived and breathed" cross-cultural responsiveness in our process of engaging with the authors, with each other, and with the co-editing work on this volume. This volume, as it turns out, is not just a work of scholarly and theoretical endeavors; it is a "living" document that we believe presents the critical topics of cross-cultural responsiveness and social justice from our and our authors' very real and lived experiences and realities over this past year or so and across our careers and professional development.

Robert and I are both AAMFT-approved supervisors and faculty members and supervisors in a CACREP-accredited master's program in Colorado. Robert is a second-generation Canadian of northern European heritage, born and raised in Canada, and he identifies as a cis-gendered, gay male. Shruti was born in India and is a first-generation naturalized US citizen who immigrated to the USA in her mid-teens. Shruti is an immigrant who has lived in several different countries other than the USA and India and identifies as a cis-gendered, heterosexual female. We are faculty members in a couple and family therapy specialization track within the counseling program at a university in a major city. We are both couple and family therapists who engage in clinical work and supervision within and outside the academic setting. We believe that sharing our personal contexts in this introduction sets the stage for what we believe is our and our authors' commitment to understanding ourselves and the clients we serve in culturally responsive and socially just ways.

Cross-cultural competence and sensitivity have been acknowledged as critical in the mental health professions since the early 1990s when the rapidly changing US demographics were brought to the attention of both mental health professionals and lay people. In recent years, there has been some debate about whether the terms cultural competence and sensitivity are adequate in addressing the complex and unique needs of increasingly diverse client populations. In fact, among scholars, clinicians, trainers, and supervisors, there is the concern that "*competence and sensitivity*" may be misleading and possibly a "passive" way of conceptualizing the training needs of mental health professionals working with diverse client populations, a way that implies that once trained to be culturally competent and sensitive, a therapist's training is done (White, Connolly Gibbons, & Schamberger, 2006).

In contrast, understanding of cross-cultural clinical work from a responsiveness and *responsibility perspective* provides a more active and process-oriented lens to not only the clinical work but also the therapist's professional development. The term responsiveness implies ongoing personal work, learning, and training in order to be responsible as a mental health provider to clients' needs (Laszloffy & Habekost, 2010). Thus, the purpose of this volume is to incorporate a culturally responsive lens rather than a "cultural competence" lens to the work of systemic therapists. We as editors of this book, along with our authors, believe that cultural responsiveness in systems therapy cannot exist without attention to social justice and privilege. Therefore, a potentially critical contribution of this volume is to connect the need to attend to and address social justice and privilege concerns when considering cultural responsiveness and responsibility in systemic therapies.

While there are numerous books on cross-cultural therapy, counseling, etc., many tend to organize this topic in ways that lend themselves to an "ethnicity/culture of the week" mentality in learning about cross-cultural competence. The authors contributing to this volume believe that the topics they are presenting will take a more nuanced and varied approach to understanding systemic therapies with diverse client populations. First, the chapters do not focus on specific ethnic groups or populations and recommended treatment, techniques, or models that ostensibly apply to these populations. The chapters of this volume include attention to cutting-edge issues in couple and family therapy. These include issues such as social justice and attention to power and privilege in couple and family therapy and in systemic EBPs, culturally responsive common factors and integrative approaches to couple and family therapy, global and international opportunities and challenges to CFT and implications for enhancing culturally responsive approaches, and cross-disciplinary challenges and opportunities to incorporating social justice and cultural responsiveness in training and supervision of CFTs.

An additional and potentially unique contribution of the proposed book will be that the chapters are presented in not only a scholarly and researched-based manner. The contributing authors each provide their particular "self-of-the-therapist" and personally contextualized brief narrative to the topic on which they focus. Our hope is that a brief glimpse into the authors' context in combination with the scholarly lens provides a message that is isomorphic to the culturally responsive way of working systemically with diverse populations (Watts-Jones, 2010) – highlighting that the authors are not just presenting professional and clinical ways of working and being culturally responsive with diverse client populations but also emulating their ability to be culturally responsive through their self-disclosure and attention to their own processes and journeys in this area. Each of the contributing authors themselves is either recent immigrants to the USA or persons of color; we identify in varied and diverse ways our gender and sexual orientation identities; we teach, practice, train, and supervise in diverse US and global contexts; and each one of us has wide-ranging years of clinical experience as systemic therapists and educators. Each author brings her, his, or their unique personal lens and lived experiences to the exploration of the diverse topics presented in this book.

The topics covered in this volume can be loosely organized and understood under several defining and identifiable themes – most importantly, a critical theme examining therapist identity, privilege, power, social justice, and, in particular, white identity and privilege is presented in this volume. Other important themes represented in this volume include the cross-cultural responsiveness and implications of utilizing and training therapists in empirically based systemic models; the cross-cultural responsiveness and adaptation of more traditional and foundational systemic models; cross-cultural responsiveness in systemic supervision and training; and the experiences, challenges, and implications for training therapists in systemic therapies and models in global and international contexts.

## Therapist Identity, Privilege, Power, and Social Justice

The volume begins with Iman and Manijeh's chapter challenging the reader to consider a true transformation and innovation in our thinking to ensure that our fields support and encourage cultural diversity and social justice. Their chapter offers a framework for supporting and including a social justice perspective in family therapy, and the authors discuss their vision of social justice that is congruent to the needs of diverse clients and working with them systemically and in culturally responsive ways. The authors also offer pragmatic and specific ideas about the inclusion of diversity and social justice in systemic practice to help therapists understand and attend to multicultural clients' dilemmas and challenges.

Cheryl's chapter provides an evocative and powerful portrayal of how the emotionality of whiteness can stifle culturally competent therapy and counseling practices. While Cheryl is not a counselor or therapist, in her expertise as a teacher educator and scholar, she brings an interdisciplinary lens to the issue of white privilege, social justice, and social justice concerns in counseling and therapy in a manner that forces us to "sit up" and listen and ultimately to act. Her use of narratives and critical race theory's counterstorytelling illustrates three various scenarios where the emotionality of whiteness enacts. Cheryl's chapter seeks to provide counselors and therapists ways in which they can understand the emotionality of whiteness, especially since a majority of counselors are white who are working with an ever-increasing diverse client population.

## Cross-Cultural Responsiveness: Implications for Utilizing and Training in EBPs

The second theme in the volume is illustrated in Robert's chapter that provides a review of the guidelines for evidence-based practices (EBPs) and some of the strengths and challenges associated with utilizing EBPs with diverse client populations. As Robert outlines in detail, EBPs have become a part of the research and clinical landscape for couple and family therapists. Developing and using evidence-based practices is seen as a natural progression of our field. Robert describes in this chapter the challenges associated with integrating science into the practice of therapy through EBPs. These challenges are often controversial and frequent and lead to debates in the field. The crux of Robert's chapter is attempting to understand EBP guidelines such as those established by Division 43 of the American Psychological Association referencing "contextual efficacy" at the third and most advanced level for determining an EBP and how these guidelines translate to cultural responsiveness. The chapter will first clarify what the current guidelines are and explore how the fields of couple and family research have explored culture and "contextual efficacy."

Senem's chapter also focuses on EBPs, specifically emotionally focused couple therapy (EFT); however, this chapter provides a unique window into the experience of Senem (a Turkey-based therapist, EFT trainer in training, EFT clinician, and supervisor) facilitating EFT training in Turkey, her country of origin. As Senem points out, the number of EFT trainings and trainers across the world has been increasing in the last decade; there is little information about the experience of

Introduction

trainers, trainees, and the training process in countries outside of what is considered the "Western world." Additionally, in her chapter, Senem speaks to her experiences assessing the effectiveness of EFT with Eastern couples and culturally responsive adaptations of EFT trainings in the Eastern context. In her chapter, she reviews the existing literature on conducting EFT trainings and therapy outside of North America and Europe. Using Turkey as an example, she describes experiences around organizing and implementing EFT trainings, EFT supervision, and therapy. Senem also provides information about evaluations by Turkish mental health professionals after the completion of their cross-cultural EFT trainings. Her chapter provides feedback from trainees that describes trainees' perspectives on the applicability of EFT within the Turkish culture. Recommendations to address language and cultural barriers in conducting international trainings and supervision are also specified in this engaging and illuminating chapter.

## Cross-Cultural Responsiveness and Use of Foundational Systemic Models

Shruti's chapter focuses on foundational systemic theory and techniques, specifically the genogram, and how she uses an integrative lens such as the common factor lens to enhance the cultural responsiveness of systemic therapies. Understanding the dynamic nature of clients' lives and their cultural realities is critical to the therapy process if the process is going to be culturally responsive. Thus, in this chapter, common factors such as therapist-client relationship, client and therapist factors, and generating hope and expectancy, which are all considered important components of effective therapy models, are presented as useful in adapting foundational systemic therapies and techniques to be more culturally responsive. Examples are provided on how to utilize clinical tools that infuse cultural responsiveness and awareness of culture and systemic work in family therapy.

## Cross-Cultural Responsiveness in Systemic Supervision and Training

In addition to systemic therapies, EBPs, and cultural responsiveness, this volume also presents therapists' and educators' experiences with culturally responsive supervision and training in systemic therapies. Nicole and Raji's co-authored chapter focuses on supervision and training and implications for client-centered advocacy in a variety of mental health settings. As the authors point out, the American Association for Marriage and Family Therapy code of ethics proposes that marriage and family therapists (MFTs) should be committed to advocacy as part of professional competency. In their chapter, the authors present the results of a study that examined the experiences of client-centered advocacy of MFT trainees and interns currently engaged in clinical training. They identify the various aspects of training and supervision that are particularly helpful in terms of educating student trainees and interns in engaging in client-centered advocacy in clinical practice. Additionally, they propose ways in which educators and supervisors can better meet the needs of students and supervisees who are engaged in client-centered advocacy throughout the training process.

Diane's chapter follows and expands on ideas presented in Nicole and Raji's chapter, exploring the definitions of cultural competence and responsiveness in the counseling and family therapy fields, and outlines professional competencies related to clinical training and supervision of counselors and family therapists in training. Diane provides a review of the education and supervision literature on cross-cultural competency and discussions of more process-oriented perspectives in the learning paradigm. In this chapter, she explores the use of active voices in the integration of cultural responsiveness and responsibility in the educator/student and the supervisee/supervisor relationships via literature, case examples, and experiential exercises.

## Experiences, Challenges, and Implications: Systemic Training in International Contexts

We would be remiss in our work in this volume only focused on the cross-cultural responsiveness and social justice issues in systemic therapies pertinent to the US mental health setting. The efforts of systemic scholars and educators in settings outside of the USA, to disseminate systemic training and ideas, are reminiscent of the early foundational days of the couple and family therapy field in the West. The mental health arena in the USA and Europe was buzzing with excitement, energy, and innovation as cutting-edge theories, such as Bowen, structural, strategic, and experiential, were being developed and introduced to psychotherapists yearning for different and effective ways of working with their clients (Gehart, 2014).

Raji's chapter focusing on exploring the cultural relevance of systemic family therapy theories and techniques to cross-cultural social contexts is an exciting example of the type of systemic training and work being done outside of the USA and Europe. Raji presents the Indian cultural context as a case example to report the results of an evaluation of a family therapy training session conducted by her in India. She introduces the framework of *globalization* and argues for the need for knowledge flow to be bi-directional, with the receiving cultures being actively engaged and reciprocal in the process of knowledge transfer. She also presents the implications of the findings from her work; these include the need for more trainings and supervised clinical work opportunities by indigenous trainers and the need to publish culturally adapted family therapy textbooks.

The final chapter by Nilufer and Yudum summarizes the history of the field of couple and family therapy in the Turkish context with its developments and challenges. While Raji highlights the inroads that systemic therapies and trainings have made in the Indian context which have been in existence for some years, the introduction of couple and family therapy treatment, education, supervision, and training in Turkey is indeed uncharted and unfamiliar territory for the field. As Nilufer and Yudum point out in their chapter, there are only seven PhD level systemically trained researchers and scholars and a number of master's level clinicians and trainers in *all* of Turkey, a country of almost 80 million people and a country that straddles two continents, Asia and Europe. A great deal of amazing training, education, and research work is being conducted in Turkey by a relatively small overall number of systemically trained clinicians and scholars. Over the last decade, the couple and family therapy field has attracted a great deal of attention from different training institutions, the public, universities, as well as the Turkish government. Nilufer and Yudum, in their chapter, provide an enlightening and useful glimpse into their experiences developing formal and credible systemic training programs to their country while also engaging in social policy change and mental health policy and law development. Their work in Turkey and those of other systemic therapists, educators, and trainers is an exciting reminder of why we are committed to this field and to its wider dissemination and implementation across diverse cultural contexts and with diverse client populations.

## Conclusion

The contributors to this volume have substantial experience as supervisors and educators and have generously shared their time and expertise and their lived experiences here. As with any endeavor such as this book, we as co-editors experienced the usual challenges and hurdles along the way, changes in authors, delayed deadlines, and navigating almost entirely opposite time zones during our collaboration! We deeply appreciate the authors' willingness to work with us on our reviewing and editing process and in contributing so meaningfully to this volume. We hope readers enjoy this book and find it useful in their reflections and professional and personal development and for supporting and engaging with clients in culturally responsive and socially just ways.

Denver, CO, USA                                                                              Shruti Singh Poulsen
                                                                                                              Robert Allan

# References

Gehart, D. (2014). *Mastering competencies in family therapy: A practical approach to theories & clinical case documentation* (2nd ed.). Belmont, CA: Brooks/Cole.

Laszloffy, T., & Habekost, J. (2010). Using experiential tasks to enhance cultural sensitivity among MFT trainees. *Journal of Marital & Family Therapy, 36*(3), 333–346. https://doi.org/10.1111/j.1752-0606.2010.00213.x

Watts-Jones, T. D. (2010). Location of self: Opening the door to dialogue on intersectionality in the therapy process. *Family Process, 49*(3), 405–420. https://doi.org/10.1111/j.1545-5300.2010.01330.x

White, T. M., Connolly Gibbons, M. B., & Schamberger, M. (2006). Cultural sensitivity & supportive expressive psychotherapy: An integrative approach to treatment. *American Journal of Psychotherapy, 60*(3), 299–316.

# Contents

Social Justice Implications for MFT: The Need
for Cross-Cultural Responsiveness . . . . . . . . . . . . . . . . . . . . . . . . . . . . . . 1
Iman Dadras and Manijeh Daneshpour

Before Cultural Competence . . . . . . . . . . . . . . . . . . . . . . . . . . . . . . . . . . . . 21
Cheryl E. Matias

Evidence-Based Practices and Cultural Responsiveness. . . . . . . . . . . . . . 41
Robert Allan

Cross-Culturally Responsive Training of Emotionally
Focused Couple Therapy: International Experiences . . . . . . . . . . . . . . . . 53
Senem Zeytinoglu-Saydam

Cultural Responsiveness in Family Therapy: Integrative
and Common Factors Lens . . . . . . . . . . . . . . . . . . . . . . . . . . . . . . . . . . . . . 69
Shruti Singh Poulsen

Client-Centered Advocacy in Education and Clinical
Training from the Supervisees' Perspective . . . . . . . . . . . . . . . . . . . . . . . . 79
Nicole Sabatini Gutierrez and Rajeswari Natrajan-Tyagi

Training and Supervision Across Disciplines to Engage
in Cross-Cultural Competence and Responsiveness:
Counseling and Family Therapy . . . . . . . . . . . . . . . . . . . . . . . . . . . . . . . . 101
Diane Estrada

Cross-Cultural Relevance of Systemic Family Therapy
and Globally Responsive Cross-Cultural Training:
An Indian Case Study. . . . . . . . . . . . . . . . . . . . . . . . . . . . . . . . . . . . . . . . . 119
Rajeswari Natrajan-Tyagi

Couple and Family Therapy Training in the Context of Turkey . . . . . . . . 135
Nilufer Kafescioglu and Yudum Akyıl

**The Future of MFT: Clinical Implications of Cross-Cultural Responsiveness and Social Justice Lens to the Field** . . . . . . . . . . . . . . . . . . 149
Shruti Singh Poulsen and Robert Allan

**Index**. . . . . . . . . . . . . . . . . . . . . . . . . . . . . . . . . . . . . . . . . . . . . . . . . . . . . . 157

# Editors

**Shruti Singh Poulsen** is an Associate Professor in the Counseling Program at the University of Colorado Denver. She teaches and supervises Master's-level students primarily in the couple and family therapy track. She has been clinically active in couple and family therapy and supervision for over 20 years. She received her doctorate from the MFT Program at Purdue University in 2003. She has been faculty at the University of Colorado Denver for over 7 years. At CU Denver, she has taught Family Therapy Theories, Family Therapy Techniques, Counseling Couples, Introduction to Sex Therapy, Internship, and Practicum; most recently, she taught an undergraduate course (Skills for Helping Professions) in Human Development and Family Relations, a new undergraduate program in her school. Her research, teaching, and service all focus on areas of multiculturalism; specifically access to good mental health care to diverse populations, and training culturally responsive and competent therapists and counselors. She is also interested in empirically based treatments and their utility with diverse client populations; to this effort, she has obtained advanced training in EFT, Gottman level I training, and training in IBCT. The majority of her scholarly work (publications and presentations) focuses on clinical work with diverse client populations with specific focus on areas such as immigration, interracial and diverse couples, and cultural implications for training and supervision.

**Robert Allan** is an Assistant Professor in the Counseling Program at the University of Colorado Denver. He teaches and supervises Master's-level students primarily in the couple and family therapy track. He came to working with people more directly in therapy after 20 years of community-based development work and developed a keen understanding of the impact of various stressors and community factors that can affect our lives. He has been helping couples, individuals, and families improve their most important relationships, health, and well-being for over 25 years now. As his clinical practice evolved, he was drawn to systemic approaches to working with people. This was a natural evolution from his community work where they drew on a range of health promotion and population health models for working with health challenges. He received his Master's in counseling from Acadia University, an interdisciplinary PhD from Dalhousie University (Canada), and did a post-grad route to become an MFT and approved AAMFT supervisor.

# Contributors

**Yudum Akyıl**  Istanbul Bilgi University, İstanbul, Turkey

**Robert Allan**  University of Colorado Denver, Denver, CO, USA

**Iman Dadras**  Alliant International University, San Diego, CA, USA

**Manijeh Daneshpour**  Alliant International University, San Diego, CA, USA

**Diane Estrada**  University of Colorado Denver, Denver, CO, USA

**Nicole Sabatini Gutierrez**  Alliant International University, San Diego, CA, USA

**Nilufer Kafescioglu**  Ozyegin University, İstanbul, Turkey

**Cheryl E. Matias**  University of Colorado Denver, Denver, CO, USA

**Rajeswari Natrajan-Tyagi**  Alliant International University, Irvine, CA, USA

**Shruti Singh Poulsen**  University of Colorado Denver, Denver, CO, USA

**Senem Zeytinoglu-Saydam**  Ozyegin University, Istanbul, Turkey

# Social Justice Implications for MFT: The Need for Cross-Cultural Responsiveness

**Iman Dadras and Manijeh Daneshpour**

> Discourse without action is dangerous because it creates the impression that progress is taking place when in fact only the words have changed. (Prilleltensky, 1997)

Multicultural sensitivity, cultural responsiveness, and cultural humility are all forms of historical determinism in order to respond to perplexing social realities of disenfranchised and oppressed groups' experiences with high prevalence of social disparities. Such disparities have been well-documented across significant domains of life. For example, ethnic minorities underutilize mental health service compared to white populations (Pole, Gone, & Kulkarni, 2008) and experience significant cultural bias regarding the process of their treatment (Schulman et al., 1999).

This chapter offers a framework for supporting and including a social justice perspective in family therapy praxis by discussing a vision of social justice that is true to the needs of families we serve. As authors of this chapter, we both have studied social sciences (first author in Iran, India, and the USA and the second author in Iran and the USA) and are academicians, researchers, and practicing clinicians and have seen the complexity of relational issues cross-culturally. We both have dealt with different kinds of social, political, and relational injustices when we lived abroad but believed that these issues are more related to the developing world's cultural context in terms of lack of sustainable laws, collectivistic values, and scarcity of resources. However, we have been shocked and then greatly motivated to examine and discuss issues related to social justice, diversity, and human suffering that are continuously and contextually happening in the USA and have tried to do a critical analysis of these phenomena. We both have extensively researched, written, and presented about lack of a social justice framework within the realm of psychotherapy in the USA and abroad. Therefore, in this chapter, we attempt to offer specific ideas about a paradigm shift in thinking about the inclusion

---

I. Dadras · M. Daneshpour (✉)
Alliant International University, San Diego, CA, USA
e-mail: mdaneshpour@alliant.edu

of diversity and social justice in practice to help clinicians understand multicultural clients' dilemmas and challenges.

First, it is critical to acknowledge that the experience of chronic stress for ethnic minorities is positively associated with health disparities caused by sociopolitical factors such as perceived racism, neighborhood poverty, family stress, acculturative stress, and maternal depression (Djuric et al., 2008). Compared to white Americans, racial and ethnic minorities report a significantly lower level of overall health. Such experiences occur due to the existing gap caused by lower socioeconomic status, lower education level, living in poverty-stricken neighborhoods, lower rates of employment, lack of access to healthcare, and providers' bias (Bahls, 2011). Further, due to chronic stress caused by daily experiences of discrimination, the prevalence of diabetes and hypertension is significantly higher among different oppressed groups such as African-Americans, Hispanics, and Native Americans (Kaholokula, Iwane, & Nacapoy, 2010; Williams & Neighbors, 2001). The US Census Bureau report revealed that 19% of African-Americans did not have any form of health insurance compared to the general population in the USA, while 20% of African-Americans are more likely than whites to experience significant mental health symptoms and diagnoses (Health and Human Services Office of Minority Health, 2012).

Furthermore, perceived discrimination and racism have been indicated as significant contributors to unhealthy coping mechanisms such as alcohol and substance use, smoking, improper nutrition, and rejection from receiving necessary medical care (Lee, Ayers, & Kronenfeld, 2009; Peek, Wagner, Tang, & Baker, 2011). Lesbian, gay, bisexual, and transgender (LBGT) individuals also experience higher risk for psychiatric disorders compared to heterosexual individuals because of higher levels of discrimination (Lehavot & Simoni, 2011; McCabe, Bostwick, Hughes, West, & Boyd, 2010).

Additionally, acculturation stress among immigrants has shown to be negatively associated with ethnic identity and self-esteem (Marin, 1993), academic achievement and depression (Cuellar, Bastida, & Braccio, 2004), psychological adjustments (Smith & Khawaja, 2011), racial micro-aggression/racism (Araújo-Dawson, 2009), substance abuse Segura, Page, Neighbors, Nichols-Anderson, & Gillaspy, 2003), and emotional well-being (Caldwell, Couture, & Nowotny, 2010). Immigrant women reported more significant experiences with depressive symptoms compared to US-born women in general (Tillman & Weiss, 2009).

## Classism and Capitalism: The Forbidden Words in the Therapy Room

Despite all the cliché and infantile attack on psychoanalysis reductionism, Sigmund Freud was among the earliest professionals who realized the limitations of psychotherapy within larger social systems. He claimed that "the vast amount of neurotic misery which there is in the world, and perhaps need not be" (Freud, 1914, p. 165). Freud was expressively disappointed for not having served the poor people. He argued that in the future "society must have an awaken[ed] conscience toward its disadvantaged citizens where treatments will be free" (p. 165). Ironically, in our current academic discourses and research practices, the issues of poverty, classicism, and economic injustices have been significantly overlooked.

Generally speaking, every individual has inherited a membership within a social class. Such category predominantly shapes and impacts individual and family experiences. Social class significantly influences human well-being either physically or psychologically (Dillaway & Broman, 2001). McDowell (2015) argues that "Social class influences the range and types of choices available to each of us, how we define ourselves, our values and expectations, and the way we organize our day-to-day lives" (p. 13). Despite the importance of the interconnectedness between social class and families' psychosomatic well-being, limited attention has been paid to these issues. The very mundane and apologist arguments of privileged therapists are that we are not economists and that it is beyond the scope of our practice. Yet, a momentary gaze into empirical evidence of economic hardship of modern age can expand our limited horizon related to the mental health hygiene in the age of economic disparities.

In the USA, 15% of people are living under the poverty line (Wolff, 2012). The top 1% of the American population earn approximately more than 38 times compared to the bottom 90% which means the top 1% accumulation is 184 times that of the bottom 90% (Saez, 2015). The income of the top 1% bracket has skyrocketed by 256% between 1979 and 2007, while the bottom 90% have experienced a very minimal growth of average income by 16.7% during the same historical period (Mishel, Gould, & Bivens, 2015), and 43.1 million people (13.5%) live below the poverty line. Among those individuals, 14.5 million (19.7%) are children under the age of 18, and 4.2 million (8.8%) are elderly 65 and older (Proctor, Semega, & Kollar, 2016).

There is a plethora of empirical studies revealing the significant impact of one's socioeconomic status on overall mental and physical health. More precisely, the poorer you are, the unhealthier you become. Faris and Dunham (1939) conducted one of the earliest studies to examine the connection between socioeconomic stress and mental health. The result indicated the prevalence of significant mental illness among the poorest neighborhood in Chicago. This was a groundbreaking study that led to other similar empirical studies including Hollingshead and Redlich (1958) in New Haven, Connecticut, and Srole et al. (1977) in Midtown Manhattan. The findings of these studies consistently convey the same concept that lower social class contributes to a higher rate of health issues both at individual and community levels. In these articles, classism is approached not only as a form of social attitude for both therapist and clients but also as a form of "social oppression" (Smith, 2005) that impacts and shapes individuals' lives negatively.

Psychotherapists are predominantly unconscious about their axiological position regarding class (Chalifoux, 1996).

Such lack of awareness can easily function as a form of countertransference called "fear of the poor" (Javier & Herron, 2002, p. 26) which leads many therapists to fail to build a meaningful relationship with their poor clients. Lorion (1974) argues that therapists' "negative attitudes" toward poor clients are potentially the most significant factors for treatment failures with this population. Jones (1974) echoes Lorion's perspective and proposes therapists' reluctance to work with poor clients as "the expression of an ugly class bias" (p. 309) (as cited in Smith, 2005). Unfortunately, a three-decades' fast-forward of clinical work with clients from lower socioeconomic status is not promising. For instance, Saris and Johnston-Robledo (2000) found a common theme after conducting a content analysis called "Poor Women Are Still Shut Out of Mainstream Psychology." Furnham (2003) claims that "the most important topics in poverty research have been almost totally neglected by psychologists" (p. 164). Regardless of researchers' intentionality, the research on poverty and mental health has mystified such unhealthy relationship through what Moreira (2003) calls "the medicalization of poverty" and Read et al. (2004) has called the "colonization of the psychosocial by the biological." Smith (2005) concludes "therapists know little more about the therapeutic experiences of poor people today than they did decades ago" (p. 687). Sue and Lam (2002) conducted an analysis of psychotherapy interventions outcomes, and their observations of clients with lower SES revealed that "despite the important influence of socioeconomic status on an individual's life, this variable has been widely ignored" (p. 414).

Because of their limited opportunity to access to mental health service, poor clients have limited chances of receiving evidence-based treatments compared to the mainstream population (Le, Zmuda, Perry, & Munoz, 2010; Miranda et al., 2005). Both academic researchers and clinicians have failed to explicitly acknowledge such invisible apparatuses of oppression and the systemic dehumanization of the poor. Therefore, understanding the existential struggles of poor clients and the discrimination that they experience due to the brutality of a class gap must be a paramount element of therapeutic endeavors. Yet, there is no consensus on how to incorporate such a mind-set into clinical practice. Zrenchik and McDowell (2012) call for adopting a "critical class consciousness" and taking action throughout the therapeutic process. Similarly, Kim and Cardemil (2012) claim that therapists must engage in a self-examination of their "unconscious classist bias." Harley, Jolivette, McCormick, and Tice (2002) suggest that therapist must be aware of how their class privilege can unconsciously harm clients.

Nonetheless, regarding classism, it appears that the self-proclaimed conscious therapist's effort to dismantle classism in the therapeutic realm remains ineffective—because the first step is a critical self-examination for therapists to realize that their expertise and knowledge derives its legitimacy from the very existence of the classist system. Such visible or invisible loyalty of the psychotherapist toward the maintenance of a classist structure is most often overlooked.

There is a significant dearth of discourses on classism and socioeconomic status in the field of couple and family therapy (Kosutic & McDowell, 2008). Since MFT as a field has not incorporated the impact of classicism and poverty into academic training, supervision, and research, it further enables the structural injustice and normalizes the internalized oppression of the clients and families who are dealing with poverty. McDowell (2015) claims that "as long as poverty is explained as the result of individual failing and wealth as the result of individual hard work and human worth, class discrimination and internalized classism will thrive" (p. 14). Similarly, Vodde and Gallant (2002) propose that there will not occur an authentic fundamental change until the root causes of the problem of oppressed clients are addressed and a collective macro-level activism initiated.

## The Ontological Birth of Multiculturalism

The discourse on the application of multiculturalism and implication of justice-oriented perspective toward therapy is not new. Yet, there has been an immensely limited conversation about why the field of mental health mandates such perspective. If it is so critical to therapeutic progress, why has it been overlooked for almost a century since the birth of the talking cure? In order to respond to the aforementioned questions, one needs to understand the ontological necessities of the emergence of multiculturalism.

Along with the existing empirical data on how minorities live in an unjust parallel universe, there are other theoretical arguments for the epistemological problem with multiculturalism as an ultimate solution to such disparities. Phillips (2007) suggests the following summation of a multicultural society:

> Multiculturalism exaggerates the internal unity of cultures, solidifies differences that are currently more fluid, and makes people from other cultures seem more exotic and distinct than they really are. Multiculturalism then appears not as a cultural liberator but as a cultural straitjacket, forcing those described as members of a minority cultural group into a regime of authenticity, denying them the chance to cross cultural borders, borrow cultural influences, define and redefine themselves (p. 14).

More radically, Ahmed (2008) argues that "multiculturalism is a fantasy which conceals many forms of racism, violence and inequality as if the organization/nation can now say: how can you experience racism when we are committed to diversity?" She further argues that multiculturalism is a fantasy in the favor of white hegemony. Ahmed (2008) discusses that a multicultural attitude simply endowed us with a politically correct language and shallow sense of coexistence while disguising the profundity of inequalities.

Žižek (2008) makes another controversial proposition. He claims that Western liberal multiculturalism has succeeded in obfuscating and disguising significant struggles of oppressed groups such as "economic exploitation, political inequalities, health disparities, and justify them through cultural differences" (p. 141). Because when we state that people's issues stem from their different cultural background, "it means we cannot change them, because it's their culture, rather than stating that the issues are political such as poverty, high unemployment rate, institutionalized and discrimination, which requires justice-based social interventions" (p. 141). Žižek

(2008) also discusses the danger of the current liberal multiculturalism which can easily turn into an oppressive force. "Political differences - differences conditioned by political inequality or economic exploitation - are naturalized and neutralized into 'cultural' differences; that is into different 'ways of life' which are something given, something that cannot be overcome" (p. 141).

Furthermore, attending multicultural trainings and workshops has become an interesting new way of buying a product and then achieving the static state of cultural competency. Nevertheless, this apolitical purchasing of multiculturalism as a commodity creates even more hindrances for minorities who are still very much misunderstood and mistreated leading to more "Otherization." Henry, Totor, Mattis, and Rees (2000) argue that multiculturalism mystifies the historical phenomena such as colonization, genocide, slavery, and diaspora that shaped the current existing life dynamics of many minority groups. Constantine and Ladany (2000) claim that "historical definition has gone virtually unchallenged by multicultural scholars and practitioners in counseling psychology" (p. 162).

Additionally, multicultural trainings emerged as responses to multiple clinical struggles. Multicultural psychotherapy for marginalized groups has been uttered for at least four decades now (Sue, Zane, Hall, & Berger, 2009). It is an empirical fact that despite experiencing higher level of psychological distress, minority clients have been underserved and drop out of therapy at much higher rates compared to the general populations (Kearney, Draper, & Baron, 2005; Sue & Sue, 2008).

For instance, many researchers argue that the majority of mental health professionals are white (Ancis & Szymanski, 2001; Fouad & Arredondo, 2007) and there is a sociohistorical mistrust within African-American communities to seek such professional support from white psychotherapists (Whaley, 2001). Gushue (2004) concludes that after participating in an extensive multicultural training, therapists' racism is still easily displayed during the course of therapy (D'Andrea, 2005). Additionally, Mindrup, Spray, and Lamberghini-West (2011) argue that fundamental theoretical approaches of psychotherapy emerged from the white male epistemology toward mental health which has significantly obscured the sociopolitical factors that position individuals and families' life condition within the larger social systems. Carter (1995) opposes the deracialized approaches of mental health professionals by stating that "more often than not, race is thought of by mental health professionals to be an unimportant aspect of personality development and interpersonal relationships. Consequently, how race influences the therapeutic process is not well understood by psychological theorists, clinicians, and clinical scholars. Race as a personality and treatment factor has, at best, been treated as marginal" (pp. 1–2). Advocates such as Sue and Sue (2008) proposed that psychotherapy could be conceptualized as "sociopolitical act," yet the very neutral language and limitation of its praxis failed in pushing the boundaries of justice discourses in the field of psychotherapy.

In summary, it is plausible to argue that the intervention of multiculturalism merely was conceptualized as a form of ethical obligations for mental health providers. The result is the promotion of another individualistic epistemology of "the Other" that mental health professionals can declare just by attending multiple trainings. This form of culturalism is indeed a theoretical mystification of the sociopolitical experience of minority clients. Akintunde (1999) argues that not only multiculturalism is pro status quo but also a very subtle enabler of white-supremacist ontological, epistemological, and axiological frameworks, since it permits the white trainees to simply become the master of "the Other's" culture. Such an "Otherization" mechanism is yet another form of privilege and entitlement for whites to continue to be the center of knowledge construction and understanding of "the Other" from their colonial gaze.

## The Subject of Multicultural Gaze

Historically speaking, white male theoreticians and researchers consciously and unconsciously (strictly Freudian) overlooked the magnificent force of sociopolitical order on the mental health status of marginalized groups. Their positionality of white privilege shaped such ontology, epistemology, and axiology which is inherently ahistorical, depoliticized, and deracialized. Since he has profited from the domination of white hegemony, and is not existentially aware of the sufferings of the oppressed, he continues to ignore how social systems transmit their inherent pathologies to underprivileged families and individuals. The existential philosopher, Sartre (1956), portrays white men's position in society as: "the White man enjoyed, the privilege of seeing without being seen; he was only a look…The white man - white because he was man, white like daylight, white like truth, white like virtue- lighted up creation like a torch and unveiled the secret white essence of beings" (p. 13). More specifically, the very position of the white theoretician and therapist created a context of negligence and distortion of his/her understanding of psychosocial etiology of mental health symptoms. McGoldrick (1998) openly acknowledges that conventional approaches of psychotherapy are significantly in favor of white men, are heterosexist, and predominantly privilege the challenges of middle and upper middle class individuals and families.

The current psychotherapeutic lens is a historical continuation of the enlightenment project, where the philosopher Descartes asserted "I think, therefore I am." Such a centrality of the knower as the primary architecture of truth has been the core assumption of psychotherapist trainings in the Western paradigm. In the so-called Cartesian dualism, there is an epistemological stance which is the separateness of the knower from known, the thinker from thought, and the observer from observed. Descartes' proposition became the rationale for objectifying the non-Western world and colonization of recourses of Others (indigenous population) whose world philosophy was not shaped by the pure instrumental reasoning (Altman, 2003). Therefore, if there will ever be a change in treating "the Other" more humanely, the Western gaze of psychotherapy must recognize its problematic way of understanding the racial Others. Accordingly, Taylor (2011) refers to the challenge of comprehending the mystery of the Other as "the great challenge of this century both for politics and social science" (p. 24). Yet, the arrogance and dogmatism of instrumental reasoning have not permitted the alternative view of "the Other." Furthermore, Gantt (2000) complains that contemporary psychotherapy has been so overwhelmingly fixated with diagnosis, techniques, and outcomes that it has failed to meaningfully develop a moral and ethical understandings of the Other's sufferings. Thus, the racial Other, as a subject of a multicultural lens, continues to be de-subjectified, in a sense that he/she does not have full range of human experiences equal to the observer, since he/she has been historically an object of the colonial gaze, reduced to a nonliving entity which is governable; does not experience pain, suffering, sadness, anger, etc.; and is subject to the colonizer/colonized relationship.

The colonized are the ones who Foucault (1980) argues are perceived as not being able to experience the full range of humanhood, "thus subjectified and are denied subjectivity." It is indeed plausible to argue that the multicultural lens is a postmodern tool for the colonizer to understand the troublesome existence of the Other, who suffers the castration and has metamorphosed into an abstract concept for experts of the Western/colonial paradigms to be analyzed, studied, or cured. The multicultural lens is an invention of the subject of knowledge who does not tolerate to bear any ambiguity about the Other, since the very unknown is an uncomfortable state of the mind for one who must know to dominate over others. No wonder, despite its theoretical incongruences, the very notion of cultural competency has received so much receptivity among mainstream psychotherapists.

## Family Therapist Cross-Cultural Responsiveness Dilemma

Family therapy field has a serious dilemma with respect to cultural responsiveness and must rehabilitate itself from the irrelevancy of the majority of implied theoretical approaches and clinical interventions to help the racial Other and must inquire a paradigm shift in understanding and providing mental health services to the Other. Some philosophers like Levinas (1969) suggest that no matter how hard the subject tries, there are always aspects of the Others that escape and resist any form of symbolization, categorization, and objectification. Therefore, instead of replacing the vexing feeling caused by the cognitive dissonance of the Other's ambiguity, a systemic thinker and therapist must expand his/her conceptualizations to understand complexity of the Other's life circumstances. Perhaps, the psychotherapist must abandon the colonial attitude of multiculturalism and emancipate himself/herself from the obsession of knowing the Other and rather focus on empowering the oppressed Other. The white therapists or those who are indoctrinated with the white ideology should engage in a form of soul-searching experience where he/she develops emotional and intellectual capacity to embrace a new form of reality, which is "there is limitation to my knowledge." Only then, a family therapist can pay attention to the other significant social realities that impact the oppressed Others through recognition of interconnectivity between race, class, politics, etc., and the therapist can utilize multiculturalism as an intervention for understanding the Other. In this way, multiculturalism will be approached as an introspective tool, where family therapists begin to view themselves from the lens of the Other. Instead of occupying the predominant position of being the omnipotent expert, psychotherapists can resign from such positions and begin to view themselves objectively, as if the Other is observing them. Such introspection is immensely lacking within the professional realm since it demands significant vulnerability on the psychotherapist's side. Therefore, neither narrowed Western paradigms nor a plethora of therapeutic models but rather family therapists' personal journey of "being the Other" can determine how the Other is viewed, understood, and conceptualized.

## Family Therapist Utilization of the Social Justice Paradigm

A social justice paradigm consciously magnifies the historical evolvements of the present social order where certain segments of society enjoy an unearned privilege at the expense of historical oppression of other disadvantaged groups (McIntosh, 1998). Seedall, Holtrop, and Parra-Cardona (2014) propose that "A social justice perspective identifies group differences in the context of social inequalities and then analyzes the source of those differences, including the interplay between disadvantage and privilege" (p. 140). Additionally, a social justice lens aims to address the institutionalization of social inequalities in maintaining such order via multiple structural methods and ideological tools such as classism, racism, and sexism (Chizhik & Chizhik, 2002). This framework intends to dismantle the systemic oppressions through empowering members of the marginalized groups by increasing their social awareness about the oppressive conditions and to create networks of support within their communities. Therefore, de-ideologization (Martín-Baró, 1985) of the social machine of oppression should be a critical pillar of social justice in MFTs' clinical work. In this way, the very internalized belief system of oppressed groups is deconstructed and an emancipatory knowledge is given back to the marginalized people in order to realize the falsehood of their problem-saturated stories. Therefore, the liberation occurs when the oppressed recognizes the false consciousness they use to justify their own life conditions. Such anti-oppressive interventions against the "oppressive condition" assist oppressed members to revise their understandings of different aspects of their lives from basic survival needs such as housing and employment to leisure, emotional well-being, and their sense of justice.

Even though the importance of discourses around social justice initiated in the 1980s by many feminist scholars (Ault-Riche, 1986; Avis, 1988; Goldner, 1985; Hare-Mustin, 1987), the family therapy field has been hesitant to make a strong sociopolitical stance against oppression in their academic and clinical training. Consequently, we have witnessed a huge gap in marriage and family therapists' awareness and advocacy for social justice and feminist issues (McGeorge, Carlson, Erickson, & Guttormson, 2006).

During early twenty-first-century conversations, there are signatures of epistemological confusion about understanding the mental health issues of the Other. For instance, Guaniapa (2003) proposes that the lack of enough multicultural course designs in family therapy programs has caused the primary issues of not having multiculturally competent trainees and therapists. There are few studies that have addressed the current struggles of the family therapy field in response to clinical application of social justice into therapeutic interventions. After reviewing 127 published articles by Journal of Marital and Family Therapy from 1999 to 2001, McDowell and Jeris (2004) found only 6.3% of published articles addressed issues related to race and racism even though the authors declare that "There is an emerging trend in MFT literature toward advocating for social justice and resisting socially unjust relationships" (McDowell & Jeris, 2004, p. 90). In a different study conducted by Kosutic and McDowell (2008) called *Diversity and Social Justice Issues in Family Therapy Literature: A Decade Review*, authors examined 1735 articles that were published between 1995 and 2008 in five major family therapy journals. The result reveals that only 0.9% of the article exclusively attempted to address social justice issues. Such findings indicate that the discourses of social justice in the MFT field are still in its infancy. Seedall, Holtrop, and Parra-Cardona (2014) conducted a content analysis of three family therapy journals (Journal of Marital and Family, Family Process, and The American Journal of Family Therapy) on addressing issues related to social justice and diversity examining a total of 769 articles between 2004 and 2011. The result indicates that only 13.5% ($n = 104$) of all articles implied a social justice perspective. Such a significant dearth of social justice theorization of mental health issues clearly symbolizes the prevalent indifferences of the family therapy field to conceptualize mental health above and beyond the conventional therapeutic models. From a clinical perspective, however, there are some articles suggesting that we should engage in more critical discourses within MFT programs and increase our awareness of the interplay of unconscious assumptions of racism, sexism, and classism on clinical interventions (Ariel & McPherson, 2000; Laird, 2000; McDowell et al., 2003).

There are similar suggestions about the problem with limited emphasis on issues of diversity and social justice in the MFT field to train students to become socially conscious clinicians. Yet, there is a limited contextualization of how those praxes can occur in our current depoliticized academia. It is very apparent that like other social science curriculums, the MFT academic programs are embedded in a Eurocentric paradigm and in favor of a white-hegemony doctrine (Aronowitz & Giroux, 1993). Other scholars have advocated for the inclusion of more critical frameworks such as critical race theory and feminism in order to counterbalance the inherent bias of the MFT trainings and interventions which are significantly shaped by patriarchy, racism, classism, and heterosexism (Carlson et al., 2006; Inman, Meza, Brown, & Hargrove, 2004; McDowell & Shelton, 2002; McGoldrick et al., 1999).

The lack of theoretical and clinical relevancy of the MFT approaches to the daily challenges of minority clients and families remains a deadlock. Hardy and Laszloffy (2002) argue that family therapy has been immensely unsuccessful in addressing the reality of oppressed groups' needs and challenges. From an ecosystemic epistemological perspective, Killian and Hardy (1998) argue that, ironically, the American Association for Marriage and Family Therapists (AAMFT) as an organization which is the epitome of systemic thinking has failed to address the existing inherent structural inequality. The AAMFT as a system has maintained a deviation-countering (static) approach not allowing a structural reconfiguration matching the change in the social demographics of our society. The unjustifiable fact that members of the marginalized groups are significantly underrepresented in AAMFT compared to the mainstream population conveys a critical message; AAMFT is "closed off from the larger system of society" (p. 216). An AAMFT statistical report indicates that in 1994, there were only 609 members out of 20,269 individuals who declared to be members of ethnic minority groups, which come to approximately 3% (Killian, & Hardy, 1998). In a more recent report, the percentage of minority membership has increased to 17% but only 9% of them are Clinical Fellows. Perhaps, the post-racial identity for members of AAMFT remains a fantasy when 82.78% of its members are white (Todd, & Holden, 2012). Killian and Hardy (1998) claim that unless a critical change such as inclusion of minorities as members of board of directors, keynote speakers, and Clinical Fellow memberships does not occur, the slogan "seeking strength and wisdom through diversity" is merely "an en vogue banner in the era of political correctness" (p. 208). Indeed, the lack of inclusion of minorities' realities of daily injustices imposes significant limitation onto the field of MFT understanding of mental health in a broader social context. Keeney (1982) eloquently proposes that "health in human ecosystems refers to a 'vital balance' of diverse forms of experience and behavior. To engage in an effort of maximization or minimization, rather than diversity, leads to an escalating sameness we have defined as pathology" (p. 126). Close to two decades ago, Killian and Hardy (1998) asked a theoretical question "Is AAMFT subject to epistemological tunnel vision? and still today one might distraughtly reply "yes". Hardy (1989) does not see any constructive effort from the AAMFT in order to embrace the shortcomings of the field related to the experiences of oppressed groups. He claims, "family therapy has successfully deemphasized the issues of oppression both with women and minorities" (Hardy, 1989, p. 8). Fishman (2008) believes that the seduction for being recognized as an empirically driven orientation has misguided the MFT field to unreasonably compete with more accepted, individualistic, and so-called evidence-based models such as CBT, abandoning its own powerful contextual and systemic understandings of human nature which does not simply fall into the positivist or post-positivist paradigms. Cushman (1995) laments the sociopolitical apathy of the psychotherapy as a field and states that this indifference to the direct relationship between the sociopolitical atmosphere and ordinary people's painful life experiences justifies the status quo even further.

To engage in a more radically unsettling discourse, Sue and Sue (2013) discuss that there is no rigorous research to indicate if psychotherapy is effective for ethnic minorities at all. For a systemic family therapist, there is an epistemological dilemma to accept the inappropriateness of depoliticized, oppressive, atomistic Western paradigms while encountering the perplexity of minority clients' life stories.

Gregory Bateson (1972) called such an error "epistemological fallacies" (p. 492), which is a systemic error leading to faulty conclusions about a phenomenon. In this case, family therapists' approaches in working with minority clients using individualistic perspectives mystify the significant interconnectivity of multiple social context, producing dysfunctional emotional symptoms in the first place. In such cases, what precisely a systemic family therapist fails to recognize is how they "join the forces that perpetuate social injustice" (Albee, 2000, p. 248).

## Sociopolitical Differentiation of Self

Derived from Bowenian family therapy, a significant focus of family therapy academic programs has been dedicated on students' increased awareness of "Self-of-the-Therapist." The core idea behind such an endeavor is to assist novice therapists to process emotional reactions to their family of origin and become emotionally mature. This is an important process in preventing obtrusive emotional reactivity while experiencing countertransference or other forms of emotions aroused by clients and families in the therapy room. Yet, limited emphasis has been directed toward a critical self-examination of therapists' positionality (i.e., social web in relation to race, class, gender, sexual orientation, etc.) on how the larger social system (economic, political, ideological) plays a role in the mental health of individuals and families (McGeorge & Carlson, 2010). Lack of a broad implication of a sociopolitical lens toward an understanding of human behavior is inherently against the core assumptions of systemic epistemology that argues human experiences are influenced by the large context of a given society. In *his masterpiece*, *The Sane Society* (1956), Fromm stated: "…many psychiatrists and psychologists refuse to entertain the idea that society as a whole may be lacking in sanity. They hold that the problem of mental health in a society is only that of the number of 'unadjusted' individuals, and not of a possible unadjustment of the culture itself" (p. 6). Fromm challenged psychotherapists' reductionist view of mental health and proposed awareness toward social advocacy and justice in the therapy room. Green (1998) raised an important question, "will we continue to only huddle in our offices waiting for individual families to request treatment, or will we move beyond family therapy to include prevention, community intervention, and family social policy within our scope of practice?" (p. 107).

## Why Address Social Oppression?

The therapist positionality and epistemology of change have been core values in the family therapy tradition. Hoffman (2002) argues that opposing the psychiatrization and institutionalization of mental health influenced the birth of the marriage and family therapy because of "pioneering psychotherapists who insisted on working against our most persistent illusion, the stand-alone self" (p. 1). However, the neutral language of systemic theory and cybernetic perspective obscures the existing power dynamic within the system which somehow normalizes the relationship between abuser and abused and oppressor and oppressed. Therefore, the notion of social justice as a central domain of therapeutic intervention remained predominantly at the margin of therapeutic work. Historically, feminist theorists disparaged the core assumptions of general systems theory for failing to address issues of power (e.g., Goldner, 1985; Hare-Mustin, 1994). It is important to note that in order to imply a counter-hegemonic approach toward oppression and racism, one cannot overlook the power imbalances that exist within social systems such as family and society (Imber-Black, 1990). After the anti-theoretical position of feminist family therapists, other scholars expanded the conversation to other forms of social oppression such as classism, racism, sexual orientation, and immigrants' maladjustment (e.g., Saba, Karrer, & Hardy, 1989). However, it must be remembered that just recently, conceptualization of the significance of environmental factors caused by the sociopolitical atmosphere has become an important discourse (e.g., Knudson-Martin & Huenergardt, 2010).

Michel Foucault's (1980) main discourses are about resisting power and dismantling any form of ruling class hegemonic structures within a society that labels human experiences through a dogmatic dichotomy of healthy/unhealthy and normal/abnormal. Foucault approaches language not simply as collaborative communication but as an effective instrument of power used by the system in order to give meaning to people's daily life experiences (Freedman & Combs, 1996). Since psychotherapy occurs through the medium of language and communication, the very characteristics of such conversations related to the issues of power and oppression can highlight or obscure the problem of the psychotherapy subject. In the same light, a social constructionist perspective proposes that reality has been shaped by power structures at the sociopolitical level and is being internalized by individuals and families.

Foucault (1980) states that those with expert knowledge in society use linguistic jargonism to subjugate and pathologize the experience of ordinary people. Such pathology-saturated stories become internalized truth, such that people judge their bodies, achievements, and personal choices based on standards set by society's judges (psychotherapist, clergy, politicians, doctors, educators, celebrities, etc.) (Nichols & Schwartz, 2008). Therefore, therapists who have anti-oppressive orientations can occupy multiple advocacy roles and should ally with the family. In this perspective, the therapist is not just a mental health professional with a set of theories and techniques to help individuals, couples, and families to improve their relationship or feel better about themselves. Rather, their aim is to support people to recognize the pathology that resides within power discourses and social inequalities.

Almeida, Dolan-Del Vecchio, and Parker (2008) dispute psychotherapists' position of neutrality and embrace the axiom that all forms of social context, either cultural or political, shape and impact client lives at multiple level including physiological, emotional, and cognitive. Waldegrave and Tamasese (1994) argue that such awareness will create a paradigm shift for therapists in their epistemology of change by making conscious efforts to empower clients and help them understand how different social contexts impact their lives.

Scholars from critical race theory and critical feminism demand professional mental health providers to dismantle structure of systemic oppression by empowering disenfranchised populations (Ortiz & Jani, 2010). Such advocacy for social justice in the realm of family therapy initiates new conversations. McDowell (2005) proposes that the therapist needs to occupy a "position of action" and assist their clients to fight against social injustice and inequalities that are negatively intervening with their life experiences as a human being. Almeida et al. (2008) challenge therapists to apply a sociopolitical perspective by "contextualizing the family's presenting crisis within larger crucibles of historical and contemporary public abuse toward marginalized groups" (p. 5). It is crucial to realize that the lack of a therapist's conscious opposition toward conditions of oppression is an act of morphostasis, perpetuating tyrannical status quo. For instance, a core idea of a critical multicultural approach is "aimed at dismantling structures and discourses that reify dominant cultural knowledge and further privilege the social positioning of those closest to the center" (McDowell, 2005, p. 1).

Furthermore, other critical approaches such as Just Therapy emphasize the importance of the therapist's epistemology of sociopolitical malaises by proposing social mobilization via conscious activism: "When therapists know that certain social and economic conditions prolong ill health, they should be active in creating public awareness concerning these issues…" (Waldegrave, 2009, p. 272). Therefore, family therapists can authentically claim to be a systemic thinker when they view human conditions above and beyond notorious pathology-oriented conceptualization or functionality of intrapsychic and interpersonal conflicts in family systems.

Akin to the aforementioned approaches, Beitin and Allen (2005) argue that "therapists must be equal in participation with those they seek to empower" (p. 13). They encourage therapists' active involvement in the community with their clients not only to grasp a better understanding of their experiences but also "join together to fight for social justice" (Beitin & Allen, 2005, p. 13). Prilleltensky (1994) opposes the conventional psychotherapeutic methods that intervene on theoretical separateness of subjects and environments. He argues that such epistemological positions are pro-oppression and reductionist, when "the individual is studied as an asocial and ahistorical being whose life vicissitudes are artificially disconnected from the wider sociopolitical context. Following this ideological reasoning, solutions for human predicaments are to be found almost exclusively with the self, leaving the social order conveniently unaffected" (p. 34).

## Preparing the Next Generation of Conscious Therapist

Many social activists and researchers contend that we need to prepare the next generation of therapists to be involved in social justice and advocacy work so they become more conscious of their sociopolitical positions inside the power structures

(McDowell et al., 2003; McGeorge et al., 2006). Specifically, we need to aid the next generation of family therapists to become aware of how systemic coercion and subjugation of clients impacts their everyday experiences, how they engage in the therapeutic process, and how they understand their own lived experiences. However, if future therapists do not understand their own societal positions and unearned privileges and only explore clients' marginalized experiences, we will not be able to move forward. We need self-reflection to dismantle our own privileges before we can embark on understanding the pain experienced by our clients (Hardy & McGoldrick, 2008; Johnson, 2006).

If we conceptualize society as a larger family and each family as an individual member, then symptom-bearer individuals and families are merely scapegoats of purposefully disguised structural dysfunctionality of the society (larger family). Therapeutic conceptualizations targeting the symptom bearers are simply epistemological fallacies which neutral therapists transform into apparatus or enabler maintaining the architecture of such inherent injustice, inequality, domination, and oppression. Thus, the socially conscious therapist is not merely an individual with a set of theories and techniques that aims to help individuals, couples, and families to improve their relationship or feel better about themselves. Rather, their aim is to support people to recognize the pathology that resides within power discourses and social injustices. In this view, therapists transform into agents of social justice which the liberation psychologist Martin-Baro describes as "…the concern of the social scientist should not be so much to explain the world as to transform it" (1994, p. 19).

# References

Ahmed, S. (2008). Editorial: The happiness turn. *New Formations, 63*, 7–14.
Akintunde, O. (1999). White racism, white supremacy, white privilege, & the social construction from modernist to postmodernist multiculturalism. *Journal of the National Association of Multicultural Education, 7*(2), 2–8.
Albee, G. W. (2000). The Boulder model's fatal flaw. *American Psychologist, 55*, 247–248.
Almeida, R., Dolan-Del Vecchio, K., & Parker, L. (2008). *Transformative family therapy: Just families in a just society*. Boston, MA: Pearson Education.
Altman, N. (2003). How white people suffer from white racism. *Psychotherapy and Politics International, 1*, 93–106.
Ancis, J. R., & Szymanski, D. M. (2001). Awareness of White privilege among White counseling trainees. *The Counseling Psychologist, 29*, 548–569.
Araújo-Dawson, B. (2009). Discrimination, stress, and acculturation among Dominican immigrant women. *Hispanic Journal of Behavioral Sciences, 31*, 96–111.
Ariel, J., & McPherson, D. W. (2000). Therapy with lesbian and gay parents and their children. *Journal of Marital & Family Therapy, 26*, 421–432.
Aronowitz, S., & Giroux, H. (1993). *Education still under siege* (2nd ed.). Westport, CT: Bergin & Garvey.
Ault-Riche, M. (1986). A feminist critique of five schools of family therapy. In M. Ault-Riche (Ed.), *Women and family therapy* (pp. 1–15). Rockville, MD: Aspen.

Avis, J. M. (1988). Reference guide to feminism and family therapy. *Journal of Feminist Family Therapy, 1,* 93–100.
Bahls, C. (2011). Health policy brief: Achieving equity in health. *Health Affairs Brief,* 1–6. http://www.healthaffairs.org
Bateson, G. (1972). *Steps to an ecology of mind.* New York, NY: Chandler.
Beitin, B., & Allen, K. (2005). A multilevel approach to integrating social justice and family therapy. *Journal of Systemic Therapies, 24,* 19–34.
Caldwell, A., Couture, A., & Nowotny, H. (2010). Closing the mental health gap: Eliminating disparities in treatment for Latinos. www.mattierhodes.org/userfiles/file/samhsa_full_report.pdf
Carlson, T. S., McGeorge, C. R., DeJean, S. D., Grams, W. A., Linde, S., & Michael, R. V. (2006). A feminist conceptual analysis of the predominant introductory textbook in couple and family therapy training. *Journal of Feminist Family Therapy, 17,* 17–39.
Carter, R. T. (1995). *The influence of race and racial identity in psychotherapy: Toward a racially inclusive model.* New York, NY: Wiley.
Chalifoux, B. (1996). Speaking up: White, working class women in therapy. In M. Hill & E. D. Rothblum (Eds.), *Classism and feminist therapy: Counting costs* (pp. 25–34). New York, NY: Harrington Park.
Chizhik, E. W., & Chizhik, A. W. (2002). Decoding the language of social justice: What do "privilege" and "oppression" really mean? *Journal of College Student Development, 43,* 792–807.
Constantine, M. G., & Ladany, N. (2000). Self-report multicultural counseling competence scales: Their relation to social desirability attitudes and multicultural case conceptualization ability. *Journal of Counseling Psychology, 47,* 155–164.
Cuellar, I., Bastida, E., & Braccio, S. M. (2004). Residency in the United States, subjective well-being, and depression in an older Mexican-origin sample. *Journal of Aging and Health, 16,* 447–466.
Cushman, P. (1995). *Constructing the self, constructing America: A cultural history of psychotherapy.* Boston, MA: Addison-Wesley.
D'Andrea, M. (2005). Continuing the cultural liberation and transformation of counseling psychology. *The Counseling Psychologist, 33,* 524–537.
Dillaway, H., & Broman, C. (2001). Race, class, and gender differences in marital satisfaction and divisions of household labor among dual-earner couples: A case for intersectional analysis. *Journal of Family Issues, 22,* 309–327.
Djuric, Z., Bird, C., Furumoto-Dawson, A., Rauscher, G., Ruffin, M., Stowe, R., … Masi, C. (2008). Biomarkers of psychological stress in health disparities research. *Open Biomark Journal, 1,* 7–19.
Faris, R. E., & Dunham, H. W. (1939). *Mental disorders in urban areas: An ecological study of schizophrenia and other psychoses.* Chicago, IL/London, UK: The University of Chicago Press.
Fishman, H. C. (2008). Wither family therapy: The next 50 years. *Context, 3,* 3.
Fouad, N. A., & Arredondo, P. (2007). *Becoming culturally oriented: Practical advice for psychologists and educators.* Washington, DC: American Psychological Association.
Foucault, M. (1980). *The history of sexuality.* New York, NY: Vintage.
Freedman, J., & Combs, G. (1996). *Narrative therapy.* New York, NY: Norton.
Freud, S. (1914). Remembering, repeating, and working through. In L. Strachey (Ed. & Trans.), *The standard edition of the complete psychological works of Sigmund Freud* (Vol. 12, pp. 145–156). London, UK: Hogarth Press.
Fromm, E. (1956). *Sane Society.* Routledge & Kegan Paul.
Furnham, A. (2003). Poverty and wealth. In S. C. Carr & T. S. Sloan (Eds.), *Poverty and psychology* (pp. 163–183). New York, NY: Kluwer Academic/Plenum Press.
Gantt, E. E. (2000). Levinas, psychotherapy, and the ethics of suffering. *Journal of Humanistic Psychology, 40,* 9–28.
Goldner, V. (1985). Feminism and family therapy. *Family Process, 24,* 31–47.

Green, R. J. (1998). Race and the field of family therapy. In M. McGoldrick (Ed.), *Re-visioning family therapy: Race, culture, and gender in clinical practice* (pp. 93–110). New York, NY: The Guilford Press.

Guaniapa, C. (2003). Sharing a multicultural course design for a marriage and family therapy programme: One perspective. *Journal of Family Therapy, 25*, 86–106.

Gushue, G. V. (2004). Race, color-blind racial attitudes, and judgments about mental health: A shifting standards perspective. *Journal of Counseling Psychology, 51*, 398–407.

Hardy, K. V. (1989). The theoretical myth of sameness: A critical issue in family treatment and training. In G. W. Saba, B. M. Karrer, & B. K. V. Hardy (Eds.), *Minorities and family therapy* (pp. 17–33). New York, NY: Haworth.

Hardy, K. V., & Laszloffy, T. A. (2002). The dynamics of a pro-racist ideology: Implications for family therapists. In M. McGoldrick (Ed.), *Re-visioning family therapy: Race, culture, and gender in clinical practice* (pp. 118–128). New York, NY: Guilford Press.

Hardy, K. V., & McGoldrick, M. (2008). Re-visioning training. In M. McGoldrick & K. V. Hardy (Eds.), *Re-visioning family therapy* (2nd ed., pp. 442–460). New York, NY: Guilford Press.

Hare-Mustin, R. (1987). The problem of gender in family therapy theory. *Family Process, 26*, 15–27.

Hare-Mustin, R. (1994). Discourses in the mirrored room: A postmodern analysis of therapy. *Family Process, 33*, 19–35.

Harley, D. A., Jolivette, K., McCormick, K., & Tice, K. (2002). Race, class, and gender: A constellation of positionalities with implications for counseling. *Journal of Multicultural Counseling and Development, 30*, 216–238.

Health and Human Services Office of Minority Health Report. (2012). http://minorityhealth.hhs.gov/

Henry, F., Totor, C., Mattis, W., & Rees, T. (2000). *The color of democracy: Racism in Canadian society* (2nd ed.). Toronto, Canada: Harcourt Brace & Company.

Hoffman, L. (2002). *Family therapy: An intimate history*. New York, NY: Norton.

Hollingshead, A. B., & Redlich, F.,. C. (1958). *Social class and mental illness: A community study*. New York, NY: John Wiley & Sons.

Imber-Black, E. (1990). Multiple embedded systems. In M. P. Mirkin (Ed.), *The social and political contexts of family therapy* (pp. 3–18). Boston, MA: Allyn B. Bacon.

Inman, A. G., Meza, M. M., Brown, A. L., & Hargrove, B. K. (2004). Student-faculty perceptions of multicultural training in accredited marriage and family therapy programs in relation to students' self-reported competence. *Journal of Marital Family Therapy, 30*, 373–388.

Javier, R. A., & Herron, W. G. (2002). Psychoanalysis and the disenfranchised: Countertransference issues. *Psychoanalytic Psychology, 19*, 149–166.

Jones, E. (1974). Social class and psychotherapy: A critical review of research. *Psychiatry, 37*, 307–320.

Johnson, A. G. (2006). Privilege, power, and difference (2nd ed). New York: McGraw Hill.

Kaholokula, J., Iwane, M., & Nacapoy, A. (2010). Effects of perceived racism and acculturation on hypertension in native Hawaiians. *Hawaii Medical Journal, 69*, 11–15.

Kearney, L. K., Draper, M., & Baron, A. (2005). Counseling utilization by ethnic minority college students. *Cultural Diversity and Ethnic Minority Psychology, 11*, 272–285.

Keeney, B. (1982). *Aesthetics of change*. New York, NY: Guilford.

Killian, K. D., & Hardy, K. V. (1998). Commitment to minority inclusion: A study of AAMFT conference program content and members' perceptions. *Journal of Marital & Family Therapy, 24*, 207–223.

Kim, S., & Cardemil, E. (2012). Effective psychotherapy with low-income clients: The importance of attending to social class. *Journal of Contemporary Psychotherapy, 42*, 27–35.

Knudson-Martin, C., & Huenergardt, D. (2010). A socio-emotional approach to couple therapy: Linking social context and couple interaction. *Family Process, 49*, 369–384.

Kosutic, I., & McDowell, T. (2008). Diversity and social justice in family therapy literature: A decade review. *Journal of Feminist Family Therapy, 20*, 142–165.

Laird, J. (2000). Gender in lesbian relationships: Cultural, feminist, and constructionist reflections. *Journal of Marital & Family Therapy, 26*, 455–467.

Le, H., Zmuda, J., Perry, D., & Munoz, R. F. (2010). Transforming an evidence-based intervention to ~ prevent perinatal depression. *American Journal of Orthopsychiatry, 80*, 34–45.

Lee, C., Ayers, S., & Kronenfeld, J. (2009). The association between perceived provider discrimination, health care utilization, and health status in racial and ethnic minorities. *Ethnicity & Disease, 19*, 330–337.

Lehavot, K., & Simoni, J. (2011). The impact of minority stress on mental health and substance abuse among sexual minority women. *Journal of Consulting& Clinical Psychology, 79*, 159–170.

Levinas, L. (1969). *Totality and infinity*. Pittsburg, PA: Duquesne University Press.

Lorion, R. P. (1974). Patient and therapist variables in the treatment of low-income patients. *Psychological Bulletin, 81*, 344–354.

Marin, G. (1993). Influence of acculturation on familialism and self-identification among Hispanics. In M. E. Bernal & G. P. Knight (Eds.), *Ethnic identity: Formation and transmission among Hispanics and other minorities* (pp. 181–196). Albany, NY: State University of New York Press.

Martín-Baró, I. (1985). La encuesta de opinión pública como instrumento desideologizador. Cuadernos dePsicología (Universidad del Valle, Colombia), VII, 93–108.

Martin-Baro, I. (1994). *Writings for a liberation psychology*. Cambridge, MA: Harvard University Press.

McCabe, S., Bostwick, W., Hughes, T., West, B., & Boyd, C. (2010). The relationship between discrimination and substance use disorders among lesbian, gay, and bisexual adults in the United States. *American Journal of Public Health, 100*, 1946–1952.

McDowell, T. (2005). Practicing with a critical multicultural lens. Introduction to a special section. *Journal of Systemic Therapies, 24*, 1–4.

McDowell, T. (2015). *Applying critical social theories to family therapy practices*. AFTA spring briefs in family therapy. New York, NY: Springer International Publishing.

McDowell, T., Fang, S.-R., Young, C. G., Khanna, A., Sherman, B., & Brownlee, K. (2003). Making space for racial dialogue: Our experience in a marriage and family therapy training program. *Journal of Marital and Family Therapy, 29*, 179–194.

McDowell, T., & Jeris, L. (2004). Talking about race using critical race theory: Recent trends in the journal of marital and family therapy. *Journal of Marital and Family Therapy, 30*, 81–93.

McDowell, T., & Shelton, D. (2002). Valuing ideas of social justice in MFT curricula. *Contemporary Family Therapy. An International Journal, 24*, 313–331.

McGeorge, C., Carlson, T., Erickson, M., & Guttormson, H. (2006). Creating and evaluating a feminist informed social justice couple and family therapy training model. *Journal of Feminist Family Therapy, 18*, 1–38.

McGeorge, C. R., & Carlson, T. S. (2010). Social justice mentoring: Preparing family therapists for social justice advocacy work. *Michigan Family Review, 14*, 42–59.

McGoldrick, M. (1998). Belonging and liberation: Finding a place called "home". In M. McGoldrick (Ed.), *Re-visioning family therapy: Race, culture and gender in clinical practice* (pp. 215–228). New York, NY: Guilford.

McGoldrick, M., Almeida, R., Preto, N. G., Bibb, A., Sutton, C., Hudak, J., & Hines, P. M. (1999). Efforts to incorporate social justice perspectives into a family training program. *Journal of Marital & Family Therapy, 25*, 191–209.

McIntosh, P. (1998). White privilege, color and crime: A personal account. In C. Richey Mann & S. Zatz (Eds.), *Images of color, images of crime* (pp. 207–216). Los Angeles, CA: Roxbury Publishing Company.

Mindrup, R. M., Spray, B. J., & Lamberghini-West, A. (2011). White privilege and multicultural counseling competence: The influence of field of study, sex, and racial/ethnic exposure. *Journal of Ethnic and Cultural Diversity in Social Work, 20*, 20–38.

Miranda, J., Bernal, G., Lau, A., Kohn, L., Hwang, W., & LaFramboise, T. (2005). State of the science on psychosocial interventions for ethnic minorities. *Annual Review of Clinical Psychology, 1*, 113–142.

Mishel, L., Gould, E., & Bivens, J. (2015). Wage Stagnation in Nine Charts. Economy Policy Report. http://www.epi.org/publication/charting-wage-stagnation/

Moreira, V. (2003). Poverty and psychopathology. In S. C. Carr & T. S. Sloan (Eds.), *Poverty and psychology* (pp. 69–86). New York, NY: Kluwer Academic/Plenum Press.

Nichols, M. P., & Schwartz, R. C. (2008). *Family therapy: Concepts and methods* (7th ed.). Boston, MA: Pearson.

Ortiz, L., & Jani, J. (2010). Critical race theory: A transformational model for teaching diversity. *Journal of Social Work Education, 46*, 175–193.

Peek, M., Wagner, J., Tang, H., & Baker, D. (2011). Self-reported racial discrimination in health care and diabetes outcomes. *Medical Care, 49*, 618–625.

Phillips, A. (2007). *Multiculturalism without culture*. Princeton, NJ: Princeton University Press.

Pole, N., Gone, J. P., & Kulkarni, M. (2008). Posttraumatic stress disorder among ethnoracial minorities in the United States. *Clinical Psychology. Science & Practice, 15*, 35–61.

Prilleltensky, I. (1994). *The morals and politics of psychology: Psychological discourse and the status quo*. Albany, New York, NY: State University of New York Press.

Prilleltensky, I. (1997). Values, assumptions, and practices: Assessing the moral implications of psychological discourse and action. *American Psychologist, 52*, 517–535.

Proctor, B. D., Semega, J. L., & Kollar, M. A. (2016). Income and Poverty in the United States: 2015 (U.S. Census Bureau Publication P60-256). http://www.census.gov/content/dam/Census/library/publications/2016/demo/p60-256.pdf

Read, J., Goodman, L., Morrison, A., Ross, C., & Aderhold, V. (2004). Childhood trauma, loss and stress. In J. Read, L. R. Mosher, & R. Bentall (Eds.), *Models of madness: Psychological, social and biological approaches to schizophrenia* (pp. 223–252). Hove, UK: Brunner-Routledge.

Saba, G. W., Karrer, B. M., & Hardy, K. V. (1989). Introduction. In G. W. Saba, B. M. Karrer, & K. V. Hardy (Eds.), *Minorities and family therapy*. New York, NY: Haworth.

Saez, E. (2015). Sticking it richer. The evolution of top incomes in the United States. https://eml.berkeley.edu/~saez/saez-UStopincomes-2015.pdf

Saris, R. N., & Johnston-Robledo, I. (2000). Poor women are still shut out of mainstream psychology. *Psychology of Women Quarterly, 24*, 233–235.

Sartre, J. P. (1956). *Being and nothingness*. New York, NY: Pocket Books.

Schulman, K. A., Berlin, J. A., Harless, W., Kerner, J. F., Sistrunk, S., Gersh, B. J., Dubé, R., Taleghani, C. K., Burke, J. E., Williams, S., Eisenberg, J. M., & Escarce, J. J. (1999). The effect of race and sex on physicians' recommendations for cardiac catheterization. *New England Journal of Medicine, 340*, 618–626.

Seedall, R. B., Holtrop, K., & Parra-Cardona, J. R. (2014). Diversity, social justice, and intersectionality trends in C/MFT: A content analysis of three family therapy journals, 2004–2011. *Journal of Marriage and Family Therapy, 40*, 139–151.

Segura, Y. L., Page, M. C., Neighbors, B. D., Nichols-Anderson, C., & Gillaspy, S. (2003). The importance of peersin alcohol use among Latino adolescents: The role of alcohol expectancies and acculturation. *Journal of Ethnicityin Substance Abuse, 2*, 31–49.

Smith, R. (2005). *Values and practice in children's services*. Basingstoke, UK: Palgrave Macmillan.

Smith, R., & Khawaja, N. (2011). A review of the acculturation experiences of international students. *International Journal of Intercultural Relations, 35*, 699–713.

Srole, L., Langner, T. S., Michael, S. T., Kirkpatrick, P., Opler, M., & Rennie, T. A. C. (1977). *Mental health in the metropolis: The Midtown Manhattan Study*. New York, NY: Harper & Row.

Sue, D. W., & Sue, D. (2008). Counseling the culturally different: Theory and practice (5th ed.). Hoboken, NJ: JohnWiley.

Sue, D. W., & Sue, D. (2013). *Counseling the culturally diverse: Theory and practice* (6th ed.). Hoboken, NJ: John Wiley & Sons.

Sue, S., & Lam, A. G. (2002). Cultural and demographic diversity. In J. C. Norcross (Ed.), *Psychotherapy relationships that work: Therapist contributions and responsiveness to patients* (pp. 401–422). New York, NY: Oxford University Press.

Sue, S., Zane, N., Hall, G. C. N., & Berger, L. K. (2009). The case for cultural competency in psychotherapeutic interventions. *Annual Review of Psychology, 60*, 525–548.

Taylor, C. (2011). *Dilemmas and connections: Selected essays*. Cambridge, MA: Belknap Press.

Tillman, K., & Weiss, U. (2009). Nativity status and depressive symptoms among Hispanic young adults: The role of stress exposure. *Social Science Quarterly, 90*, 1228–1250.

Todd, T., & Holden. (2012). AAMFT's all members survey. Family Therapy Magazine, September/October. (pp. 10–60).

Vodde, R., & Gallant, J. P. (2002). Bridging the gap between micro and macro practice: Large scale change and a unified model of narrative-deconstructive practice. *Journal of Social Work Education, 38*, 439–458.

Waldegrave, C. (2009). Cultural, gender and socioeconomic contexts in therapeutic social policy work. *Family Process, 48*, 85–101.

Waldegrave, C., & Tamasese, K. (1994). Some central ideas in the "just therapy" approach. *Family Journal, 2*, 94–103.

Whaley, A. L. (2001). Cultural mistrust and mental health services for African Americans: A review and meta-analysis. *The Counseling Psychologist, 29*, 513–531.

Williams, D., & Neighbors, H. (2001). Racism, discrimination, and hypertension: Evidence and needed research. *Ethnicity & Disease, 11*, 800–816.

Wolff, E. N. (2012). *The asset price meltdown and the wealth of the middle class*. New York, NY: New York University.

Žižek, S. (2008). *Violence: Six sideways reflections*. London, UK: Profile Books.

Zrenchik, K., & McDowell, T. (2012). Class and classism in family therapy praxis: A feminist, neo-marxist approach. *Journal of Feminist Family Therapy, 24*, 101–120.

# Before Cultural Competence

## A Therapy Session on Exploring the Latent and Overt Emotionalities of Whiteness

Cheryl E. Matias

### So Why Am I Here?

Counseling and therapy are about "a purposeful private conversation" between two people: one who is to "reflect on and resolve a problem" and another who is to "assist in that endeavor" (McLeod, 2007, p. 7.). In this intimate relationship, there are unspoken considerations between the client and the counselor or therapist: trust, understanding, and emotional investment. Yet rarely are those unspoken qualities self-interrogated. Indeed, it is commonplace for one to acknowledge that trust, understanding, and emotional investment are essential and must be readily available when engaging in effective therapy. What is not so clearly understood is how does privilege, specifically white privilege, influence how one defines, applies, and enacts notions of trust, understanding, and emotional investment? Simply, just as culture impacts how we display love for one another, privilege can also impact how we define, enact, and develop trust with one another. In a field, whereby a majority of therapists are white, the question becomes *how do therapists—especially those who are white—understand their own emotionality of whiteness embedded within their white privilege to fully develop trust, understanding, and emotionally invest in their clients of Color,*[1] *especially when those clients are bereft with racial traumas?* Essentially, what must therapists do before cultural competence?

This chapter draws upon the theorizations of the emotionalities of whiteness in teacher education (see Matias, 2016a) to illuminate how such a theory can also apply to the field of therapy. I do so not to demonize particular therapists within the field nor do I intend to derail all the work around cultural competency done thus far.

---

[1] In this chapter I recognize how language has been used to dehumanize People of Color while humanizing whites. As such, I capitalize People of Color or of Color.

C. E. Matias (✉)
University of Colorado Denver, Denver, CO, USA
e-mail: Cheryl.matias@ucdenver.edu

Instead, I theorize emotionalities of whiteness to exemplify how teacher education *and* therapy alike have similar hopes of diversity, inclusion, and effectiveness, but may, perhaps, fall short in that endeavor when the emotionalities of whiteness are not considered. Employing a similar application of psychoanalytic analyses on race such as Cheng (2001) or Fanon (1967), this chapter theoretically explores the emotional dimensions of whiteness and suggests that if such emotionalities are left intact, they, in the end, still pervert even the most trained individual in cultural competency. Suffice it to say, the amount of culturally competent training will not reduce racial biases if latent or overt emotionalities of whiteness remain unrecognized. Therefore, in order to dig straight into the deep emotionalities that first silenced multiculturalism, the therapists must first entertain the existing hegemonic emotional condition that perched itself atop other emotions and, in doing so, overlooked the necessity of culturally competent therapy in the first place.

## Where Am I Coming from?

There are many theories that help shape how I understand racial dynamics; however, for this particular chapter, I predominantly draw from philosophy of race, psychoanalysis of race, and critical whiteness studies (CWS).

First, philosophy of race offers a phenomenological approach to race whereby it acknowledges the racial interpellations between and of each racialized individual. In a field like therapy or counseling where it is necessary to have self-awareness in order to both understand the other and to develop trust with the other; the inclusion of phenomenology then becomes essential. Moustakas (1994) asserts, for instance, the following:

> Ultimately both person and social knowledge are needed to arrive at valid understandings of reality, but I must first be attuned to my own being, thinking, and choosing before I can relate to others' thoughts, understandings, and choices. I must arrive at my own sense of the nature and meaning of something, make my own decisions regarding its truth and value before I consider the point of view of others (p. 62).

Since understanding oneself is necessary to understand the other, then white culturally competent therapists must first understand their own white existence before they can empathize with the racialized identities of their clients of Color. Simply put, this is similar to Helms' (1990) demand that folks "who intend to lead others into the jungle of racial conflict, will first have to take the journey herself or himself" (p. 219).

Second, psychoanalysis of race also informs my understanding of race precisely because, as Cheng (2001) suggests that

> ...psychoanalysis could illuminate the race question: not insofar as it elucidates private desires and psychology, but because psychoanalysis understand those private desires to be enmeshed in social relations (p. 27).

Just as something as innate as desires can be enmeshed in social relations, so too can one's beliefs on trust, understanding, and emotional investment. Therefore, if therapists/counselors aspire to be culturally competent, then a thorough investigation on their own understandings must be had; lest they be at the mercy of imposing one's own perspective, experience, and identity upon another.

Finally, CWS is a transdisciplinary field that steers away from oft-used quandaries about race like "How does it feel to be a person of color" and moves toward an inquiry of "What does it mean to be White in U.S. society" (Leonardo, 2013, p. 83). And, since "whiteness is everywhere in the U.S. culture, but it is very hard to see" (Lipstiz, 2006, p. 1), it becomes ever more pressing to unveil how whiteness might embed itself even within a discourse of cultural competence and our very emotions.

## How Do I Go About Telling You About This Problem?

Critical race theory (CRT) "challenges the ways which race and racial power are constructed and represented in American legal culture and in, more generally, American society as a whole" (Crenshaw, 1995, p. XIII). Of recent, CRT has moved into other fields like education (see Taylor, Gillborn, & Ladson-Billings, 2009) in the hopes of "illuminating our thinking about school inequity" (Ladson-Billings, 2009. p. 33). In the same vein, the application of CRT to the field of counseling can provide more equitable practices, especially for clients of Color. Although I do not draw too heavily on CRT in analyzing the emotionalities of whiteness in therapy, I do however employ CRT methodological application of *counterstorytelling* to illustrate my theoretical postulations.

To clarify, counterstorytelling is one particular method within CRT that is "aimed at coming to a better understanding of the role of race and racism in American life" (Love, 2004, p. 228). It draws upon the tradition of storytelling to unveil how normative rhetoric, discourses, and epistemologies are laden with majoritarian stories (Solórzano & Yosso, 2002) and, thus, is in need of stories that counter that dominating perspective. Fortuitous is this method because in its application to unveil how the emotionalities of whiteness impact the hope for culturally competent counseling, one can begin to see how the rhetoric of cultural competency can also, inadvertently, embed the hegemony of whiteness. Below I begin with explicating terminologies and concepts used throughout the chapter so that a common lingua franca is employed.

## What Words Will I Use to Tell You My Issue?

Common parlance of race often relates to People of Color (PoC), their racial experiences, and enactments of racism. This is seen when folks try to describe their experiences with race and often are limited to expressions like "that's racist." In this chapter I metaphorically flip the racial coin by using terminologies specific to whiteness. I do so to redirect our understanding of race from the oppressive nature of racism on PoC and toward an understanding of how whiteness, when enacted, contributes—whether directly or indirectly—to that oppressive nature. This is not to say that one does not need a thorough understanding of how *racial microaggressions* (Sue et al., 2007), *racial battle fatigue* (Smith, Allen, & Danley, 2007), or *stereotype threat* (Steele & Aronson, 1995) impact PoC. Alas, failing to recognize the gravity of racial trauma of PoC is, in and of itself, counterintuitive to the purpose of therapy. With that said if I, as a racially just educator, am to be fierce enough to stop such trauma, then my speech must directly speak to that which perpetrates the trauma. This is analogous to making sure the psychology of the abused is understood alongside with the psychology of the abuser. For if I, as an intervener, am truly committed to stopping the abuse, I need not focus too narrowly on the abused. Indeed, I need to also investigate the abuser by using specific terminologies and concepts that best capture their psychosocial condition. Since racial trauma *is* trauma because it "confront[s] human beings with the extremities of helplessness and terror" (Herman, 1997, p. 33), there must be language to explicate the perpetration of such terror. Below is a list of terminologies I employ to explicate the extent that emotionality of whiteness impacts the development of trust, understanding, and emotional investment needed to "resolve" the racial traumas of clients of Color.

## Whiteness

"If Blackness is a social construction that embraces Black culture, language, experiences, identities, and epistemologies, then whiteness is a social construction that embraces white culture, ideology, racialization, expressions, and experiences, epistemology, emotions, and behaviors. Unlike Blackness, whiteness is normalized because white supremacy elevates whites and whiteness to the apex of the racial hierarchy" (Matias, Viesca, Garrison-Wade, Tandon, & Galindo, 2014, p. 290). Whiteness is hegemonic and need not be consciously enacted. Additionally, whiteness can also inhabit the mindsets of behaviors of PoC, albeit through a different mechanism of survival and codependence (see Fanon, 1967).

## White Privilege

A set of unearned assets provided to those who are racially identified as white under a white supremacist society at the expense of People of Color (i.e., higher real estate equity due to redlining and racial covenants, familial wealth due to profiteering off the historical labor of slaves, employment advantages due to racial discrimination in the workplace).

## White Supremacy

A state and, more accurately, globally sanctioned existence whereby those who are racially deemed white are given material, legal, emotional, ideological, epistemological, historical, political, and educational benefits at the expense of People of Color.

According to Allen and Howard (2012), white supremacy "functions hegemonically, meaning it requires some degree of complicity from those whom it oppresses in order to exist" regardless to whether or not a person intends to or actively, consciously, and/or directly supports white supremacist agendas. Therefore, when I use the term, I do not refer only to commonplace notions of white supremacists like Neo-Nazis, Klu Kux Klan, or any other coded white supremacist groups like the Alt-right. Instead, I refer to US society that was built off the backs of Native American stolen land and genocide, African-American slave labor, and centuries of discriminatory laws and practices that as systematically denied People of Color equal access to the "American Dream" that white immigrants were afforded.

## Whites

Refers to a group of people who are racially deemed white only by whites themselves. Though there are white individuals who experience varying degrees of racialization, they are all, nonetheless, given systematic white privilege in a white supremacist society. For example, whites who are not fearing police because, whether they want to admit it or not, know that most police brutalities occur against Black and Brown individuals and not against them. Having the racial demarcation of "white" is noteworthy for many reasons. First, court cases such as United States v. Bhagat Singh Thind (261 US 204) or Takao Ozawa v. United States (260 US 178) clearly demonstrate that People of Color, regardless to the ever-changing definition of what constitutes white, will never be deemed white. Second, this demarcation is paramount in a white supremacist nation state because those who are legally "white" are afforded privileges, rights, legality, citizenship, and access over those who are not (see Treaty of Guadalupe, anti-miscegenation laws, Jim Crow, FHA housing act, 1940 G.I. Bill, etc.). Third, since those privileges have been accrued by whites for so long, generations of whites thereafter barely recognize (or refuse to recognize) the material benefits their families once received from being deemed white. Hence, whites then rely heavily on Horatio Alger stories of American individualism, hard work, and/or "pull up your own bootstraps" rationales to provide an alternative explanation of their material accumulation.

## Emotionalities of Whiteness

These are feelings that are routinely expressed or felt by whites when they engage in the following:

1. Interracial race talk.
2. Experience, witness, or listen to racial trauma of People of Color.
3. Learn about whiteness, white supremacy, and white privilege.

Some of these emotional sentiments include guilt, sadness, shame, denial, anger, silence, shock, defensiveness, or "sentimentalized emotions[2]" (see Matias & Zembylas, 2014). Because they are so routinely expressed, it becomes a pattern of behaviors that are *not* strictly innate (or without social influence) for the individual. Instead, these emotions are socially reproduced; hence racialized emotions. These racialized emotions stem from similar racialized experiences as white bodies within a white supremacist society. Since whiteness is hegemonic and white supremacy upholds that hegemony, white emotionalities are purported above the emotionalities of People of Color. Read another way, PoC's emotions regarding their racial traumas become only three fifths of a white person's emotions regarding their discomfort with race because whiteness elevates the interests of whites above PoC. As such, white emotionalities become a strategic mechanism employed to silence the realities People of Color experience with race. This will be discussed more below.

The aforementioned vocabulary contains a few concepts and terminologies that best explicate how whiteness may impact the hopes of culturally competent therapy. Despite each term's rigid definition, they must also be understood with fluid connectivity. Metaphorically speaking, how does one fully grasp the concept of a valley without juxtaposing it to the concept of mountains? Therefore, conceptualizing each terminology in isolation denies the necessary understanding one needs in order to understand the larger racial picture. Below I include a chart from Chap. 12 of *Feeling White: Emotionality, Whiteness, and Education* (Matias, 2016a) that best captures how each concept are intimately intertwined with one another.

**Operations of Power in Institutionalized White Supremacy** *not an exhaustive list*

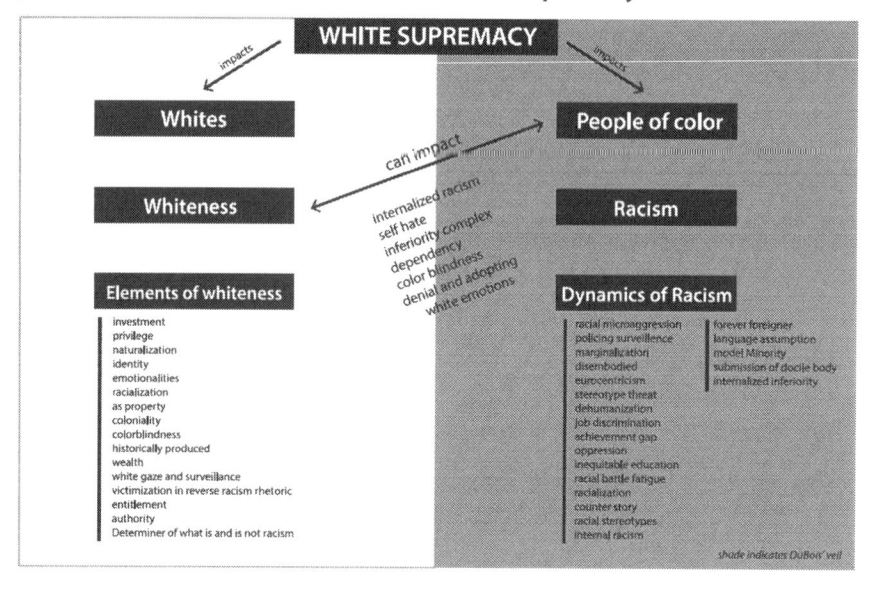

| Whites | | People of color |
|---|---|---|
| Whiteness | internalized racism / self hate / inferiority complex / dependency / color blindness / denial and adopting white emotions | Racism |
| **Elements of whiteness** | | **Dynamics of Racism** |
| investment | | racial microaggression |
| privilege | | policing surveillance |
| naturalization | | marginalization |
| identity | | disembodied |
| emotionalities | | eurocentricism |
| racialization | | stereotype threat |
| as property | | dehumanization |
| coloniality | | job discrimination |
| colorblindness | | achievement gap |
| historically produced | | oppression |
| wealth | | inequitable education |
| white gaze and surveillance | | racial battle fatigue |
| victimization in reverse racism rhetoric | | racialization |
| entitlement | | counter story |
| authority | | racial stereotypes |
| Determiner of what is and is not racism | | internal racism |
| | | forever foreigner |
| | | language assumption |
| | | model Minority |
| | | submission of docile body |
| | | internalized inferiority |

*shade indicates DuBois' veil*

---

[2] Emotions that are expressed in one way but are felt in another. For example, publicly expressing pity for African-Americans but deeply feeling disgust for them.

## So Here's What I Have to Say About Whiteness and Therapy. Will You Listen?

The increasing diversity in the United States has led to several complications between mental health providers and diverse clients. Because almost 84%[3] of psychology workforce are white and are unfamiliar with cultural and linguistic nuances of People of Color, there exist, as Sue (1998) suggests, "cultural and linguistic mismatches that occur between clients and providers" (p. 441). Counseling, much like therapy, has now responded with a marked need for cultural competence. Cultural competence, according to Sue (1998), "is the belief that people should not only appreciate and recognize cultural groups but also to be able to effectively work with them" (p. 440). Yet, in this increased demand for multiculturalism (Sue, 2001), counseling programs overlooked the underlying issue as to why they have not considered multicultural or culturally competent counseling in the first place. Perhaps, for argument's sake, since the majority of counselors, therapists, and psychologists are racially white, the hegemonic dominance of whiteness is left intact thus rendering counseling at the mercy of white privilege (Ancis & Szymanski, 2001). Furthermore, since, as Wildman and Davis (2008) suggest, white privilege "is not visible to its holder," those white therapists may not be able to see how their own practices, communiqué, and commonplace understandings are embedded within their own racial privilege (p. 114). Stated another way, how can one begin to acknowledge a different racial reality if the white lens that is commonly used to perceive reality filters out racial reality? Therefore, a thorough understanding of white privilege and hegemonic whiteness in a field dominated by white therapists is essential in order to effectively support clients of Color, especially when clients of Color are experiencing traumatic racial microaggressions (Nadal, Griffin, Wong, Hamit, & Rasmus, 2014).

However, I digress a bit to address another misconception that periodically arises when explaining how hegemonic whiteness works to silence racial realities of People of Color. Often when engaging in discussion on the dynamics of whiteness, such as the oft-employed excuse of colorblindness, laypeople will erroneously equate whiteness to white people. To be clear, such terms are not synonymous to me, nor are they to many other race scholars. Whiteness, for clarity's sake, can also inhabit the mindsets and behaviors of PoC, albeit through a different operating process than whites. Whereas whites bask in their said "epistemological ignorance of race" (Mills, 2007) in order to turn a blind eye to racial benefits and privilege that were afforded to them, PoC who subscribe to whiteness do so in the hopes that they too can earn privileges and benefits in becoming honorary whites (see Bonilla-Silva, 2003), a misguided survival mechanism that will produce an inferiority-dependent complex (see Fanon, 1967). To better understand this phenomenon, I draw from Black feminist scholar Patricia Hill Collins' critique on the white feminist movement. Namely, Collins (1986) claims white women are seen as obedient dogs, whereas

---

[3] See http://www.apa.org/workforce/publications/13-demographics/index.aspx.

Black women are considered obstinate mules in the face of white patriarchy. Yet what must be considered is beyond favoritism of a dog over a mule or, for that matter, a house slave over a field slave, the dynamics is such that regardless of who is favored or receives honorary status, they are nonetheless still oppressed under white supremacy and white supremacist patriarchy (see bell hooks, 1994). In observing that whiteness can inhabit both white therapists and therapists of Color, it then becomes necessary to address whiteness itself.

In order to see past the ocular of whiteness, which is necessary to debunk racial biases, there must be a thorough investigation of whiteness (see Case, 2007). Aspects of whiteness such as colorblind racism (Bonilla-Silva, 2006), possessive investment of identity politics (Lipsitz, 1998), and white privilege (McIntosh, 2001) have been explored; however, what has not been investigated are the latent and overt emotionalities of whiteness, many of which sustain a white supremacist ideology (Matias, 2016a). Take, for instance, how some white Americans felt (and still feel) prejudice against People of Color simply because they felt PoCs were not as pure as whites. Although thought of as mere prejudicial feelings, this widespread feeling undergirded the swift adoption of anti-miscegenation laws. As such, the emotionalities of whiteness have dangerous implications if left intact and unchecked. And, these are the very dangerous emotional conditions that predate the current emotional cry for cultural competence. Notwithstanding such danger, below I explore some elements within the emotionalities of whiteness that pertain to counseling and therapy.

Most curious, yet simultaneously telling, to race scholars is how routinely these emotionalities of whiteness are expressed among whites writ large and how rarely expressers self-acknowledge them. If "therapy 101" recommends that in order to heal one must first recognize the trauma, then understanding how rarely emotionalities of whiteness are self-acknowledged becomes suspect. Given that whites rarely identify white emotionalities and, that therapists are predominantly white, one needs to question the aptitude of white therapists who intend to serve clients of Color.

Take, for instance, the field of US teacher education whereby 86% of teachers are white (NCES, 2012) and a majority of K-12 students are of Color, thus necessitating culturally responsive pedagogy (Villegas & Lucas, 2002). However, understanding culturally responsive pedagogy is remiss if considerations of race and whiteness are not present (see Matias, 2013). When simply teaching about race, particularly, whiteness, white teacher candidates (and anyone who is indoctrinated with whiteness ideology) internalized the content and develop feelings of defensiveness. Common emotional outbursts include tears, fist poundings, or statements like "I never owned slaves" or "Stop making me feel guilty!" Although the internalization is, in and of itself, quite interesting because these white teacher candidates suppress their connectivity to the content but express the opposite, what is even more interesting to note is people who routinely express defensiveness are the same individuals who adamantly profess they do not see race. In fact, some go as far as to overly pontificate their friendships with or support of People of Color (Matias, 2016b). The quandary left unanswered is if one truly does not see race or self-proclaims to be a "white ally," then why is s/he having such a deep emotional reaction to merely studying about it?

Thandeka (1999) offers one psychoanalytic analysis of white childhood that provides a possible explanation for these emotional outbursts. Whites, since childhood, have been racialized to be whites by their white parents and white communities through an unhealthy white kinship. This racialization, as Thandeka suggests, begins when white children bear witness to race, racial incidents, and racial hypocrisies but are denied that racial reality when white parents shush their children's observations of race. Essentially, this shushing makes the white child learn "to silence and then deny its own resonant feelings toward racially proscribed others" which in the long run forces the child to develop "an antipathy towards its own forbidden feelings *and* to the persons who are the objects of these forbidden desires: the racial other" (p. 24). The white child conforms to this hypocrisy of bearing-witness-to-race-but-not-admitting-to-it simply "to remain within the community" (p. 24), lest be ostracized from the community and be labeled, as Ignatiev and Garvey (1996) suggest, a race traitor.

As the white child grows into a white adult, this deeply buried racial experience must be emotionally safeguarded. Thandeka (1999) argues "white shame functions as a psychological guard…whose sole duty is to keep the emotions of the resident of this realm in check" (p. 27). This shame results in part because white adult knows they are, in fact, "someone who is living a [white] lie" (p. 34) each time they pretend to not see race. Thandeka's analysis provides a formidable understanding as to why whites, though claiming to never see race, may feel shame when it comes to race. Or, stated another way, it explains as to why the white teacher candidates may internalize the content of race and whiteness while denying race has any relevance.

Needless to say, white racialization into the world of whiteness *is* a racial trauma, yet I would be remiss to equate that trauma to the racial traumas of People of Color. Let me further illuminate this point by using gender instead of race. Although men and women both experience genderization under a system of patriarchy, they experience it at opposite ends; one experiences male privilege and the other experiences sexism, rape culture, or gender stereotypes. Therefore, claiming that "the reality is that men are hurting" under patriarchy because they are forced to deny their feelings is *not* the same as women who are hurting due to sexualization, sexism, rape culture, or gender stereotypes (Hooks, 2004, p. 6).

The notion that whites, too, *are* traumatized by race and that such traumatization is *not* equitable to the traumas felt by People of Color, leaves us at a contentious point of departure. If a therapist is too consumed by shame to acknowledge their own racialization into whiteness, how then are they to empathize or acknowledge the gravity of racial trauma for their diverse clientele? Otherwise, if therapists are too shamed to acknowledge their own emotionalities of whiteness, then how might that impact their ability to develop trust and understanding and emotionally invest in clients who may have experienced racial trauma from the same kinds of people? On the flipside, how then are diverse clientele to trust their therapists with experiences with racism if their therapists may, perhaps, refuse to understand their own racialization processes?

To illustrate how the emotionality of whiteness can impact the relationship between diverse individuals desperately seeking support from white individuals inside a predominantly white space, I offer two counterstories stemming from my own experiences as one of the few female faculty of color inside a predominately white school of education. In fact, I was the first ever tenure-line faculty of color hired specifically and solely for an urban community teacher education program that was committed to cultural responsivity, urban education, and social justice.[4] Need I remind my readers that I do not relay these counterstories to demonize particular individuals; rather, in sharing my counterstories, I illustrate the necessity of recognizing the impacts of emotionality of whiteness, especially for those folks who believe they are aiding, supporting, or allying with diverse peoples. Below are counterstories of my attempts to bring racially just education to teacher education; yet, in those attempts I was bombarded with intoxicating white emotionalities of guilt, defensiveness, shame, anger, and sadness, so much so that I no longer attempt in that space.

## Counterstory #1

During my first 2 years as a professor at the university, I experienced extreme "whitelash."[5] For example, in one of my yearlong teacher education seminars, I was the only person of color in the classroom. Since the program was committed to social justice, I took 45 min of one class session of one semester to discuss critical race theory and how it might support antiracist teaching practices. After that yearlong course, I haphazardly found out four white female teacher candidates took initiative to circulate a petition in an attempt to get me fired, claiming, I "focus too much on race." On my student evaluations I had feedback like "who does she think she is," "I don't care if she has a PhD," and "never in my life have I seen students treat a professor so badly."

In another instance, my doctoral student (a Latino male) was teaching my teacher education foundation course that was predominately with white female teacher candidates. After the class read one of my articles, he asked me to guest lecture to further explain the article. During this lecture, there was a white female teacher candidate, who later revealed in her class survey that she was 19, never took a class on race, and rarely had relationships with People of Color. While explaining my article that was published in the premier internationally recognized journal on race, ethnicity, and education, she interrupted me and shouted in front of the entire lecture hall, "I mean, after reading this, I was like who the fuck does this bitch think she is?!" Clearly, emotionalities of whiteness are embedded in so much racial entitlement that it feels no obligation to even *check yo'self* (see Matias, 2013).

---

[4]To be transparent I admit that the program no longer exists and that my tenure line has now been moved into a non-degree granting servicing program with no program budget.
[5]See http://www.thefreedictionary.com/whitelash.

These are just some of my experiences with how the emotionalities of whiteness racially traumatized me. In fact, the trauma deepened because when I sought support from my white colleagues (all except one), their responses were either of the following:

1. Remain emotionally frozen—as if a deer in headlights (see Matias, 2016c)—and change the topic quickly
2. Minimize the racializing aspect of the situation by claiming all students are entitled nowadays to all professors—similar to #alllivematters versus #Blacklivesmatter minimizing maneuvers.

Therefore, in recognizing how emotionalities of whiteness provide the context for which racial traumas happen to People of Color, one can then understand my fear when I was instructed to deliver a talk about my research to dozens of white classroom teachers and principals. Based on patterns within the emotionalities of whiteness, I knew emotional outbursts would occur in order to silence, belittle, and/or threaten me as they have done in the past. In fact, this maneuver is more popularly recognized as emotional abuse whereby the perpetrator purposefully uses acts that intimidate, infantilize, or humiliate in order to belittle the dignity, respect, identity, and humanity of another person.

However, in order to stay committed to developing trust and understanding with my white colleagues, I knew I had to communicate this fear to them. Essentially, my attempt to open up to my colleagues of that which I fear most was a cry, so to speak, to solicit support and understanding from those who self-identify as white allies—allies who are supposed to support People of Color. In identifying as such, I, as a person of Color, should be able to trust them with issues of race. However, instead of listening to me, several of my white colleagues emotionally reacted with whiteness. That is, instead of listening to my fear and understanding where they come from (literally instead of being an ally), they selfishly (as the emotionalities of whiteness often are) fixated on their own feelings of guilt of being white and because they too were intimidated by my research on race.

Several times, a few of them felt defensive and shouted condescending questions like "What are *you* so afraid of?" One white male was so consumed with rage that he physically moved his chair away from the table he sat in front of in order to face me directly. Then he threw his hands in the air while displaying a demeanor that suggested "Oh my God, what now?" A white female colleague could not physically contain her guilt and shame such that she stood up from her chair and sat atop a table with her arms crossed and fidgeted the entire time. Another white female colleague began to tear up but was obviously exasperated and annoyed with my honesty. Instead of listening to me she remarked "Wait, I just don't understand what you're afraid of? I mean, I study race too and I'm not scared." In saying this, she inadvertently re-centered her white self, ignoring that there are stark differences in being white and being a Person of Color in a white supremacist society.

During this time, there was one Black male doctoral student present who attempted to support me. He, a self-identified Negro man, fully understood as to why I may be intimidated, especially since that same intimidation was happening in the room. Meaning, my fear of emotional outbursts stemming from the emotionalities of whiteness was manifesting in that very space while whites "allies" refused to acknowledge how they were engaging in it. He began with, "Look, I may not have a doctoral degree but I understand where Cheryl's coming from." Before he could finish, the white man with his arms in the air interjected and mocked, "Now wait. I don't have a doctoral degree either." At this interjection, the Black male doctoral student took a deep break and said as calmly as possible, "And it's obvious you don't need one." This comment was made in recognition that every single female at that meeting had doctoral degrees and that he, himself, was earning his own doctoral degree. All had a doctoral education, except for the white male. Yet, despite lacking a doctoral degree, this white male had the same, if not more, institutional power to decide on curricula, faculty agendas, and his vote counted the same as any more qualified female in the room. To that, the white man rolled his eyes and shut up.

I was in such disbelief in how potent the emotionalities of whiteness were that I withdrew, remained silent for the rest of the meeting, and felt further disillusioned of their potential "allyship." Put simply, I was never heard because all that was listened to was their own issues with race. Racial trauma was ignored.

## Counterstory #2

During my third year in the academy, I was a part of a collaborative research team investigating how graduates from our urban teacher education program truly understood race. Though I was not the lead investigator, I was highly welcomed into this space because of my expertise in race. The team consisted of three faculties of Color and one female doctoral student of Color and was led by a white female. Before the findings were finalized, the white female decided to present the preliminary findings with the doctoral student at a teacher education faculty meeting against the advice of the faculty of Color on the team. During this presentation, the white female professor reported how the few teacher candidates of Color in the program had experienced racism with a few professors inside the program. She showed slide after slide of verbatim transcriptions.

Before she could finish, a white male instructor from the program was so consumed with denial that he interrupted her, claiming he could not believe this information and that he needed "data" to prove racism was actually happening inside the program. In order to clarify whether or not this was indeed data, I asked the white female professor if these were verbatim transcriptions of the interviews she conducted. After she confirmed they were, I let the program know I corroborate with these findings and have often felt oppressed. Upon hearing this, the emotionalities of whiteness ran rampart. True to the most common expression within the emotionality of whiteness, most white professors froze. They looked down at their laptops, disengaged in the conversation, pretended not hear anything, and some even walked out to use the restroom. The white male was so entrenched in guilt and denial that

Before Cultural Competence 33

he began to emotionally project his feelings onto me. At the top of his lungs he screamed, "There you go again. How the hell am I oppressing you?! You are oppressing me." He then performed another aspect of whiteness. Because guilt makes one feel "bad," the individual will then try to reaffirm their "goodness" in various ways. Some ways to reconcile this feeling is to make another person look worse or to over-exaggerate "good" aspects of oneself. And, these were the exact two avenues this white male took. After attempting to make me look like the oppressor, he started pontificating his involvement in the 1960s Civil Rights March and his "many" friendships with African-Americans. Then a self-identified, lesbian white female professor jumped in. Despite the fact that she sat right in front of the presenters, she turned all the way around so that her back faced the presenters and she faced me at the back of the room. Staring at me angrily she yelled, "It's not all about race. Gay people are killing themselves, you know?" In her white guilt and shame, she deflected. First, she assumed I was straight. This is a common misconception in whiteness in that since whiteness centers itself, those who ascribe to it are unable to see intersectional identities when it comes to People of Color.[6] Second, her demand to quickly change the topic from race to gay issues was an attempt to reconcile her shame (see Allen, 2009). A shame that manifested because she, too, may have possibly contributed to the experiences these teacher candidates of Color had within the program. Finally, bear in mind that I was not the one presenting the information about racism. Yet, by corroborating with the data presented, and being the symbolic Brown marker in the room, the emotionalities of whiteness were fixated on me. Again, these self-professed white "allies" missed the opportunity to learn from their students, colleagues, and from the data about how racial trauma manifests in People of Color simply because their emotionalities of whiteness were too overwhelming.

Although the two counterstories offered take place in the field of teacher education, there are many parallels to the field of therapy, especially if one professes to be committed to cultural competence. What can be deduced here is that before a teacher, professor, or therapist can claim to be culturally competent, there must be a thorough investigation of the self first and foremost: for the reasoning behind cultural competence is about improving relationships between providers (who are predominantly White) and clients of Color. In order to improve that relationship, one need not only master the cultural and linguistic checklist for the cultural other. Instead, one must see how their privileged position in race has already influenced how they interact, think, behave, and feel around the cultural other. Until that happens, how is one to build trust, understanding, and emotionally invest in their clients' emotional needs if they cannot attend to, or even recognize, for that matter, their own?

---

[6] For example, when actress Patricia Arquette asked People of Color to support her and other white feminists in an effort against sexism and other gender discrimination in the film industry at the Academy Awards, she inadvertently ignored the intersectional identities of PoC who also experience gender and race discrimination in the same field.

## Are You Serious About Offering the Best Culturally Competent Therapeutic Practices? Will You Consider These Strategies?

There are many ways to improve the cultural competence of therapy and therapists. The litany of research often fixates on understanding the cultural and linguistic nuances of diverse groups of people. Yet, missing in that equation is understanding the white self and its relations to whiteness. Though not exhaustive, below are considerations one must reflect on to begin a deeper journey into cultural competence.

## Checking Emotionalities of Whiteness

As illustrated in the two counterstories above, the emotionalities of whiteness must be checked before assuming one can support People of Color. So how does one check their emotionalities of whiteness if such feelings have never been checked before? Of course, such checking rarely takes place when living within a white supremacist nation state that has historically demoralized, discriminated, ostracized, and traumatized People of Color who have tried. In thinking of how much one checks themselves before they wreck themselves (see Matias, 2013), there are few concepts to consider in popular culture.

One, common parlance pokes fun at white privilege claiming when one loses white privilege it feels like racial oppression. Instead of relying on that erroneous analogy that wrongly places victimization on the racially privileged, consider how losing unearned racial privilege may bring one closer to humanity, a feeling that will free one from shame, guilt, defensiveness, anger, and denial. Matias and Allen (2013) explicate this sense of freedom in their postulation of how loving whiteness to death frees one to finally have humanizing love for one another. Take, for instance, the notion of love. Because practicing, giving, receiving, and interpreting love is so inextricably bound to society's prescription of what love constitutes, love then becomes contrived. Therefore, one must check their understanding of love in order to more fully love. The same can be said for checking whiteness. If, as Ignatiev and Garvey (1996) suggest, "treason to whiteness is loyalty to humanity" (p. 10), then checking whiteness at the door becomes an attempt to become more loyal to humanity. However, this feels quite awkward for someone who has had racial privilege all their life.

In my classes I play a game with my students who are a majority white. In the class I ask them why they would not talk to Uncle Joe, a fictitious white male character, about racism at the dinner table. As the students respond, I scribe their answers on the board. Common answers are as follows:

- He'll yell at me and I don't want that
- He'll totally disregard me

- He'll tell me to prove it
- He'll say that racism is outdated; a thing of the past
- He'll deny everything I say
- He'll get angry
- He won't listen to me

I then tell them as they read through the readings that focus on whiteness they will, at times, feel like Uncle Joe. However, if they are truly committed to learning, they must resist the urge to react and shut down as Uncle Joe would have done, for to do so would block the learning. I remind them these things in wanting to become a white ally.

1. You will feel the emotionalities of whiteness arise within you, and it will make you feel vulnerable, not in control, and scared. Your face will probably redden and you may feel the urge to deflect, project, deny, remain silent, change the topic, or emotionally shut down altogether.
2. When you feel them, realize it, learn how they come about, and explore their characteristics or visceral manifestations. Allow yourself the time to become better acquainted with how the emotionalities of whiteness feel.
3. Once you are in complete recognition of these feelings, reframe them. Instead of feeling the need to regain control using racially demeaning mechanisms such as silencing, intimating, or belittling, reframe these uncomfortable feelings as doing your part in shouldering your fair share of the racial burden. That is, racism burdens People of Color with racial traumas every day, and whites, who often perpetrate these traumas, are at a loss as to how to be better allies to stop the trauma. Despite how uncomfortable it makes you, continually shouldering that burden that consists of bearing witness to racial traumas better develops trust. I tell my class, if two lovers truly care and empathize with one another, then during a heated quarrel they will not get up and leave the table just because the argument becomes too emotionally discomforting. Instead, to show human connectivity each partner demonstrates their commitment to each other by staying at the table to share the burden of hurt. That is what I am asking of you.
4. Once you have reframed how to deal with your emotionalities of whiteness, listen as a way to learn. Do not re-center whiteness by talking about your intent, justifications for your actions, or your feelings because this is not about you. Instead, listen to the impact of your actions, words, emotional outburst, or behaviors on a person of Color.

## Building Racial Empathy

Empathy, as Patel (2016) argues, can "all too easily become parking lots for emotionality and white fragility" (p. 83). In fact, empathy, used wrongly, becomes a narcissistic display of false caring (Matias & Zembylas, 2014) if the social locations of the one giving empathy and the one receiving empathy are not addressed. Furthermore, disregarding how the larger societal construct positions those individual locations is half-assed at best. To exemplify false empathy at its finest, I draw from the recent trend to wear safety pins post-Trump election to signify someone is an "ally" to marginalized people, particularly, People of Color, immigrants, and Muslims.[7] Though such an act appears empathetic on the surface, it quickly transforms into narcissistic displays of false caring and empathy when the aggrandizing becomes bigger than the work needed to be done in order to be an ally. That is, unless they emotionally invest in learning what does it mean to be white and understand the relevancy of whiteness then they cannot pretend to be an ally. Needless to say, a pedagogical process is required to reteach those who have for too long practiced false racial empathy. Here is a five-step exercise white therapists can practice with willing friends of Color to expand their repertoire of racial empathy.

1. Pick a racialized situation you and your friend of Color both experienced. Describe the situation, its chronology, impacts, and details.
2. Explain your own role, thoughts, emotions, and behaviors in that particular situation. *Why did you react this way? Where did those emotions stem from?* Make explicit your intentions behind your reactions.
3. Attempt to describe how a person of color may have felt and behaved. *Do you believe it to be the same or different? How so? Why do you think they may have behaved or felt this way?* Beyond your intent, speculate as to the impact of your reactions to the racialized situation. For example, if your reaction(s) was to get really quiet in the face of the racialized situation or to be overly gregarious about the situation, how could that have been interpreted by a Person of Color? Before you answer the last question consider the history of how People of Color have been treated in US society?
4. Ask for clarifications. *What was their response and reaction to the racialized situation? How did they feel about your reactions?* Despite how difficult it may be to hear the impact of your actions, remain calm and listen. After all, this is a learning experience.
5. Describe what you could have done to be a better ally. Then ask your friend of Color if those suggestions would have been a better way to support them. Learn how it may have or how it may have not.

---

[7] The notion that People of Color, immigrants, and Muslims need particular safe spaces came from racist, anti-immigrant, and anti-Muslim comments made during Donald Trump's presidential campaign, namely, the blatant disregard for People of Color and his association with the alt-right (who are, at times, affiliated with Neo-Nazi groups); his ideas of building a wall to keep out immigrants, particularly Mexican immigrants; and his idea to mandate forced registration of all Muslim Americans.

## What Happens If You Don't Consider and Truly Listen to My Needs? What Happens If You Do?

According to Leonardo (2009), whiteness is both everywhere and nowhere simultaneously, meaning it surrounds us in invisible ways but manifests itself in concrete ways. However, ignoring whiteness, specifically the emotionalities of whiteness, becomes a dangerous game that thickens the fakeness of white masks while burying more deeply a chance for freedom in developing humanizing relationships. And in this condition, how then are therapists to develop trust, understanding, and emotionally invest in their diverse clientele? Clearly stated, if one hopes to become a culturally competent therapist, then one must first examine that which comes before cultural competence: whiteness. Upon this introspective examination, counselors, therapists, and psychologists can then unveil their own emotional racial biases and, by doing so, have a fuller incorporation of culturally competent practices. And, only when a therapist emotionally invests in painfully self-investigating their own racial traumas first can clients of Color feel safe enough to allow them to assist in theirs.

*Being that you've finally heard me, may I reschedule for another session?*
*I think I can trust you now.*

**Special Note** To T. B. and other therapists who have already done the work of deconstructing their own emotionalities of whiteness for the sake of themselves and their clients and to not being afraid to confront them.

## References

Allen, R. L. (2009). What about poor White people. In *Handbook of social justice in education*. New York, NY: Routledge.

Allen, R. L., & Howard, N. (2012). Racial supremacy. In H. Anheier & M. Juergensmeyer (Eds.), *The encyclopedia of global studies* (Vol. 4, pp. 1428–1430). Los Angeles, CA: Sage Publishing.

Ancis, J. R., & Szymanski, D. M. (2001). Awareness of white privilege among white counseling trainees. *The Counseling Psychologist, 29*(4), 548–569. https://doi.org/10.1177/0011000001294005

Bonilla-Silva, E. (2003). New racism, color-blind racism, and the future of whiteness in America. In A. Doane & E. Bonilla-Silva (Eds.), *White out: The continuing significance of racism* (pp. 271–284). New York, NY: Routledge.

Bonilla-Silva, E. (2006). *Racism without racists: Color-blind racism and the persistence of racial inequality in the United States*. Maryland: Rowman & Littlefield Publishers.

Case, K. A. (2007). Raising white privilege awareness and reducing racial prejudice: Assessing diversity course effectiveness. *Teaching of Psychology, 34*(4), 231–235. https://doi.org/10.1080/00986280701700250

Cheng, A. A. (2001). *The melancholy of race: Psychoanalysis, assimilation, and hidden grief*. New York: Oxford University Press.

Collins, P. H. (1986). Learning from the outsider within: The sociological significance of black feminist thought. *Social Problems, 33*(6), s14–s32.

Crenshaw, K. (1995). *Critical race theory: The key writings that formed the movement*. New York, NY: The New Press.

Fanon, F. (1967). *Black skin, white masks [1952]*. (C. L. Markmann, Trans.). New York, NY: Grove Press.
Herman, J. L. (1997). *Trauma and recovery: The aftermath of violence--from domestic abuse to political terror* (Vol. 551). New York: Basic Books.
Hooks, B. (1994). *Teaching to transgress*. New York, NY: Routledge.
Hooks, B. (2004). *The will to change: Men, masculinity, and love*. New York, NY: Washington Square Press.
Ignatiev, N., & Garvey, J. (Eds.). (1996). *Race traitor*. New York, NY: Routledge.
Ladson-Billings, G. (2009). What is critical race theory doing in our nice field of education? In E. Taylor, D. Gillborn, & D. Ladson-Billings (Eds.), *Foundations of critical race theory in education* (pp. 17–36). New York, NY: Routledge.
Leonardo, Z. (2009). *Race, whiteness, and education*. New York, NY: Routledge.
Leonardo, Z. (2013). *Race frameworks: A multidimensional theory of racism and education*. New York, NY: Teachers College Press.
Lipsitz, G. (1998). *The Possessive Investment of Whiteness: How White People Profit From Identity Politics*. Philadelphia: Temple University Press.
Love, B. (2004). Brown plus 50 counter-storytelling: A critical race theory analysis of the "Majoritarian achievement gap" story. *Equity & Excellence in Education, 37*(3), 227–246. https://doi.org/10.1080/10665680490491597
Matias, C. E. (2013). Check yo'self before you wreck yo'self and our kids: Counterstories from culturally responsive white teachers?... To culturally responsive white teachers. *Interdisciplinary Journal of Teaching and Learning, 3*(2), 68–81.
Matias, C. E., & Allen, R. L. (2013). Loving whiteness to death: Sadomasochism, emotionality, and the possibility of humanizing love. *Berkeley Review of Education, 4*(2), 285–309.
Matias, C. E. (2016a). *Feeling white: Whiteness, emotionality, and education*. Boston, MA: Sense Publishers.
Matias, C. E. (2016b). White skin, black friend: A Fanonian application to theorize racial fetish in teacher education. *Educational Philosophy and Theory, 48*(3), 221–236. https://doi.org/10.1080/00131857.2014.989952
Matias, C. E. (2016c). White Tundra. In N. D. Hartlep, & C. Hayes (Eds.), *Unhooking from Whiteness. Constructing Knowledge (Curriculum Studies in Action)*. Rotterdam: SensePublishers.
Matias, C. E., Viesca, K. M., Garrison-Wade, D. F., Tandon, M., & Galindo, R. (2014). "What is critical whiteness doing in OUR nice field like critical race theory?" applying CRT and CWS to understand the white imaginations of white teacher candidates. *Equity & Excellence in Education, 47*(3), 289–304. https://doi.org/10.1080/10665684.2011.933692
Matias, C. E., & Zembylas, M. (2014). 'When saying you care is not really caring': Emotions of disgust, whiteness ideology, and teacher education. *Critical Studies in Education, 55*(3), 319–337. https://doi.org/10.1080/17508487.2014.922489
McIntosh, P. (2001). Unpacking the invisible knapsack. In M. Andersen & P. Collins (Eds.), *Race, class, and gender* (pp. 95–105). Belmont, CA: Wadsworth.
McLeod, J. (2007). *Counseling skill*. New York, NY: McGraw-Hill International.
Mills, C. (2007). White ignorance. In S. Sullivan & N. Tuana (Eds.), *Race and epistemologies of ignorance* (pp. 11–37). New York, NY: SUNY Press.
Moustakas, C. (1994). *Phenomenological research methods*. Thousand Oaks, CA: Sage Publications.
Nadal, K. L., Griffin, K. E., Wong, Y., Hamit, S., & Rasmus, M. (2014). The impact of racial microaggressions on mental health: Counseling implications for clients of color. *Journal of Counseling & Development, 92*(1), 57–66. https://doi.org/10.1002/j.1556-6676.2014.00130
National Center for Education Statistics. (2012). *Fast facts: Teacher trends*. New York, NY: Institute of Educational Sciences/U.S. Department of Education. Retrieved from: http://nces.ed.gov/fastfacts/display.asp?id=28
Patel, L. (2016). The irrationality of antiracist empathy. *English Journal, 106*, 81–84.

Smith, W. A., Allen, W. R., & Danley, L. L. (2007). "Assume the position... You fit the description" psychosocial experiences and racial battle fatigue among African American male college students. *American Behavioral Scientist*, *51*(4), 551–578. https://doi.org/10.1177/0002764207307742

Solórzano, D. G., & Yosso, T. J. (2002). Critical race methodology: Counter-storytelling as an analytical framework for education research. *Qualitative Inquiry*, *8*(1), 23–44. https://doi.org/10.1177/107780040200800103

Steele, C. M., & Aronson, J. (1995). Stereotype threat and the intellectual test performance of African Americans. *Journal of Personality and Social Psychology*, *69*(5), 797–811. https://doi.org/10.1037/0022-3514.69.5.797

Sue, D. W. (2001). Multidimensional facets of cultural competence. *The Counseling Psychologist*, *29*(6), 790–821. https://doi.org/10.1177/0011000001296002

Sue, D. W., Capodilupo, C. M., Torino, G. C., Bucceri, J. M., Holder, A., Nadal, K. L., & Esquilin, M. (2007). Racial microaggressions in everyday life: Implications for clinical practice. *American Psychologist*, *62*(4), 271–286. https://doi.org/10.1037/0003-066X.62.4.271

Sue, S. (1998). In search of cultural competence in psychotherapy and counseling. *American Psychologist*, *53*(4), 440–448. https://doi.org/10.1037/0003-066X.53.4.440

Taylor, E., Gillborn, D., & Ladson-Billings, G. (2009). *Foundations of critical race theory in education*. New York, NY: Routledge.

Thandeka. (1999). *Learning to be white: Money, race, and god in America*. New York, NY: Continuum International Publishing Group.

Villegas, A. M., & Lucas, T. (2002). Preparing culturally responsive teachers rethinking the curriculum. *Journal of Teacher Education*, *53*(1), 20–32. https://doi.org/10.1177/0022487102053001003

Wildman, S., & Davis, A. (2008). Making systems of privilege visible. In P. S. Rothenberg (Ed.), *White privilege* (pp. 109–116). New York, NY: Worth Publishers.

# Evidence-Based Practices and Cultural Responsiveness

**Robert Allan**

There are a number of considerations to explore when discussing evidence-based practice. To start with, there are various terms used to describe the research about evidence-based approaches to couple and family therapy (CFT), such as empirically supported treatments, evidence-based psychological practices, empirically validated treatment, and principles of empirically supported interventions, among others. In this chapter, I will use the term evidence-based practice (EBP) as an umbrella term to encompass a range of CFT approaches developed with the assistance of efficacy and effectiveness research. I am trained in evidence-based approaches to working with couples and families and use them in my therapy and supervision practice. I also train and educate others in evidence-based approaches and about EBPs in general. As an immigrant, gay man, and someone who is passionate about social justice, I also have lived realities of what it is like to not be included in decisions that are made about what is best for me. The latter also informs my therapy, supervision, and education practices.

The American Psychology Association (APA) took steps to identify what constitutes an EBP in 1995 by defining criteria for empirically validated treatments. These criteria included at least two studies demonstrating efficacy, defined as being superior to a pill or to a psychological placebo or to another treatment or equivalent to an already established treatment. Alternatively, a large series of smaller studies demonstrating efficacy was also acceptable. For either scenario, experiments had to be conducted with treatment manuals, the characteristics of the research participants had to be clearly specified (i.e., a single diagnosis), and the effects must have been demonstrated by at least two different investigators. The APA also defined "probably efficacious treatments" as two experiments showing that treatment is more effective than a wait list control group or a larger study or a series of smaller studies meeting all of the previously mentioned criteria except the requirement to have the effects demonstrated by more than one investigator (American Psychological Association (APA), 1995).

Central to understanding these criteria is efficacy and effectiveness research, with the former viewed as more in line with empirically validated treatment research. Efficacy research contrasts one kind of CFT to a comparison group under well-controlled conditions (Seligman, 1995). The ideal efficacy study will include the following criteria as outlined by Seligman (1995):

1. The patients are randomly assigned to treatment and control conditions.
2. The controls are rigorous: Not only are patients included who receive no treatment at all, but placebos containing potentially therapeutic ingredients credible to both the patient and the therapist are used in order to control for such influences as rapport, expectation of gain, and sympathetic attention (dubbed nonspecifics).
3. The treatments are manualized, with highly detailed scripting of therapy made explicit. Fidelity to the manual is assessed using videotaped sessions, and wayward implementers are corrected.
4. Patients are seen for a fixed number of sessions.
5. The target outcomes are well operationalized (e.g., clinician-diagnosed DSM-IV disorder).
6. Raters and diagnosticians are blind to which group the patient comes from.
7. The patients meet criteria for a single diagnosed disorder, and patients with multiple disorders are typically excluded.
8. The patients are followed for a fixed period after termination of treatment with a thorough assessment battery (p. 965).

Another option for exploring whether a CFT approach has a therapeutic impact on a couple or family is to do an effectiveness study.

Effectiveness research is the study of how CFT participants fare under the actual conditions of treatment in the field (Seligman, 1995). There are five elements that characterize how CFT is actually done in the field that are missing from efficacy research. First, it is rare to have a fixed number of sessions for CFT in real life. Generally, a therapist would set goals with a couple or family and assess progress toward those goals and the quality of the therapeutic alliance, and therapy would end when some or all aspects of the goals have been accomplished. Second, therapy is self-correcting; if one approach does not work, a therapist might choose to try another approach and not simply stick to a scripted manual waiting for clients to improve. A third difference between efficacy research and CFT in the field is that patients often actively shop for a therapist. A fourth and oft-noted difference is that patients usually have more than one presenting problem. Finally, another difference in a therapist's practice as compared to efficacy research is that there is concern for general improvement as well as improvement in a specific disorder and relief of specific symptoms. Effectiveness research provides an opportunity to incorporate one or many aspects of real-life practice and may be an important step for transportability research and dissemination research.

Transportability research explores the movement of efficacious treatments to usual-care settings. There are three broad questions one can consider in transportability research (Schoenwald & Hoagwood, 2001): What is the intervention? Who, and under what circumstances, can the intervention in question be conducted? What is the effect for clients and systems? Transportability research is a precursor to dissemination research, which examines whether a treatment approach produces the desired outcomes under conditions faced by the ultimate consumers of the treatment. It is both reasonable and ethical to attempt a broader distribution and to evaluate the impact of these distribution efforts, to develop strategies to raise awareness of the treatment among potential consumers, and to identify consumers likely to reject, adopt, or adapt it (Schoenwald & Hoagwood, 2001).

The field of couple and family therapy research has explored the role of EBPs for practitioners as well as developed EBPs. An article in a prominent CFT research journal proposed a set of guidelines for EBPs for couple and family therapy (Sexton et al., 2011). The article was co-authored by influential researchers in the field who had developed these guidelines when working together on a subcommittee of APA's Division 43 (Family Psychology). In 2007, they submitted an "official recommendations" report to Division 43 with an outline for guidelines for evidence-based treatments for CFTs. The proposed guidelines consist of three levels of evidence-based practice ranging from "evidence-informed" to "evidence-based." The three levels are intended to provide "both a hierarchical index of confidence that a treatment model 'works' and a comparative index of clinical applicability" (Sexton et al., 2011, p. 382).

The third or highest level of EBPs in this model has three additional categories of evidence that are intended to further "demonstrate effectiveness by considering model-specific change mechanisms, superior performance when compared with other viable treatment options, and generalizability to a diversity of client populations and clinical settings" (Sexton et al., 2011, p. 382). The authors go on to suggest that the categories in the third level are intended to be more "contextual" than hierarchical and provide guidelines for researchers about what questions to consider regarding the use and implementation of a model.

Interestingly, Sexton et al. (2011) suggest that evidence should include at least two outcome studies with research coming from multiple sites and go on to indicate that to be evidence-based, couple or family interventions should include:

(a) Clear specification of the content of the treatment model (e.g., treatment manual)
(b) Measures of model fidelity (therapist adherence and/or competence)
(c) Clear identification of client problems
(d) Substantive description of the service delivery contexts in which the treatment is tested
(e) The use of valid measures of clinical outcomes (p. 385)

These criteria are very similar to the APA guidelines released in 1995, and while suggesting elsewhere that there are contextual factors that are important to attend to, they do not attend to how EBPs can design research to attend to these factors.

Another consideration rarely attended to in the research literature is the author or researcher's location and whether we are required to disclose this as part of an ethical research practice. EBPs are increasingly being sought by funding agencies, particularly state funding agencies in the United States, as the reason for funding a program. For example, the University of Colorado's Centre for the Study and Prevention of Violence has developed an extensive Blueprints for Violence program that focuses on determining if a program can be listed as evidence-based. Being listed by the Blueprints program can be a key criterion for a state to fund a CFT program. Some of the researchers involved with APA's Division 43 subcommittee that created the recommendations for evidence-based CFT treatments are strongly aligned with CFT practices that offer extensive training programs run much like a business. To draw a crude analogy intended to highlight the potentially more difficult aspects of this work, can this be compared to pharmaceutical companies having the only say in research guidelines for drug trials on humans? We know the reality is that pharmaceuticals have enormous influence, but there do seem to be some measures in place to mitigate that influence. While worth mentioning, this question is beyond the scope of this chapter and has been briefly noted elsewhere in the literature as "allegiance issues" (Sprenkle, 2012). More relevant for this chapter are the practice considerations for CFTs that EBPs bring to the fore. The next section will focus on the benefits, challenges, and social justice considerations for CFT practitioners and researchers.

## Practice Considerations for Couple and Family Therapists

As previously noted, the role of EBPs in all aspects of mental and health care are growing. As Alexander, Sexton, and Robbins (2000) note:

> The philosophy and guidelines embedded in the empirically validated and supported treatment movement have come to define the practical application of current (CFT) intervention…the evolution of this movement is at the hub of several social, professional, and historic forces that are converging. (p. 23)

There is a sense of hope about the possibilities for EBPs in the development of the CFT field, both for the people receiving a service as well as for practitioners and researchers who can increasingly feel confident that their work is supported by research. While there are short-comings of the randomized controlled trial (RCT) methodology that is required for a practice to become evidence based, RCTs are still seen as the "gold standard" for intervention methodology research (Sprenkle, 2012). Further, "if CFTs want to have their discipline taken seriously by the external world (including other disciplines, governments, insurance companies, and other third-party payers), they will have to continue producing high-quality RCTs" (p. 4). It is therefore critical that CFTs pay attention to the benefits of EBPs in their practice.

What follows is a list of a number of the benefits of the evidence-based movement for CFTs. Efficacy studies are seen as the best "scientific instrument" for telling us whether an intervention is likely to work with a given disorder (Seligman, 1995). Clinicians have a clinical, ethical, and legal responsibility to attend to the results of RCTs (Persons & Silberschatz, 1998). Knowing about and understanding EBPs in general are important for CFTs who work across disciplines because "whether in medicine, education, or mental health, the culture of evidence based practice pervades almost every aspect of our public lives" (Midgley, 2009, p. 323). Developing evidence-based CFT practices is seen as a natural progression and evolution of our field, a maturing of sorts from anecdotal clinical reports to "conceptual and methodological sophistication" of CFT research and clinical practices (Sexton & Alexander, 2002).

Continuing with the benefits of EBPs, for CFTs the knowledge of, or certification in, an EBP provides a professional reputation and legitimacy as well as a knowledge base for practitioners. CFTs also have an ethical responsibility to ensure our work is as beneficial as possible and there are opportunities to promote a research culture within an evidence-based approach and promote stronger researcher-practitioner alliances. For program managers, funders, and government departments, there is an increased pressure to allocate resources on an explicit rational basis and in consideration of consumer rights, which again means attending to the results of research (Morago, 2006; Plath, 2006). There is also the hope that EBPs will improve the quality of the service, potentially influence policy makers to increase access to CFT, and allow for faster and better training. The culture of EBP is intended to have a heuristic value as well "to encourage further development of guidelines and lists of effective treatments; they do not have to be perfect to be useful for the field" (Elliott, 1998, p. 118). In keeping with disciplines interested in empirical research, there is a notion that unless it has been studied using an RCT, "we have no compelling evidence that it is effective and we cannot be certain it is not harmful" (Persons & Silberschatz, 1998, p. 126). While there are a number of benefits of evidence-based research for therapists to consider, there are other perspectives on the role of EBPs in the field of couple and family therapy that enrich the dialogue and bring forth a range of compelling reasons to explore the issue further.

These other perspectives challenge the focus on EBP and how the research is done as well as raise social justice considerations for CFTs. What follows is an outline of the challenges associated with EBPs and the related research. The challenges associated with integrating science into the practice of CFT through EBPs "have always been controversial, resulting in frequent, passionate, and at times divisive debates in the field" (Sexton et al., 2011, p. 378). While characterizing the debate as passionate and divisive might suggest that some may want to raise unnecessary challenges, these challenges are integral to the development and evolution of the field. For example, connected to a singular framework (Wendt Jr., 2006), the narrow epistemological band of empiricism that asserts that "we can only know, or know best, those aspects of our experience that are sensory" (Slife, Wiggins, & Graham, 2005, p. 84) limits what and who engages in that dialogue. Empiricism is "merely one epistemology or philosophy among many, each with inherent strengths, limitations, and biases" (Wendt Jr., 2006, p. 91). CFT practitioners apply a broad range of "experiential knowledge and strategies that are hardly mentioned in the text books" (Malterud, 2001, p. 398). EBPs emphasize evidence for interventions over evidence for assessment and planning and do not sufficiently conceptualize how practice expertise and service users' values can be included (Gilgun, 2005). As Seligman (1996) noted, "experiments resemble real therapy only slightly" (p. 1072) and lack an ability to reflexively engage in noting what is seen as well as what is not seen (Burke, 1954).

Another challenge for therapists to consider is that EBPs have been criticized for promoting a view of decision making that is deterministic, which is inconsistent with the reflective process noted as integral to ethical CFT practice (Coulter, 2011). Further, as Staller (2006) noted, the "monolithic notion of best evidence—at the exclusion of other competing informative evidence—is reductionistic and dangerous" (Staller, 2006, p. 512). Henry (1998) raises six concerns about the "benign but naive scientific efforts" of EBPs that, when "coupled with political and paradigmatic agendas" (p. 127), need to be considered by researchers and CFTs. The first is that an EBP approach fundamentally sacrifices a traditional approach in favor of a medical model of questionable utility for the phenomena under study. Secondly, it has the potential to decrease the quality of CFT training in favor of technical approaches that limit the understanding of training to a set of steps much like a recipe book. Third, it "may give even greater power to third-party payers as de facto untrained supervisors" (p. 127). Fourth, it may actually discourage research in some areas such as couples or families presenting with multiple problems or personality disorders. Fifth, the research findings distributed are of little value to consumers' best interest. Finally, it "entrenches an outdated research paradigm that militates against the discovery of new knowledge" (p. 127). Another aspect of the EBP dialogue for CFTs to consider is social justice considerations.

The social justice aspects of the evidence-based dialogue in CFT explore the role of our professional associations, who has been included and excluded from research, whose needs are served by research and programs, how EBPs are constructed, who is included in the dialogue as well as a number of other areas. What follows is a brief outline of some of the social justice issues for CFTs to consider, starting with professional associations that regulate the various practitioners who practice CFT and "have political, social, and economic functions and interests" (Gambrill, 2010, p. 307–8). One of the roles afforded to the helping professions in our mental and health-care systems is social control (Gambrill, 2010). Practitioners who naively ignore this role, attributing it to something their employer does but they have nothing to do with, run the risk of absent-mindedly replicating some of the very mechanisms that led a couple or family to seek services in the first place. One of the more troubling aspects of the empirically supported treatment enterprise is the "systematic discrimination against certain classes of research, treatment, and patients" (Elliott, 1998, p. 118), in particular, non-English research, qualitative research, and research with ethnic minorities and children.

A leading proponent of APA's empirically validated treatment project through the 1990s was Diane Chambless who wrote that "We know of no psychotherapy treatment research that meets basic criteria important for demonstrating treatment efficacy for ethnic minority populations" (Chambless et al., 1996, p. 2). Furthermore, the "dearth of culturally cross-validated measures makes even beginning such research problematic" (Chambless et al., 1996, p. 2). CFT practice cannot be guided by research findings alone; it relies on multiple values, tacit judgment, local knowledge, and a range of skills (Hammersley, 2004). This contrasts the notion of the clinician as "an institutional subject who is presumed both to know the truth of disease and to have the moral and intellectual authority to prescribe treatment" (Holmes, Murray, Perron, & Rail, 2006, p. 183). How we know what works and for whom will always be debated by therapists, researchers, and the people who seek services. Some researchers advocate for an "intentional practice" where CFTs' work should reflect what they know is most likely to be helpful (Allan & Ungar, 2014), recognizing that there will always be tension between practice and theory, positivist and other research paradigms, and social, political, and pragmatic considerations.

The hope expressed in the literature is that RCTs have the potential to be externally valid, can include qualitative components to add richness and relevance, and can be used to study common factors. Many of the problems noted with RCTs are not rooted in the paradigm itself, but rather how they are used and misinterpreted to make claims that are too far reaching (Laska, Gurman, & Wampold, 2013; Sprenkle, Davis, & Lebow, 2009). There is a need to improve research by doing more in real-life settings that approximate actual practice and not overinterpreting results of RCTs by attributing the reasons for which interventions work for specific problems or populations (Sprenkle, 2012). The overreliance on evidence as solely determined by APA's guidelines makes it difficult for "scholars to express new and different ideas in an intellectual circle where normalisation and standardisation are privileged in the development of knowledge" (Holmes et al., 2006, p. 182). EBPs present a range of benefits, challenges, and social justice considerations for CFTs and researchers alike.

Some of the benefits of EBPs that CFTs cannot ignore are that they are a given of present-day practice and research. EBPs present an opportunity to improve service, training, and save programs money. The key challenges with EBPs are the lack of epistemic agility that informs them and the lack of recognition of the role of the therapist and consumer. While social justice considerations raise questions about whom EBPs serve and highlights the stark absence of research ability or actual research with non-English speaking populations and diverse populations. Another possibility for EBPs noted by Gambrill (2010) is to help narrow the gap between what a CFT knows and what they can do. According to Gambrill, the authority of a CFT can be replaced by a well-informed couple or family who can make decisions about whether the intervention is useful. The role of the therapist becomes that of openly explaining what they are doing, being aware of EBPs, and working with couples and families to work toward outcomes that they themselves find meaningful. The next section will focus on whether EBPs have been culturally responsive and in what ways.

## Cultural Responsiveness and Evidence-Based Practices

Cultural responsiveness is contingent on the relationship developed between a therapist and the couple or family and is necessary for the clients' cultural needs to be incorporated into therapy. All mental health professional organizations have codes of ethics requiring their members to be culturally sensitive, take into account multicultural and diversity considerations, and be aware of and respect cultural or attend to cultural norms. Often there are guidelines offered by these organizations that outline the competencies or best practices that facilitate a therapist being culturally responsive (e.g., American Psychological Association (APA), 2012; Ratts, Singh, Nassar-McMillan, Butler, & McCullough, 2015). Curiously, these codes of ethics and guidelines have not made a substantial impact on the fields of couple and family research. What follows is a brief review of the research outlining the relevance of cultural responsiveness in therapy and how the research has attended to these factors.

The research about the need for culturally responsive therapists and the challenges for preparing therapists to be culturally responsive is well documented. Ethnic and sexual minority populations in the United States are underserved and face barriers to accessing culturally relevant mental health services (Meyer, 2013; Substance Abuse and Mental Health Services Administration (SAHMSA), 2015). Researchers have documented the need for training programs to better prepare therapists for working with lesbian, gay, and bisexual clients (Carlson, McGeorge, & Toomey, 2013; Henke, Carlson, & McGeorge, 2009; Rock, Carlson, & McGeorge, 2010). There is a need for culturally adapted prevention parenting programs that focus on diverse populations (Baker, Arnold, & Meagher, 2011). The research supporting the benefit of underserved ethnic and sexual minority populations receiving culturally adapted interventions is well documented (Barrera, Castro, Strycker, & Toobert, 2013; Canino & Alegria, 2008; Smith, Domenech Rodríguez, & Bernal, 2011). Along with extensive case study and conceptual articles, there is no shortage of research writing about the necessity for couple and family therapists to be culturally responsive. Despite the attention given to the need for cultural responsivity, there is a dearth of outcome research targeting ethnic and sexual minorities in couple and family research let alone how evidence-based couple and family therapy practices can be culturally adapted.

While completed 20 years ago, one content analysis of couple and family journals found that 0.006% of the 13 out of 217 articles focused on gay, lesbian, and/or bisexual issues (Clark & Serovich, 1997). A 2017 search using the words gay, lesbian, or bisexual of SAMHSA's National Registry of Evidence-Based Programs and Practices produced two results of 468 programs or 0.004%. A content analysis of three top couple and family research journals from 2004 to 2011 resulted in more than 70% of the journal articles not attending to one aspect of diversity (Seedall, Holtrop, & Parra-Cardona, 2014). The field of couple and family research has conceptualized EBPs as taking context into consideration for the most effective of treatments (Sexton et al., 2011). Further, scholars advocating for the cultural adaptation of EBPs emphasize the need for research aimed at clarifying which specific components of adapted interventions are found to be most relevant by the recipients of interventions (Castro, Barrera, & Holleran Steiker, 2010). Finally, there is a need for first person accounts of culturally adapted EBPs to clarify which aspects are most meaningful for the recipients of these interventions.

One approach to using EBPs in my own clinical and research work while attending to contextual issues is to consider cultural adaptations of evidence-based approaches. An example of a conceptual approach in my own work is researching what cultural adaptation strategies are used by therapists who identify as using a specific evidence-based approach. I also write about how to adapt an approach for a specific population (e.g., Allan & Johnson, 2016). The research about cultural adaptations of EBPs is nascent and promising (Griner & Smith, 2006), and there is considerable evidence that culture and context influence almost every aspect of treatment and diagnostic processes (Alegría & McGuire, 2003; Canino & Alegria, 2008; Comas-Díaz, 2006). My clinical and supervision experience parallels the growing body of research that investigates the need to attend to cultural factors for the very reason that EBPs were developed in the first place which is to be more effective and have better clinical outcomes.

For some couple and family therapists and researchers, having the systematic approach offered by EBPs provides structure and accountability in their work. For others, the risk of adopting a one-size-fits-all approach risks limiting the competence of their interventions and intervention research. Couple and family therapists who are culturally responsive move away from cataloguing differences in culture to understanding culture and how it shapes couples and families and informs therapy (Ryder, Ban, & Chentsova-Dutton, 2011). Disorder or pathology is understood as behavioral and cultural and as much a part of a couple or family's social ecology. Claims of efficacy are often cited as a critical reason for why couple and family therapists need to be culturally responsive (e.g., Bernal, Jiménez-Chafey, & Domenech Rodríguez, 2009; McKleroy et al., 2006; Smith et al., 2011). Couple and family therapists would be wise to heed this advice and consider the contextual aspects of evidence-based guidelines put forth by APA's Division 43 (Sexton et al., 2011). These contextual aspects are integral to what makes EBPs effective. Further practitioners and researchers need to consider whether an evidence-based approach to their work is a continual exploration and understanding of what aspects of their work need to be culturally adapted.

# References

Alegría, M., & McGuire, T. (2003). Rethinking a universal framework in the psychiatric symptom–disorder relationship. *Journal of Health and Social Behavior, 44*, 257–274. http://www.jstor.org/stable/1519778

Alexander, J. F., Sexton, T. L., & Robbins, M. S. (2000). The developmental status of family therapy in family psychology intervention science. In H. A. Liddle, D. A. Santisteban, R. F.

Levant, & J. H. Bray (Eds.), *Family psychology intervention science* (pp. 17–40). Washington, DC: American Psychological Association.

Allan, R., & Johnson, S. M. (2016). Conceptual and application issues: Emotionally focused therapy with gay male couples. *Journal of Couple & Relationship Therapy*., (Online first). https://doi.org/10.1080/15332691.2016.1238800

Allan, R., & Ungar, M. (2014). Developing a measure of fidelity for an ecological approach to family therapy. *Journal of Family Psychotherapy, 25*(1), 1–16. https://doi.org/10.1080/08975353.2014.881688

American Psychological Association. (1995). Task Force on Promotion and Dissemination of Psychological Procedures, Division of Clinical Psychology, Training in and dissemination of empirically-validated psychological treatments: Report and recommendations. *The Clinical Psychologist, 48*, 3–23.

American Psychological Association, Division 44/Committee on Lesbian, Gay, and Bisexual Concerns Joint Task Force on Guidelines for Psychotherapy with Lesbian, Gay, and Bisexual Clients. (2012). Guidelines for psychological practice with lesbian, gay, and bisexual clients. *American Psychologist, 67*(1), 10–42. https://doi.org/10.1037/a0024659

Baker, C. N., Arnold, D. H., & Meagher, S. (2011). Enrollment and attendance in a parent training prevention program for conduct problems. *Prevention Science, 12*, 126–138. https://doi.org/10.1007/s11121-010-0187-0

Barrera, M., Castro, F. G., Strycker, L. A., & Toobert, D. J. (2013). Cultural adaptations of behavioral health interventions: A progress report. *Journal of Consulting and Clinical Psychology, 81*, 196–205. https://doi.org/10.1037/a0027085

Bernal, G., Jiménez-Chafey, M. I., & Domenech Rodríguez, M. M. (2009). Cultural adaptation of treatments: A resource for considering culture in evidence-based practice. *Professional Psychology: Research and Practice, 40*, 361–368. https://doi.org/10.1037/a0016401

Burke, K. (1954). *Permanence & change: An anatomy of purpose*. Los Altos, CA: Hermes Publications.

Canino, G., & Alegria, M. (2008). Psychiatric diagnosis—Is it universal or relative to culture? *Journal of Child Psychology and Psychiatry, 49*, 237–250. https://doi.org/10.1111/j.1469-7610.2007.01854.x

Carlson, T. S., McGeorge, C. R., & Toomey, R. B. (2013). Establishing the validity of the affirmative training inventory: Assessing the relationship between lesbian, gay, and bisexual affirmative training and students' clinical competence. *Journal of Marital and Family Therapy, 39*(2), 209–222. https://doi.org/10.1111/j.1752-0606.2012.00286.x

Castro, F. G., Barrera, M., & Holleran Steiker, L. K. (2010). Issues and challenges in the design of culturally adapted evidence-based interventions. *Annual Review of Clinical Psychology, 6*, 213–239. https://doi.org/10.1146/annurev-clinpsy-033109-132032

Chambless, D. L., Sanderson, W. C., Shoham, V., Bennett Johnson, S., Pope, K. S., Crits-Christoph, P., … McCurry, S. (1996). An update on empirically validated therapies. Unpublished manuscript retrieved from http://www.apa.org/divisions/div12/est/newrpt.pdf

Clark, W. M., & Serovich, J. M. (1997). Twenty years and still in the dark? Content analysis of articles pertaining to gay, lesbian, and bisexual issues in marriage and family therapy journals. *Journal of Marital and Family Therapy, 23*(3), 239–253. https://doi.org/10.1111/j.1752-0606.1997.tb01034.x

Comas-Diaz, L. (2006). Latino healing: The integration of ethnic psychology into psychotherapy. *Psychotherapy: Theory, Research, Practice, Training*, (4), 436–453. https://doi.org/10.1037/0033-3204.43.4.436

Coulter, S. (2011). Systemic family therapy for families who have experienced trauma: A randomised controlled trial. *British Journal of Social Work, 41*(3), 502–519. https://doi.org/10.1093/bjsw/bcq132

Elliott, R. (1998). Editor's introduction: A guide to the empirically supported treatments controversy. *Psychotherapy Research, 8*(2), 115–125. https://doi.org/10.1080/10503309812331332257

Gambrill, E. (2010). Evidence-informed practice: Antidote to propaganda in the helping professions? *Research on Social Work Practice, 20*(3), 302–320. https://doi.org/10.1177/1049731509347879

Gilgun, J. (2005). Evidence-based practice, descriptive research and the resilience-schema-gender-brain functioning (RSGB) assessment. *British Journal of Social Work, 35*(6), 843–862. https://doi.org/10.1093/bjsw/bch216

Griner, D., & Smith, T. B. (2006). Culturally adapted mental health intervention: A meta-analytic review. *Psychotherapy: Theory, Research, Practice, Training, 43*, 531–548. https://doi.org/10.1037/0003-066X.63.3.146

Hammersley, M. (2004). Some questions about evidence-based practice in education. In G. Thomas & R. Pring (Eds.), *Evidence-based practice in education* (pp. 133–149). New York, NY: Open University Press.

Henke, T., Carlson, T. S., & McGeorge, C. R. (2009). Homophobia and clinical competency: An exploration of couple and family therapists' beliefs. *Journal of Couple and Relationship Therapy, 8*(4), 325–342. https://doi.org/10.1080/15332690903246101

Henry, W. (1998). Science, politics, and the politics of science: The use and misuse of empirically validated treatment research. *Psychotherapy Research, 8*(2), 126–140. https://doi.org/10.1080/10503309812331332267

Holmes, D., Murray, S. J., Perron, A., & Rail, G. (2006). Deconstructing the evidence-based discourse in health sciences: Truth, power and fascism. *International Journal of Evidence-Based Healthcare, 4*(3), 180–186. https://doi.org/10.1111/j.1479-6988.2006.00041.x

Laska, K. M., Gurman, A. S., & Wampold, B. E. (2013). Expanding the lens of evidence-based practice in psychotherapy: A common factors perspective. *Psychotherapy, 51*(4), 467–481. https://doi.org/10.1037/a0034332

Malterud, K. (2001). The art and science of clinical knowledge: Evidence beyond measures and numbers. *Lancet, 358*(9279), 397–400. https://doi.org/10.1016/S0140-6736(01)05548-9

McKleroy, V. S., Galbraith, J. S., Cummings, B., Jones, P., Harshbarger, C., Collins, C., … Carey, J. W. (2006). Adapting evidence-based behavioral interventions for new settings and target populations. *AIDS Education and Prevention, 18*(4 Suppl. A), 59–73. https://doi.org/10.1521/aeap.2006.18.supp.59

Meyer, I. H. (2013). Prejudice, social stress, and mental health in lesbian, gay, and bisexual populations: Conceptual issues and research evidence. *Psychology of Sexual Orientation and Gender Diversity, 1*(S), 3–26. https://doi.org/10.1037/2329-0382.1.S.3

Midgley, N. (2009). Editorial: Improvers, adapters and rejecters the link between 'evidence-based practice' and 'evidence-based practitioners'. *Clinical Child Psychology and Psychiatry, 14*(3), 323–327. https://doi.org/10.1177/1359104509104045

Morago, P. (2006). Evidenced-based practice: From medicine to social work. *European Journal of Social Work, 9*(4), 461–477. https://doi.org/10.1080/13691450600958510

Persons, J. B., & Silberschatz, G. (1998). Are results of randomized controlled trials useful to psychotherapists? *Journal of Consulting and Clinical Psychology, 66*(1), 126–135. https://doi.org/10.1037/0022-006X.66.1.126

Plath, D. (2006). Evidenced-based practice: Current issues and future directions. *Australian Social Work, 59*(1), 56–72. https://doi.org/10.1080/03124070500449788

Ratts, M. J., Singh, A. A., Nassar-McMillan, S., Butler, S. K., & McCullough, J. R. (2015). *Multicultural and social justice counseling competencies*. Retrieved from http://www.multiculturalcounseling.org/index.php?option=com_content&view=article&id=205:amcd-endorses-multicultural-and-social-justice-counseling-competencies&catid=1:latest&Itemid=123

Rock, M., Carlson, T. S., & McGeorge, C. R. (2010). Does affirmative training matter? Assessing CFT students' beliefs about sexual orientation and their level of affirmative training. *Journal of Marital and Family Therapy, 36*(2), 171–184. https://doi.org/10.1111/j.1752-0606.2009.00172.x

Ryder, A. G., Ban, L. M., & Chentsova-Dutton, Y. E. (2011). Towards a cultural-clinical psychology. *Social and Personality Psychology Compass, 5*(12), 960–975. https://doi.org/10.1111/j.1751-9004.2011.00404.x

Schoenwald, S. K., & Hoagwood, K. (2001). Effectiveness, transportability, and dissemination of interventions: What matters when? *Psychiatric Services, 52*(9), 1190–1197. https://doi.org/10.1176/appi.ps.52.9.1190

Seedall, R. B., Holtrop, K., & Parra-Cardona, J. R. (2014). Diversity, social justice, and intersectionality trends in C/MFT: A content analysis of three family therapy journals, 2004–2011. *Journal of Marital and Family Therapy, 40*(2), 139–151. https://doi.org/10.1111/jmft.12015

Seligman, M. E. (1996). Science as an ally of practice. *American Psychologist, 51*(10), 1072–1079. https://doi.org/10.1037/0003-066X.51.10.1072

Seligman, M. E. P. (1995). The effectiveness of psychotherapy: The consumer reports study. *American Psychologist, 50*, 965–974. https://doi.org/10.1037/0003-066X.50.12.965

Sexton, T., Gordon, K. C., Gurman, A., Lebow, J., Holtzworth-Munroe, A., & Johnson, S. (2011). Guidelines for classifying evidence-based treatments in couple and family therapy. *Family Process, 50*(3), 377–392. https://doi.org/10.1111/j.1545-5300.2011.01363.x

Sexton, T. L., & Alexander, J. F. (2002). Family-based empirically supported intervention programs. *The Counseling Psychologist, 30*(2), 238–261. https://doi.org/10.1177/0011000002302003

Slife, B. D., Wiggins, B. J., & Graham, J. T. (2005). Avoiding an EST monopoly: Toward a pluralism of philosophies and methods. *Journal of Contemporary Psychotherapy, 35*, 83–97. https://doi.org/10.1007/s10879-005-0805-5

Smith, T., Domenech Rodrıguez, M. M., & Bernal, G. (2011). Culture. *Journal of Clinical Psychology, 67*, 166–175. https://doi.org/10.1002/jclp.20757

Sprenkle, D. H. (2012). Intervention research in couple and family therapy: A methodological and substantive review and an introduction to the special issue. *Journal of Marital & Family Therapy, 38*(1), 3–29. https://doi.org/10.1111/j.1752-0606.2011.00271.x

Sprenkle, D. H., Davis, S. D., & Lebow, J. (2009). *Common factors in couple and family therapy: The overlooked foundation for effective practice*. New York, NY: Guilford Press.

Staller, K. M. (2006). Railroads, runaways, & researchers: Returning evidence rhetoric to its practice base. *Qualitative Inquiry, 12*(3), 503–522. https://doi.org/10.1177/1077800406286524

Substance Abuse and Mental Health Services Administration. (2015). *Racial/ethnic differences in mental health service use among adults*. HHS publication no. SMA-15-4906. Rockville, MD: Substance Abuse and Mental Health Services Administration.

Wendt, D., Jr. (2006). The unevaluated framework of APA's policy on evidence-based practice in psychology (EBPP). *The New School Psychology Bulletin, 4*(1), 89–99.

# Cross-Culturally Responsive Training of Emotionally Focused Couple Therapy: International Experiences

**Senem Zeytinoglu-Saydam**

I am a couple and family therapist, currently living and working in İstanbul. I completed my doctoral studies in couple and family therapy in the USA and moved back to Turkey, my home country. Currently, I am an assistant professor at a private university, where I collaborated with my colleagues to establish the first master's program in couple and family therapy in Turkey. At the university, I teach undergraduate and graduate courses in the Department of Psychology and provide supervision. I also have a private practice in Istanbul. Currently, I am the only EFT-certified therapist, supervisor and organizer of EFT trainings in Turkey. In this chapter, I will describe how my own interest and expertise in emotionally focused couple therapy (EFT) evolved into organizing trainings and building an EFT community in my home country.

Emotionally focused couple therapy is a relatively short-term, structured, and evidenced-based therapy approach designed for working with couples (Johnson, 2004). Since the model is based on working with primary emotions and attachment needs in relationships, it can be applied to families or other relationship difficulties. EFT conceptualizes relational difficulties as partners getting stuck in negative interactional cycles stemming from unmet attachment needs and unexpressed and vulnerable primary feelings. This negative cycle causes each partner to feel disconnected from each other and alone in their relationship and creates an inability to talk about their issues without the conversation escalating into a fight (Johnson, 2004). EFT's structured approach for reducing relational difficulties is comprised of several interventions: highlighting the conflict issues in the relationship; describing the negative interactional cycle in terms of secondary and primary emotions and unmet attachment needs; identifying and heightening the vulnerable, unexpressed, primary feelings underneath the partners' destructive behaviors; creating a new definition for the

---

S. Zeytinoglu-Saydam (✉)
Ozyegin University, Istanbul, Turkey
e-mail: senem.zeytinoglu@ozyegin.edu.tr

© Springer International Publishing AG, part of Springer Nature 2018
S. Singh Poulsen, R. Allan (eds.), *Cross-Cultural Responsiveness & Systemic Therapy*, Focused Issues in Family Therapy, https://doi.org/10.1007/978-3-319-71395-3_4

negative interactional cycle with the underlying vulnerable feelings; encouraging acceptance of these vulnerable feelings within and between partners; and restructuring the relationship with these new positions and helping the partners to create new solutions (Sandberg & Knestel, 2011).

EFT is an evidenced-based model found to be effective and efficient in working with couples' issues. Furthermore, learning EFT seems to create positive long-term and short-term effects for trainees in their personal and professional lives. Montagno, Svatovic, and Levenson (2011) describe that after completing the EFT externship, participants reported an increased knowledge and competence in the model. As they continued to use the model, their emotional processing skills increased, leading to higher self-compassion. The participants also reported a positive impact on their own romantic relationships and their understanding of life experiences and relationships with others. Sandberg and Knestel (2011) underline that trainees specifically stated the benefit of focusing on the process, recognizing secondary emotions and asking about primary emotions. The majority of the trainees highlighted EFT interventions' positive impact on their clients after they started using the model. Yet, some participants also stated that it is an ongoing learning process and, at times, they feel frustrated.

Even though there are several studies conducted on EFT with different clinical populations in North America and Europe, research on the model with Eastern populations is still limited. Since I currently live and work in İstanbul, Turkey, I searched for literature on using EFT with Middle Eastern couples and Turkish couples specifically. The literature search I conducted yielded a few studies conducted in Iran, mostly related to the impact of EFT in reducing couples' negative symptoms. For example, Soltani, Molazadeh, Mahmoodi, and Hosseini (2013) investigated the effectiveness of EFT on increasing the intimacy between the partners using pre- and posttest assessments and compared the results with a no-treatment control group. The participants were recruited from two counseling centers in the city of Shiraz and grouped consisting of seven couples each. The couples in the experimental group received eight to ten sessions of EFT, with each session lasting two hours. The results yielded increased intimacy in couples' emotional, psychological, sexual, physical, relationship, and intellectual experiences. Investigating the effectiveness of EFT with couples facing marital conflict, Ahmadi, Zarei, and Fallahchai (2014) used a pretest, posttest, and no-treatment control group design with 15 couples in each group. Participants were recruited through the consultation centers in Bandar Abbas City. Couples in the experimental group received nine sessions lasting an hour and half each. The difference in marital conflict for the experimental group was significantly lower than the control group. Exploring the effectiveness of the model with infertile couples, Soltani, Shairi, Roshan, and Rahimi (2014) created an experimental and a control group consisted of six couples each. Both groups included three infertile women and three infertile men with their partners who applied for treatment to a fertility center in Tehran. The couples were chosen through convenience sampling since they presented with high levels of stress, depression, and anxiety. The experimental group received the EFT treatment, while the control group did not receive any treatment. The treatment lasted for 10 weeks. Based on the posttest results, the experimental group's anxiety, stress, and depression showed a significant decrease compared to the control group. Even though these studies are valuable since they seem to be the first ones published on the effectiveness of EFT with the Middle-Eastern couples, the sample sizes were very small, and the studies did not focus on the training aspects and experiences of the therapists delivering the EFT interventions. Furthermore, to date, there is no literature on the experience of conducting EFT trainings outside of North America and Europe. For this reason, I will describe in this chapter experiences around conducting emotionally focused couple therapy training in the Turkish context to emphasize the pivotal points for organizing and offering trainings in a culturally responsive and applicable manner. I will also highlight the trends around marriage and divorce in Turkey, clarifying the need for cultural adaptations of EFT to the Turkish culture.

## Trends of Marriage and Divorce in Turkey

Marriage and divorce trends in the Turkish population show changes across time and across the country's diverse geographical locations. In order to understand the changing trends and the current needs, a countrywide quantitative research on the family structure is conducted every 5 years with the initiative of the Ministry of Family and Social Policy in Turkey (Aile ve Sosyal Politikalar Bakanlığı, 2011). The findings of this research, last conducted in 2011, shed light into the practices of, attitudes toward, and ideals related to marriage.

According to the findings of the countrywide 2011 study, people marry at a very early age in Turkey. For almost one fifth of the population, the age of first marriage is below 18, while more than half of the population marry between the age of 18 and 24. The incidences of arranged marriages with the consent of the parties are high (42%), even though many people continue to choose their partners independently, especially with increased levels of education and socioeconomic status. Demir (2013) highlights that the meaning of "arranged marriages" has changed in Turkey over time. Couples whose marriages were being arranged used to be introduced to each other by elder family members with a promise to get married after a couple of meetings. Currently, arranged marriage entails being introduced to one another for the purpose of marriage without a specific timeline on the "dating" relationship. Sadly, there is still a significant percentage of the population, 12% of women and 6% of men, who are forced to marry a partner based on their family's choice.

The family's approval of marriage partner choice remains crucial in the Turkish population. Over 80% of the married partners meet their spouse through their families and neighborhood connections. Only 14% of individuals report meeting their spouse through friends or work (Aile ve Sosyal Politikalar Bakanlığı, 2011). How people meet their spouses differs based on geographical regions; northern and eastern areas of Turkey are known to be more traditional and conservative; marriages among blood relatives and arranged marriages (usually first cousins), and even "forced" marriages without the partner's consent, are more common here than in other areas of Turkey. Therefore, the main motivation for marriage lies around meeting the demands of the families rather than emotional connection.

Overall, participants of the countrywide 2011 survey conducted by the Ministry of Family and Social Policy report a high level of marital satisfaction. Ninety-five percent of the participants describe their marriages as good or very good. Men rate their marital satisfaction higher than women. Yet, we need to approach this finding with a grain of salt as it is "shameful" and inappropriate to complain about your partner outside of your close circles (Bianchi, Milkie, Sayer, & Robinson, 2000). Based on research and survey findings, three major sources of conflict in marriages are distribution of parenting responsibilities, distribution of expenses, and stresses due to financial difficulties. People who belong to a higher socioeconomic class report more problems related to the distribution of parenting responsibilities (Aile ve Sosyal Politikalar Bakanlığı, 2011).

In many marital relationships in Turkey, in times of relational conflict, and in line with the main negative interactional positions highlighted in EFT, the most common response is to keep quiet, stonewall, and yell. Seventy-five percent of the partners surveyed reported keeping quiet and stonewalling. When gender differences around interactional positions are investigated, women report being more likely to keep quiet and stonewall and men are more likely to scream, yell, leave, or show physical aggression. These reactions are in line with the Turkish societal expectations around how women and men should act when faced with a disagreement.

When faced with a conflict, most couples (62%) in Turkey do not think to get help from outside sources for their difficulties. Twenty-three percent reported they would ask guidance from the elder members of their families and 6% from their children. Only 3% of the participants cited mental health providers as a possible source of guidance and support. Yet, this finding does not seem to apply to couples in İstanbul, the largest city in Turkey. Eight percent of couples surveyed who lived in İstanbul reported seeking mental health services as a viable option for marital difficulties. Furthermore, this percentage rose as socioeconomic status and educational level increased.

Based on the findings, being in love, having similar family structures, and being religious and employed are the most desirable factors sought in a partner. Personal qualities such as being well-groomed, loyal, family-oriented, reliable, honest, sensitive, generous, and patient are all reported as very important when considering marriage. Factors such as acting appropriately in public and supporting the spouse against one's own family were also cited as important by almost all the participants. These qualities and expectations clarify a need for emotional connection in Turkish couples entering marriage. Fundamental attachment needs such as being able to rely on and trust your partner and feeling your partner's love are defined as important factors for many Turkish couples to consider when deciding on marriage.

Even though the divorce rates show a small increase since the last time this comprehensive research was conducted in Turkey in 2006, this increase becomes even more apparent when related to the socioeconomic status of the participants. The highest SES level of the Turkish population has the highest divorce rate. Demir (2013) states that, like the USA, 40% of divorces in Turkey occur in the first 5 years of the marriage. The most common reason cited for divorce in 2011 was "irresponsible or indifferent attitude" for both men and women followed by inability to support the family and adultery. For strategies around dealing with conflict, the behavioral tendencies of yelling, keeping quiet, and stonewalling are in line with the pursuer-withdrawer dynamic described in EFT (Johnson, 2004). Physical violence for women and disrespectful behavior toward the husband's family for men are also common reasons for divorce. When asked about remarriage, more men than women expressed a desire to remarry. This difference is consistent even if the participants have children. More men with children report thinking about remarriage than women. The latter report to be hesitant about remarriage due to the societal stigma around being a divorced woman. Thus, even after they go through divorce, Turkish couples and Turkish men in particular do not give up on the idea of marriage.

Based on these findings, there seems to be a need for effective couple therapy starting from the premarital stages of the relationship or in the beginning of married life in Turkey. Turkish people marry very young, usually with the encouragement or the approval of their families, with partners who have similar family structures as them. In our clinical experience, most of the couple's issues arise as they move through the life cycle changes, like couples everywhere. Expectations of each partner change over time, yet their need for emotional connection stays the same. When the main reason cited (lack of emotional connection) for divorce is considered, Turkish couples like any other couple need accessibility, responsiveness, and engagement from their partners, given these are the core components of attachment. The content of their issues, their cognitive appraisals, and action tendencies may differ from the Western world, yet, in our clinical experience, their core feelings and needs are like couples elsewhere. Currently, most couple therapy approaches being taught and used in Turkey are based on cognitive interventions or psychodynamic perspectives. Cognitive interventions without bringing the vulnerable feelings into the room do not create long-lasting solutions, and many couples cannot afford to stay in therapy as long as psychodynamic approaches often require. Thus, EFT, with its focus on vulnerable emotions and attachment needs and its relatively short-term structure approach, offers a unique solution for couples' relationship issues.

My desire to bring EFT trainings to Turkey emerged when I continued onto the core skills training during the third year of my doctoral program through the Philadelphia Center for EFT. Our trainer, who was born and raised in Asia and conducted most of her EFT trainings in that continent, talked about couples' issues she had witnessed in the Eastern world. I was really touched by her international experience since mostly in the USA, discussions around social justice and multiculturalism are limited to the underrepresented populations within the USA. Even though I completed my graduate level of training in programs focused on multiculturalism, I had seen that most of the faculty members' thinking, experience, and advocacy were around racial and ethnic minorities living in the USA. For this reason, witnessing how a therapy model is taught and conducted outside of the Western world was new to me. Furthermore, I felt the need for a couple intervention model that would help me to work through the feelings of anger and aggressive comments made by partners and family members in sessions. Anger outbursts and ultimatums were frequent reactions that I had experienced in my sessions both with Turkish and Western clients. Thus, I asked the trainer if she would be interested in offering trainings in Turkey once I moved back there after completing my doctoral work.

## Conducting EFT Trainings and Supervision in Turkey

Based on the International Center for Excellence in Emotionally Focused Therapy (ICEEFT) guidelines, EFT trainings are conducted in two levels: externship and advanced core skills. Externship takes place over the course of 28 h, which is divided over 4 days. Since it is an introductory course, it does not have an upper limit for the number of trainees. Advanced core skills training on the other hand is a more focused and advanced level of training, designed mostly around intervention strategies and supervision. Core skills training is a total of 48 h over several weekends. The quota for the advanced core skills training is 8–16 trainees. Based on this structure, it makes sense to organize an externship first and then move on to planning a core skills training if there is enough interest from the externship participants.

Based on ICEEFT rules, we (me and the trainer from Philadelphia) first needed to check if there were any active EFT trainings in Turkey. When we learned that there were none, we applied to the ICEEFT board to get the formal approval for conducting the first EFT externship in İstanbul in 2014. Once we received the approval from ICEEFT, we got to work. Although I was the main organizer of the trainings, I had a very supportive, hardworking, and efficient partner in Turkey, whose doctoral degree is also in family therapy. We were both teaching at the same clinical psychology program's couple and family therapy track at the time we started organizing the trainings. When organizing trainings in the Eastern world, there are a few critical issues to consider: logistics, language of the training and the training materials, cost of the training, and credibility of the training and training announcements.

### *Logistics*

As the organizers of the training, and since my Turkish colleague and I were faculty members at the same university, we decided to hold our trainings at this university. This was also convenient because the university had a clinic that had rooms with one-way mirrors. We decided that this setup would make it easier to have the live sessions required for the externship.

Since live sessions were a new concept in Turkey and did not take place in many trainings, it was a struggle to find a Turkish couple fluent in English who would agree to come in for a session knowing that they would be watched by a group of people through a one-way mirror. The couple needed to be Turkish and fluent in English for two reasons: (a) I wanted the trainees (from other parts of the world in addition to Turkey) to see how a Turkish couple would respond to EFT given the model's English-language base, and (b) they needed to speak English well enough to explain themselves elaborately and understand what the US-trainer therapist was saying. One of the difficulties was to find a couple who could speak English fluently enough to explain themselves in a therapeutic setting. Another challenge in finding a couple willing to participate in the live session process was that therapy is still considered a taboo issue in Turkey, evoking feelings of shame. Furthermore, people usually had the fear of potentially having an acquaintance behind the one-way mirror as they shared their troubles and vulnerable feelings. Yet, we knew that for delivering a culturally responsive training, it was crucial for the trainees to experience EFT conducted with a Turkish couple. We expected that the trainees might have doubts about the effectiveness of the model with Turkish couples and how the Turkish couples would respond to the interventions since the common models used in Turkey are more cognitive or psychodynamic based. We also wanted the trainees to see an example of what the trainer-therapist might work with in terms of issues specific to the Turkish culture (e.g., over-involvement of the in-laws). We wanted to show the trainees how EFT works with a Turkish couple to increase their belief in the cross-cultural responsiveness of the model. For this reason, we started the search for a client couple as early as possible while we were organizing the trainings. Our search of 2 months involved emailing professional groups for referrals, asking the signed-up participant trainees to bring one of their cases, and even asking our acquaintances. Finally, our extensive search yielded a Turkish couple fluent in English and who wanted to come to a one-session couple therapy with our trainer.

## *Announcing and Establishing the Credibility of the Training*

Our trainings were announced using the Google groups for mental health professionals and through universities' clinical master's programs and Facebook. Even though ICEEFT is a well-known organization in North America and Europe, most Turkish mental health professionals are not familiar with it. Plus, to this day, there are other EFT trainings conducted in Turkey by local professionals who have never been officially trained and credentialed in EFT through ICEEFT. For this reason, we needed to lay out the uniqueness and legitimacy of this training as we were announcing it. In our flyers, we made it a point to explain what ICEEFT and ICEEFT-approved trainings mean, and we explained how a certificate-of-training completion by ICEEFT would be valid and valued internationally.

## *Language of the Training and Training Materials*

Even though many undergraduate and graduate psychology programs in Turkey provide their courses in English, most mental health professionals in Turkey do not understand or speak the language well enough to attend a 4-day training in English. Delivering all the training materials in English could also be a hurdle for recruiting potential trainees. For this reason, one of our primary issues was to decide whether we would translate all the materials into English and provide translation during the training either by a professional company or by a therapist fluent in both languages and trained in EFT. To make the training applicable to all trainees during and after the training, all the training materials were translated to Turkish including the transcription of the training tape. We decided to do the translation for the group of professionals who expressed a need for it in the beginning of the externship. However, currently, we provide translation for the whole group since it gives the trainees more time to process what they have heard and learn the Turkish terminology and way of speaking as they conduct EFT. Based on the trainees' feedback, they find having an EFT-trained translator very helpful, and based on our experience, translating what the trainer said after she completed a few sentences did not create a time constraint for the training as the trainer was also willing to work with the translator. As we translated what the trainer said in the moment, we could also model how to use the therapeutic interventions in our native tongue. Emotionally focused therapy interventions require simple words and imagery (i.e., RISSC; Johnson, 2004). Yet, direct translation of the English words to Turkish as they are used in a session may lose their simplicity and sound theatrical. For this reason, it was helpful to share with the trainees our experience regarding the use of certain words in our native tongue in a simple and natural way and how to use "lighter" words, such as worried instead of scared, when necessary. At times, trainees also asked questions regarding the cultural issues that came up with certain interventions, such as difficulty supporting men to be vulnerable in sessions, couples focusing on parenting issues to distract from their lack of intimacy, and asking for a "prescription" to solve their issues rather than allowing themselves to become vulnerable with one another. At those times, my colleague and I asked the trainer about her experiences with similar issues and, at times with the permission of the EFT trainer, shared our ideas and experience as EFT-trained professionals practicing couple therapy in Turkey. For this reason, we opted for translating the training ourselves rather than hire a translator who was not trained or familiar with the concepts and the EFT approach.

## *The Cost of the Trainings*

When we first started conducting EFT trainings in Turkey, the Turkish lira's worth was almost half of a US dollar. Currently, the lira is almost a quarter of a US dollar due to the economic crisis in our country. Even as we first started to build the budget, we needed to consider possible fluctuations in the currency in the upcoming months since these fluctuations were very likely to happen in developing countries. For this reason, our first move was to ask for a fee adjustment from our US-based EFT trainer. We asked for the adjustment based on a couple of things; first we checked the price of similar trainings conducted in Turkey to set a price for ours and considered the possible fluctuations of the currency. In countries that are not economically stable, high prices create major problems for recruitment. Based on our venue, we had an estimate for the number of trainees. We also checked the prices for the flight and accommodations. After we created our budget, we decided on our adjusted fee. At this time, we really appreciated the experience of working with someone who is used to giving trainings in the Eastern world for adjusted fees due to changes in the currency; this was an important consideration, cultural and economic, given our desire to hold the trainings in Turkey for primarily a Turkish training audience.

## *New Developments*

When we started organizing the EFT trainings, we decided to hold them in a university setting to increase their legitimacy, ensure easy access to clinical psychology students since students in Turkey are more likely to sign up for trainings than working professionals, and benefit from the one-way mirror room settings existing in our on-site clinic. We arranged the trainer's accommodation in a hotel close to the university. However, another consideration that has come up in the last several years, due to the frequent bombings in İstanbul, was the decision to arrange for a hotel much closer to my and my colleague's homes to have access if there was another attack and the roads were closed. Our trainer has been very understanding, accommodating, and supportive of us throughout the political situation and terrorist attacks in Turkey.

Moving forward, it became difficult to find classrooms in the university and to arrange the clinic for live sessions since the students in the clinical psychology program continue to see their clients 7 days a week. The trainees also reported that the classrooms were not very comfortable because occasionally we had to be in a different classroom for each training session. Furthermore, there had been a few attacks to the university campus in the past years, and once, the administration had to shut down the campus because of a terrorist threat. For this reason, we began holding and are currently holding the trainings and all EFT-related activities in the psychotherapy center in which I (SZS) work, which is a relatively safer venue. At this time, we use a webcam for the live session as the trainer is seeing the couple. We reflect it on the projection screen via the computer in the training room. This also creates a comfortable therapy setting for the live session clients since the webcam is less visible and intrusive than the one-way mirror. Since we have been having live sessions for the past few years, finding a couple to participate in a live session has become relatively easier since we ask the couples already participating in the live session for referrals of other potential couple clients. They might recommend their friends who might benefit from the live session experience and participation. At times, a couple that participated in a live session in a previous year's training might ask to come again for the next externship because they had benefited from the live session experience.

## Training Feedback Related to Cultural Barriers

At the end of each training, the trainees are asked to fill out evaluation forms. Overall, for the past 4 years, the trainees have consistently reported finding the training informative, enlightening, and helpful for their work. For the purposes of this section, I will describe the trainees' constructive feedback regarding their possible reservations about applying EFT in the Turkish cultural context.

The most common doubt raised by trainees is utilizing EFT with male clients. Some trainees expressed that it would be difficult for men to show their emotions during therapy since culturally they are taught not to be vulnerable or show vulnerability, especially in front of women. Trainees had concerns around using RISSC (using and repeating the clients' words and using a soft voice, simple words, and imagery) and increasing the emotional intensity in the room; trainees reported believing that it would threaten the male clients and would disrupt the therapeutic alliance with them. They highlighted that "shame" is a very dominant feeling in Turkish culture, and clients are likely to become defensive once the feeling of shame comes up. Trainees highlighted that it would be difficult for women to express their needs and for the men to accept it especially in couples with low socioeconomic status because they may be more traditional in their gender roles, which requires the women to accommodate and men to dominate. Trainees asserted that when women in the Turkish culture become what is perceived as demanding, usually the families would intervene, asking them to be more "reasonable." For this reason, it might be difficult for women to identify and express their needs without some encouragement and approval from the families of origin around expressing her needs and feelings. Refraining from and avoiding conflict are the favored conflict management styles in Turkish culture (Cingöz-Ulu & Lalonde, 2007), so, for women, it would be too aggressive to complain about their spouses to an unfamiliar third party. Furthermore, culturally, enduring the pain around relationship conflict without openly complaining and making sacrifices accordingly is glorified for women. According to some trainees, it would be difficult for clients, both male and female, to express negative emotions. Congruent with their dominant conflict management styles, Turkish people do have a difficult time expressing negative emotions in relationships such as sadness, anger, fear, and disgust due to both the characteristics of the feeling and social expectations (Bolak Boratav, Sunar, & Ataca, 2011).

Some trainees reported that it would be difficult to ensure client retention in the therapy process since EFT does not offer the clients solutions in the first session. Culturally, Turkish people are used to a hierarchical approach in therapy where they get advice from an expert in their field, an authority figure. For this reason, validating and reflecting without offering a solution might lead them to think that the therapist is not an expert on his/her field and does not have the answers. A similar concern was around the therapist expressing his/her own feelings in the session, which is part of a collaborative approach, and yet, this would diminish the authority of the therapist in the eyes of the clients.

The last issue brought up by the trainees was domestic violence since intimate partner and relational violence is common, but rarely reported in Turkey. The trainees needed more information on how to assess relational violence and how to intervene using an EFT perspective, with couples dealing with intimate partner violence. Questions around this issue included how to assess intimate partner violence with EFT and any modality of therapy to be used; individual or couple, if there is intimate partner violence. Trainees did not know if there are certain recommended ways to ask about the violence using EFT and if the therapist would still see the client as a couple and move forward with the interventions when there is ongoing violence.

## *Recommendations to Trainees in Dealing with Cultural Barriers*

Engaging male clients in couple therapy has generally been a concern for therapists regardless of the model they use (Shepard & Harway, 2012). Therefore, it is understandable that trainees are worried about how to apply a technique based on emotions with Turkish men. Yet, as they start practicing EFT, they find that male clients, as any other client population in other cultural settings, usually respond well to validation and reflection and that it does help build the therapeutic alliance since feeling heard and understood seem to be a universal desire for human beings. Reflection also helps to slow down the process and focus on the core issues of the couple's relationship. In our own clinical experience and what we shared with trainees, men find reflection helpful since the therapist does not seem to get tangled up in content and "waste time with trivial details." In our trainings, we explain to the trainees that in terms of the RISSC intervention, male clients usually react suspiciously to someone using a soft voice since they are not used to "experts" and "authority figures" speaking in a soft voice; therefore, we recommend that they adjust their voices as they move forward with the therapy process. This would require them to use a higher- or louder-pitched tone of voice as they are reflecting the secondary feelings such as anger and lowering their tone of voice as they move down to more vulnerable feelings. We also suggest using less intense words to describe their emotional experience in the beginning (e.g., cautious instead of scared) and gradually move onto more vulnerable emotions.

Using guilt and shame is a frequently used parenting strategy in the Turkish culture (Kagitcibasi, Sunar, & Bekman, 1988). In line with the trainees' concern, shame is a feeling that usually evokes defensive in people. Thus, it is important for the therapist to delve into the feelings of shame slowly to build the therapeutic relationship, so that the couple believes the therapist is working for the benefit of the relationship rather than siding with one party. Paying attention to the facial expressions and body language becomes crucial when exploring shame. Based on our clinical experience, Turkish men tend to have a "guilty smile" as feelings of shame come up. In the trainees' eyes, this might seem as entitlement for their behavior, which might make the trainee therapist angry with the client during the session. For this reason, it would be important for the EFT supervisors and trainers to describe this as a common reaction to shame in preparing the therapists and to engage role-play strategies to explore this reaction deeper. Questions around difference in emotional reactions do come up during the trainings and supervision, so we pay attention to addressing these questions and using case examples, at times from trainees' own cases, when we conduct role-plays. Since both our trainers are from cultures somewhat similar to Turkey and I am born and raised in Turkey, we do provide examples and model how to reflect, validate, and reframe culturally unique emotional reactions.

Expressing their needs and desires might be difficult for Turkish women as well. Yet, in our and our trainees' experience when women come to therapy, it is usually their last resort. For this reason, they are open to exploring their own needs to ameliorate their relationship. As stated in the previous section, women usually consult with their family members or their children when they have relationship issues, before consulting with a therapist. Therefore, women usually come to couple therapy on the following occasions: their children are having emotional or behavioral issues, they are advised by the family members to seek counseling, or they would like to seek counseling regardless of the family's advice because their dissatisfaction with their relationship is severe. We explain to the trainees that in the first scenario, usually the couple's issues become clear during the assessment phase and the couple is then invited for counseling. At this time, it might take some time for the women to figure out what they need from their partner and they might be hesitant about it since they would not want to "rock the boat." It is also important to assess if the woman has become a "drained pursuer" with no hope that the relationship would improve, which would explain her difficulty around expressing her needs.

Answering another concern of the trainees, we emphasize in our training that it is vital to always assess for violence as we start couple therapy in Turkey both in couple and individual sessions. In Turkey, intimate partner violence is common, but underreported. Since there might also be a shame for both parties, around reporting the violence, asking how bad the fights get would be a more useful way than asking if there is ongoing violence in the relationship since Turkish people favor an indirect communication style and might find direct questioning around a sensitive issue offensive (Zeyrek, 2001); direct questioning might lead the couple to shut down and disrupt the therapeutic relationship. Even if there is no ongoing violence in the relationship, if there were incidents in the past, it is helpful to do a nonviolence contract in a couple therapy session. Furthermore, Turkish people have survived a number of political traumas in the past years, so we emphasize to the trainees that it is important to get information on the history of violence and assess for anxiety, depression, and PTSD in both partners. We share our clinical experiences with the trainees that many clients suffer from depression and anxiety following a terrorist attack. Referral for individual therapy and/or psychiatric consultation may be needed for further stabilization.

In Turkey, clients' primary goal is to get an expert opinion when seeking advice from a therapist. Therefore, we emphasize to our trainees the need to specify what we mean by a "collaborative approach." In EFT, we assume that the clients are experts on their own experiences, feelings, and needs, so as the trainees identify the clients' appraisals, feelings, and needs, they are constantly checking in with their clients about how they describe their experience and assume a collaborative approach. We encourage the trainees to present this collaborative process to their clients as vital for identifying the problem. Yet, as we get both partners' behaviors, appraisals, feelings, and needs and describe them as their cycle, we do get into an "expert" role, showing them that their actions, even though they make sense based on their perceptions and feelings, do not help the relationship. In our trainings and supervision, we emphasize that, at times in sessions, we hold an "expert" role, holding the mirror to the source of their negative interactional cycle, labeling it as "the core of the issue," identifying what works and what does not work and direct them empathically to showing more of their vulnerable sides to each other. The trainees can also highlight to their clients that once they are able to talk about their problems from a stance of vulnerability, they can come up with solutions on their own. Through this process, we help the trainees to hold a "both/and" approach in holding collaborative and expert positions.

Usually, men enter couple therapy with a belief that if they cannot solve the problem in the relationship, nobody else can. After validating this belief, empathizing with the time and effort they had spent on solving the issues in their relationship and normalizing that sometimes solutions are hard to find when you are part of the negative cycle, it is important for the trainees to highlight that their main job is to figure out why clients cannot solve their issues and what does not work as they desperately try. As we emphasize this, we ask the trainees to once again assume the expert role, the relationship consultant with experience of showing clients what does not work so they can change their relationship dynamics themselves. With regard to offering solutions, as the trainees identify and externalize the cycle, it does become a solution for couples to stop the cycle. Trainees can start highlighting the cycle and externalizing it piece by piece starting from the first session to show clients what is not working in their relationship and why.

Even though the EFT trainings are very helpful and create a strong foundation in the learning process, Sandberg and Knestel (2011) state that ongoing supervision and continuous support are needed for the trainees. For this reason, we decided to move forward with building the EFT community in Turkey, offering case consultations and supervision. Our efforts around community building will be described in the next section.

## Building a Community

We have been organizing EFT trainings in Turkey since 2014. Currently, we collaborate with two trainers; a US-based trainer with whom we started this process and a trainer geographically closer to Turkey. To date, we have conducted four externships and two core skills trainings. After completing the trainings, we invite people to join our Google group where we discuss cases and share upcoming EFT events and resources.

Since becoming a supervisor in training, I also hold monthly supervision and case consultation groups in which the goal is to strengthen our EFT skills in multiple ways: watching videos and training tapes, doing role-plays, sharing cases, and doing case formulations. The trainees involved in these groups are already trained in EFT, so they can bring their cases for supervision, provide video or audio tapes of their sessions, and receive supervision as we watch their tapes. Since most of our trainees are practicing in Turkey with Turkish couples right now, they present their cases and bring in their tapes for supervision or case consultation. This provides me the opportunity to focus on unique cultural issues and model and conduct role-plays on how to approach Turkish couples in therapy. However, the trainees do not have to be actively working with couples to attend these meetings. Our main goal is to practice case formulation using the EFT framework, identifying the cycle, using RISSC, and conducting interventions. We do role-plays in every meeting and discuss culturally specific issues when using EFT, such as difficulty around expressing negative emotions, difficulty for men to be vulnerable, and refraining from conflict. I try to help the trainees with common impasses experienced in EFT sessions, such as freezing when the emotional intensity in the room is high, resorting to problem solving, talking faster and in a more high-pitched tone, and "sugarcoating" the difficulties. At this point, I find it vital to work on increasing trainees' self-compassion since working with couples and learning a new therapy model are both difficult. If they need further help, trainees can also seek individual and group supervision based on their specific cases.

Currently, we have a website (www.duyguodaklicifterapisi.com) which clarifies all the rules and regulations enforced by ICEEFT related to receiving training and supervision in EFT and outlines EFT resources in English and in Turkish. Additionally, we have active Facebook, LinkedIn, and Instagram accounts to attract people interested in EFT and to also share weekly, related videos, resources, international trainings, and updates from the Turkish community. Per ICEEFT guidelines, there has to be a certified supervisor in the area in order for the community to be official (Building and Successfully Growing EFT Centers & Communities, 2017). A community is built based on ICEEFT rules and regulations to get officially linked to ICCEFT. For this reason, along with the trainees interested in taking an active role in the management of this community, we developed our mission statement and short-term goals. Currently, we are in the process of receiving official recognition from ICEEFT. In order to legitimize ourselves in Turkey, we are also moving forward with becoming a local association. Our next steps include linking ourselves officially with ICEEFT; increasing the number of certified EFT therapists and supervisors; becoming a local EFT association; developing our website further to include more EFT resources, direct contact to therapists, and news on the ongoing activities; and organizing EFT events open to public.

## Conclusion

As I look back on our process when writing this chapter, it is the relationships, the people who believe in our ability to make this happen and support us that make it possible. There are still challenges around organizing trainings due to terrorist attacks and fluctuations in foreign currency, which highlights the necessity of having a local trainer in Turkey. Moving forward, aside from developing our community further and increasing the number of certified supervisors and therapists, our next steps involve doing more extensive clinical research in working with Turkish couples using EFT, developing guidelines for working through challenges of strict gender norms, refraining from expressing negative feelings, and talking about conflict.

## References

Ahmadi, F. S., Zarei, E., & Fallahchai, S. R. (2014). The effectiveness of Emotionally Focused Couple Therapy in resolution of marital conflicts between the couples who visited the consultation centers. *Journal of Educational and Management Studies, 4*(1), 118–123. Retrieved from http://jems.science-line.com/attachments/article/21/J.%20Educ.%20Manage.%20Stud.,%204(1)%20118-123%202014.pdf

Aile ve Sosyal Politikalar Bakanlığı. (2011). Türkiye'de Aile Yapısı Araştırması 2011, Ankara.

Bianchi, S. M., Milkie, M. A., Sayer, L. C., & Robinson, J. P. (2000). Is anyone doing the housework? Trends in gender division of household labor? *Social Forces, 79*(1), 191–228. https://doi.org/10.2307/2675569

Bolak Boratav, H., Sunar, D., & Ataca, B. (2011). Duyguları Sergileme Kuralları ve Bağlamsal Belirleyicileri. *Türk Psikoloji Dergisi, 26*(68), 90–101. Retrieved from http://www.turkpsikolojiyazilari.com/PDF/TPD/68/06.pdf

Building and successfully growing EFT Centers & Communities. (2017). Retrieved from https://members.iceeft.com/files/BuildingAnEFTCommunity.pdf

Cingöz-Ulu, B., & Lalonde, R. N. (2007). The role of culture and relational context in interpersonal conflict: Do Turks and Canadians use different conflict management strategies? *International Journal of Intercultural Relations, 31*(4), 443–458. https://doi.org/10.1016/j.ijintrel.2006.12.001

Demir, S. A. (2013). Attitudes towards concepts of marriage and divorce in Turkey. *American International Journal of Contemporary Research, 3*(12), 83–88. Retrieved from http://www.aijcrnet.com/journals/Vol_3_No_12_December_2013/14.pdf

Johnson, S. M. (2004). *Creating connection: The practice of emotionally focused couple therapy* (2nd Ed). New York: Brunner/Routledge.

Kagitcibasi, C., Sunar, D., & Bekman, S. (1988). *Comprehensive preschool education project: Proje Raporu.* Ottawa, Canada: International Development Research Centre.

Montagno, M., Svatovic, M., & Levenson, H. (2011). Short-term and long-term effects of training in emotionally focused couple therapy: Professional and personal aspects. *Journal of Marital and Family Therapy, 37*(4), 380–292. https://doi.org/10.1111/j.1752-0606.2011.00250.x

Sandberg, J. G., & Knestel, A. (2011). The experience of learning Emotionally Focused Couples Therapy. *Journal of Marital and Family Therapy, 37*(4), 393–410. https://doi.org/10.1111/j.1752-0606.2011.00254.x

Shepard, D., & Harway, M. (2012). *Engaging men in couple therapy.* New York, NY: Routledge.

Soltani, A., Molazadeh, J., Mahmoodi, M., & Hosseini, S. (2013). A study on the effectiveness of Emotional Focused Couple Therapy on intimacy of couples. *Procedia – Social and Behavioral Sciences, 82*, 461–465. https://doi.org/10.1016/j.sbspro.2013.06.293

Soltani, M., Shairi, M. R., Roshan, R., & Rahimi, C. (2014). The impact of Emotionally Focused Therapy on emotional distress in infertile couples. *International Journal of Fertility and Sterility, 7*(4), 337–344. Retrieved from https://www.ncbi.nlm.nih.gov/pmc/articles/PMC3901179/

Zeyrek, D. (2001). Politeness in Turkish and its linguistic manifestations: A socio-cultural perspective. In A. Bayraktaroglu & M. Sifianou (Eds.), *Linguistic politeness across boundaries: The case of Greek and Turkish* (pp. 43–74). Amsterdam: John Benjamins Publishing Company.

# Cultural Responsiveness in Family Therapy: Integrative and Common Factors Lens

**Shruti Singh Poulsen**

I became a family therapist almost 25 years ago, because the systemic lens and perspective resonated with how I already viewed the world and with my beliefs about how people function and grow. Within my cultural context (Asian Indian), I already felt "at home" thinking and functioning systemically. My formal education and training as a family therapist provided me with the structure, the language, and the scholarly framework to understand and apply a way of being and working clinically that I already adhered to as a person. However, with the formal training in family therapy also came questions about what all this meant for practicing in a context that was diverse, multicultural, and demographically varied. Wrapped into these questions was also the awareness of myself as a diverse, multicultural being with cross-cultural identities and experiences. I am a woman of color, an immigrant who was born in India who has lived in several other countries in addition to India and the United States, a partner in a long-lasting interracial and interethnic heterosexual marriage, a parent of biracial young adult children, a scholar and teacher, and of course, a family therapist. All these cultural identities and experiences, and others that are not listed, have led me to reflect deeply about the models of systemic therapy, both foundational and contemporary, that I "grew up" with as a family therapist – how do they apply to someone like me, what resonates for me as a person and a clinician, why or why not, and what do these models mean to my clients who themselves come from diverse, multicultural contexts and experiences and identify in multiple different ways?

These questions and my attempts at understanding myself and my work as a culturally responsive therapist have led me to an appreciation for using an integrative lens to my understanding and application of systemic therapy models. In particular, I am drawn to the common factors lens (Sprenkle & Blow, 2004) because it resonates

S. Singh Poulsen (✉)
University of Colorado Denver, Denver, CO, USA
e-mail: Shruti.Poulsen@ucdenver.edu

with my understanding of myself as a person as well as a family therapist working in diverse contexts with diverse, cross-cultural clients. During my doctoral studies, I learned about the common factors lens and I also learned about being integrative in my use of the various systemic models (foundational, postmodern, and empirically based) to which I was exposed. While several of the foundational, postmodern, and empirically based models that I learned resonated with me, I felt limited as a cultural being, identifying in multiple ways culturally, to stick to only one model. I also found individual models, limiting and limited when considering how to use them cross-culturally with culturally diverse clients. While a common factors lens is not intended to replace any model or to diminish the important clinical contributions of historical and contemporary models to our work, the lens has helped me understand my own work and how I integrate aspects of different models in ways that can be therapeutically effective and culturally responsive. A challenge of using a common factors lens is that its origins and development are not rooted in attunement to cross-cultural responsiveness or working with culturally diverse clients. In the 14 years since the completion of my doctoral degree, I have spent a great deal of time reflecting and analyzing my own clinical work, the systemic models and techniques I use, and how I can use the common factors lens as a guide to my understanding and application of systemic therapies in ways that support cross-cultural responsiveness, both for my clients and for my own self-understanding. As a doctoral student, I "fell in love" with the foundational systemic tool, the genogram, especially the cultural genogram, as a process for deeper understanding of myself and my clients. The more that I have used variations of the genogram in my practice, the more evident it has become to me that the tool is effective in its ability to tap into an integrative way of working that is also culturally responsive. In this chapter, I attempt to describe how I use a common factors lens in implementing the genogram and cultural genogram to enhance systemic work to be more culturally responsive and respectful.

## Cultural Responsiveness: Why an Integrative Approach Makes Sense

Our clients are not unidimensional, and their experiences are not unidimensional. I and they are an integration and intersection of identities and lived experiences (D'Aniello, Nguyen, & Piercy, 2016). To know someone deeply and clearly is to be able to access these experiences and identities and meanings that people bring to their sense of self and to their experiences in their relationships. One model of therapy is not sufficient, nor are multiple models applied in eclectic or haphazard ways, enough. A theoretically sound and integrative approach is useful in working with clients in all their diversity and uniqueness (Lee, 2012; White, Connolly Gibbons, & Schamberger, 2006). I have found in my clinical work that a common factors lens offers a way to use systemic models and techniques, especially foundational ones, to enhance cross-cultural responsiveness and ultimately practice in socially just ways.

Attunement to several factors, therapeutic relationship, client and therapist factors, and engendering hope are considered important elements of effective therapy models (Sprenkle & Blow, 2004). I use genograms to support systemic therapy work in understanding the lived realities of clients and their diverse social locations. Understanding the dynamic nature of clients' lives and their cultural realities is important to the therapy process; I believe the common factors lens allows me to be integrative in the family therapy approaches I use in my work and also be culturally responsive in my work.

I believe that utilizing a foundational approach such as the genogram can cultivate and expand culturally responsive conversations for clients and therapists, when they are implemented using a common factors lens. Genograms are invaluable as a clinical tool in understanding clients' lived realities and their diverse social locations; a common factors lens can enhance the clinical utility and cultural responsiveness of such a systemic tool.

## Common Factors: Cross-Cultural Responsiveness and Integrative Lens

Common factors are described as the "common mechanisms of change, which cut across all effective psychotherapy approaches" (Sprenkle & Blow, 2004, p. 114). These "common mechanisms of change" are variables that are associated with positive clinical outcomes. They are not specific to any particular approach; they are common across several or all approaches (Morgan & Sprenkle, 2007). While current literature identifies a number of possible common factors that can be found across effective and successful psychotherapies (Stamoulos et al., 2016), in my clinical work, I focus on primarily client factors, therapist factors, the therapeutic relationship, and promoting hope and expectancy. The common factors lens enables an integrative and holistic approach to clinical practice (Hubble, Duncan, & Miller, 1999; Sprenkle, Davis, & Lebow, 2009). Paying attention to client factors, therapist factors, the therapeutic relationship, and promoting hope and expectancy are critical to systemic therapies in general and certainly a useful framework when attempting to be integrative and culturally responsive in our systemic work.

When I utilize the common factors lens in my systemic work, I emphasize the integrative and cultural responsiveness potential of the common factors that have been shown to be effective in client change processes. There are also common factors that are specific to systemic models which are important to pay attention to regardless of which systemic techniques and tools I am using – relational conceptualization, managing relational patterns, and expanded treatment systems and relational alliance (Sprenkle et al., 2009). As systems theorists and clinicians, we tend to understand and incorporate in our work factors such as a relational conceptualization, managing relational patterns, and attending to the expanded treatment systems and the relational alliance; in many ways, it is "a given" that systems therapists attend to these systemic common factors in our work. In my systemic practice, attunement to the systemic-specific common factors lens and the general common factors lens has led to my own and my clients' deeper understanding and a more flexible approach to systemic therapy that supports cross-cultural responsiveness.

## *Using the Genogram and Cultural Genogram*

The genogram and the cultural genogram have long been staples of systemic therapy processes and part of clinical assessment, treatment, and in developing clinical and cultural understanding of clients' lived experiences (Hardy & Laszloffy, 1995; Lim, 2008; Keiley et al., 2002; Magnuson & Shaw, 2003). The "basic" genogram focuses on primarily family-of-origin interactional, structure, organization, history, and patterns (McGoldrick, Gerson, & Petry, 2008). The cultural genogram includes all the variables in a "basic" genogram as well as explorations of cultural elements such as immigration history, racial and ethnic background, and intergenerational experiences within the macro-systemic contexts of oppression, racism, privilege, and power (Hardy & Laszloffy, 1995). Genograms are used not only for data gathering and assessment; using the genogram or cultural genogram with clients can have a profound impact on their development and change process and on the client-therapist relationship (Lim, 2008). In working with my clients on their genograms, I might describe the experience at times as challenging, scary, intrusive, and intense; however, more often than not, I and my clients also experience construction of their genogram as part of the therapy process, to be transformative and effective in gaining deeper empathy, connection, and contextual understanding. Clients report that the genogram process is often a catalytic experience that provides them an opportunity to examine and understand in a culturally meaningful way, previously held notions, assumptions, and values about oneself and the world around them. Clients' experience of the genogram also can lead to supporting their ability to make decisions about different ways of being and relating and existing in their larger contexts once they have more in-depth knowledge of their own experiences, context, culture, and background.

Genograms and the cultural genogram have been adapted for a variety of uses in not only the therapy setting; in the training setting, they are frequently used to enhance a therapist trainees' understanding of systemic concepts as well as an understanding of the self and one's larger systems and contexts, especially culture (Magnuson & Shaw, 2003). Genograms and the cultural genogram used with clients provide a framework for deepening the client-therapist trust and alliance and also in engendering hope in the therapy process. When I construct a genogram with my clients, usually early in the therapy process, it provides a structure and organization to the therapy process. This structure creates safety for the client even when I am asking vulnerable questions. The structure to ask vulnerable questions starting early in the therapy process contributes to developing the therapeutic alliance. I and my clients generally experience the use of the genogram and cultural genogram as ways to strengthen the therapeutic alliance, especially when the genogram process occurs early in the therapy setting. Clients report that doing the genogram helps them gain an appreciation for their own challenges and that my willingness to ask them difficult questions early in the therapy process demonstrates a commitment on my part to provide a safe holding space for clients' exploration and change process. Some examples of the types of difficult questions I ask are asking about clients' experiences, understanding, and awareness of difficult physical and mental health concerns in their life as well as in their family of origin or questions about how difficult emotions were expressed in their family of origin or how anger and conflict were handled. Clients report that my incorporating questions about their cultural contexts into the genogram process is particularly meaningful to them in developing empathy for themselves and other members of their systems and to a deeper understanding of their own lived experiences and realities. In particular, questions focusing on clients' experiences with macro-systems such as oppression, racism, power, and privilege seem to generate empathy for themselves and their systems. In working with clients with immigration experiences, experiences as partners in same-sex relationships, or experiences as a person of color, I incorporate questions that attempt to get to richness and lived realities of those experiences and client identities. My experience as the therapist using the genogram and incorporating a cultural lens, has helped enhance my cultural "expertise" and responsiveness to my clients' experiences and realities. The cultural responsiveness of the genogram and cultural genogram allows me to understand client behavior in context, with attention to the complexity and diversity of their systems and their lived experiences. The process helps me go beyond the most immediate and "obvious" systems the client is part of; it helps me gain an understanding of the many levels of contexts within which clients exist and function.

The cultural lens in using the genogram is a process that I try to implement with all my clients. It can be challenging at times to use the cultural genogram: how to organize the process and how to depict or notate specific information (Shellenberger et al., 2007). Having practiced the genogram construction process multiple times in my own systemic training process, I have explored my own ethnic and cultural heritages and generational family patterns. By constructing my own genograms, interviewing and constructing the genograms of my fellow supervisees and trainees, and sharing my own cultural and relational genogram diagrams in the training setting, I have experienced firsthand the cultural responsiveness of this process and tool. I occasionally share with my clients my experiences of doing my own genogram when I am explaining the process to them in the therapy setting; clients seem to appreciate that I am using the tool not from a detached, clinical distance but from a personally experienced perspective. The response from clients that I receive and the impact the process has on clients and the client-therapist relationship can be quite profound and useful in moving the therapeutic process forward. I highlight to my clients that when I as the therapist do not share a common culture with them, the genogram process helps protect me, the client, and the therapy process from misunderstanding a client's culture, family, and lived experiences. Most importantly, I have found that the use of the genogram reduces the potential for clients feeling disrespected or unsafe or for them to receive care that is not appropriate for them given their cultural experiences and context (Shellenberger et al., 2007).

My use of the genogram emphasizes for me that it is a clinical, systemic process that is congruent with common factors elements that support positive therapy outcomes especially with culturally diverse client populations. Studies on the use of the genogram with African-American (McCullough-Chavis & Waites, 2016) and Asian-American clients (Lim & Nakamoto, 2008) demonstrate that the use of the cultural genogram and the genogram is effective in rapport and trust building (common factor, the therapeutic alliance) particularly with client populations that historically have not felt at ease with psychotherapy and thus have felt misunderstood, pathologized, and marginalized. Lim and Nakamoto (2008) emphasize that the use of the genogram has been found to be culturally resonant with Asian cultures, that the genogram process honored diversity, felt congruent to cultural values and experiences, and provided a context in which clients could share and explore areas of their lived experiences that might not be culturally sanctioned in other settings.

Currently, many therapy and counseling training institutions emphasize and promote postmodern sensibilities and sensitivities to issues of power, privilege, oppression, and social location as important in socially just clinical practice (Kosutic et al., 2009). Given this context for the training therapists receive, a common factors lens to utilizing foundational systemic models can be effective in incorporating these postmodern ideals and values. I believe that using the common factors lens as an umbrella over the genogram and cultural genogram process can be a part of socially just and culturally responsive practice, as well as meeting the parameters of "best" clinical practices. This lens can support bringing voice to the voiceless and making visible the invisible; being silenced and feeling invisible may be often what clients from marginalized and historically oppressed groups are experiencing. Thus, it is imperative for systemic therapists to bear witness and validate their clients' lived realities in as much depth as possible. In particular, three of the four common factors, therapeutic relationship, client as a factor, and expectation and hope, are salient to the culturally responsive use of the genogram and cultural genogram.

## *Therapeutic Relationship as a Factor*

When I keep at the forefront of my mind the therapeutic relationship as a common factor as major element in effective therapy, I find that using the genogram reduces my anxiety about the process of "getting to know" my client "better" and helps me to engage in deeper cultural explorations. I want my clients to feel safe and hopeful about the therapy process before I can present them with more challenging questions and explorations that may be perceived as "intrusive" by clients – often these "more challenging questions and explorations" are an important part of better understanding my clients' cultural and social contexts and also a way to begin to establish that safety. As a systemic and culturally responsive therapist, I explicitly use the genogram work with my clients to ensure that cultural safety and responsiveness emerge from the very beginning of therapy process. The therapeutic alliance is supported and grows from my willingness to explicitly open the therapy setting to challenging questions and explorations from the very beginning of the process.

According to Falender, Shafranske, and Falicov (2014), self-assessment and difficult conversations are integral components of culturally responsive clinical work and culturally responsive systemic therapies. At times, I have the concern that jumping into the genogram process with all of the "intrusive" questions might lead to distancing in the therapist-client relationship and connection. However, the question that often emerges for me, is what else would I propose to do or how else would I propose to establish this sense of safety, of therapeutic alliance and relationship with my client? Additionally, I consider the possibility that it is these very same "more challenging questions and explorations" that might be the very mechanism by which safety, alliance, and hopefulness about the process are facilitated. In particular, I remind myself that working with our diverse clients may actually require that we get to these challenging, possibly intrusive explorations much sooner in the therapy process in order to impart the clear message that these areas of explorations are not forbidden, taboo, or extraneous and that they matter critically to providing a safe and open environment in which clients can engage in their change process (Falender et al., 2014). The genogram process with my clients has the potential to result in much greater and deeper therapeutic alliance and connection between me and my clients. Clients feel heard, understood, validated, and respected when provided with the space and structure of a genogram and cultural genogram.

## *Client as a Factor*

The genogram technique of data collection and exploration is one that meets the parameters of good ("best") clinical practice, i.e., a common factors lens. Genograms allow for an expanded understanding of clients' lived experiences, cultural contexts, and familial and relational contexts; thus, even the most "barebones" genogram can often provide a great deal of insight and information regarding the lives and contexts of our clients, of what they are experiencing the other 167 h of the week that they are not in one's therapy office. It is an invaluable tool in obtaining a rich, in-depth understanding of client factors, characteristics, resources, and experiences. I find that when I use the genogram as a tool to gather information about a client and their contexts and what is important to them in their systems, I am much more likely to be mindful about the impact of their larger systemic contexts, ones such as racism, heterosexism, and other "isms" that are often "invisible" in the therapy setting, but very much part of clients' lived experiences and realities that are having an impact on what the client reports as their "presenting problem." Additionally, attunement to the details of the genogram allows me to facilitate clients' access to resources, supports, strengths, and resilience in themselves as individual systems and in their larger systems.

## *Expectation and Hope as a Factor*

Models and therapy techniques that have built-in methods of engaging and connecting with clients and generate a sense of positive outcome in the process tend to be associated with positive therapeutic outcomes (Sprenkle et al., 2009). The genogram process, in my experience, is one such process that can engender a sense of hopefulness and expectation of a positive outcome when clients can visualize themselves as part of something bigger, that they are not alone, and that there are indeed important and legitimate contexts for their experiences. Seeing in the genogram's stark, visual representation, one's intergenerational history and patterns, and the larger systemic forces of oppression can be immensely evocative and painful for our clients. However, I have found that it can also facilitate a sense of hopefulness in clients as they see in a very tangible way, how they as individuals and as part of larger systems have managed, adapted, and grown because of their challenging circumstances. While there may be the experience of pain in seeing systemic and cultural experiences laid out so overtly, clients also can gain a sense of competence and mastery when their experiences are contextualized in empathetic and courageous ways in their genogram.

## Conclusion

The genogram and cultural genogram are just one systemic foundational tool that is part of the repertoire of systemic tools that I use in my practice. It is also one example of how I employ the common factors lens to my systemic work, whether it is the genogram or another systemic technique. While the common factors lens has been touted as an effective lens for being integrative in using systemic therapies, its potential as a culturally responsive lens and way of working systemically with diverse client populations have been less emphasized or explored. A common factors lens to culturally responsive systemic work may appear challenging as the research and application of this lens is not rooted in cross-cultural awareness, and there is no template or step-by-step method that guides the process. However, what I have found most useful about utilizing this lens is that it allows me to adapt and use flexibly the systemic models and techniques that are at the foundation of couple and family therapy and that help me navigate as a clinician an increasingly diverse and complex clinical world.

# References

D'Aniello, C., Nguyen, H. N., & Piercy, F. P. (2016). Cultural sensitivity as an MFT common factor. *The American Journal of Family Therapy, 44*(44), 234–244. https://doi.org/10.1080/01926187.2016.1223565

Falender, C. A., Shafranske, E. P., & Falicov, C. J. (2014). Diversity & multiculturalism in supervision. In C. A. Falender, E. P. Shafranske, & C. J. Falicov (Eds.), *Multiculturalism and diversity in clinical supervision: A competency-based approach* (pp. 3–28). New York, NY: Guilford Press.

Hardy, K. V., & Laszloffy, T. A. (1995). The cultural genogram: Key to training culturally competent family therapists. *Journal of Marital & Family Therapy, 21*, 227–237. https://doi.org/10.1111/j.1752-0606.1995.tb00158.x

Hubble, M. A., Duncan, B. L., & Miller, S. D. (1999). *The heart & soul of change: What works in therapy*. Washington, DC: American Psychological Association.

Keiley, M. K., Dolbin, M., Hill, J., Karuppaswamy, N., Liu, T., Natrajan, R., … Robinson, P. (2002). The cultural genogram: Experiences from within a marriage and family therapy training program. *Journal of Marital and Family Therapy, 28*, 165–178. https://doi.org/10.1111/j.1752-0606.2002.tb00354.x

Kosutic, I., Garcia, M., Graves, T., Barnett, F., Hall, J., Haley, E., … Kaiser, B. (2009). The critical genogram: A tool for promoting critical consciousness. *Journal of Feminist Family Therapy, 21*, 151–176. https://doi.org/10.1080/08952830903079037

Lee, E. (2012). A working model of cross-cultural clinical practice (CCCP). *Clinical Social Work Journal, 40*, 23–36. https://doi.org/10.1007/s10615-011-0360-3

Lim, S. L. (2008). Transformative aspects of genogram work: Perceptions & experiences of graduate students in a counseling training program. *The Family Journal: Counseling & Therapy for Couples & Families, 16*, 35–42. https://doi.org/10.1177/1066480707309321

Lim, S. L., & Nakamoto, T. (2008). Genograms: Use in therapy with Asian families with diverse cultural heritages. *Contemporary Family Therapy, 30*, 199–219. https://doi.org/10.1007/s10591-008-9070-6

Magnuson, S., & Shaw, H. E. (2003). Adaptations of the multifaceted genogram in counseling, training, & supervision. *The Family Journal: Counseling & Therapy for Couples & Families, 11*, 45–54. https://doi.org/10.1177/1066480702238472

McCullough-Chavis, A., & Waites, C. (2016). Genograms with African American families: Considering cultural context. *Journal of Family Social Work, 8*, 1–19. https://doi.org/10.1300/J039v08n02_01

McGoldrick, M., Gerson, R., & Petry, S. (2008). *Genograms: Assessment & intervention*. New York, NY: W. W. Norton.

Morgan, M. M., & Sprenkle, D. H. (2007). Toward a common-factors approach to supervision. *Journal of Marital & Family Therapy, 33*, 1–17. https://doi.org/10.1111/j.1752-0606.2007.00001.x

Shellenberger, S., Dent, M. M., Davis-Smith, M., Seale, J. P., Weintraut, R., & Wright, T. (2007). Cultural genogram: A tool for teaching & practice. *Families, Systems, & Health, 25*, 367–381. https://doi.org/10.1037/1091-7527.25.4.367

Sprenkle, D. H., & Blow, A. J. (2004). Common factors and our sacred models. *Journal of Marital and Family Therapy, 30*, 113–129. https://doi.org/10.1111/j.1752-0606.2004.tb01228.x

Sprenkle, D. H., Davis, S. D., & Lebow, J. L. (2009). *Common factors in couple & family therapy: The overlooked foundation for effective practice*. New York, NY: Guilford Press.

Stamoulos, C., Trepanier, L., Bourkas, S., Bradley, S., Stelmaszczyk, K., Schwartzman, D., et al. (2016). Psychologists' perceptions of the importance of common factors in psychotherapy for successful treatment outcomes. *Journal of Psychotherapy Integration, 26*(3), 300–317. https://doi.org/10.1037/a0040426

White, T. M., Connolly Gibbons, M. B., & Schamberger, M. (2006). Cultural sensitivity & supportive expressive psychotherapy: An integrative approach to treatment. *American Journal of Psychotherapy, 60*(3), 299–316.

# Client-Centered Advocacy in Education and Clinical Training from the Supervisees' Perspective

**Nicole Sabatini Gutierrez and Rajeswari Natrajan-Tyagi**

As the field of managed healthcare transitioned to the recovery model in recent years, it brought with it a focus on client-centered advocacy (Bilynsky & Vernaglia, 1998; Stylianos & Kehyayan, 2012). The recovery model inherently promotes advocacy, as it defines recovery as a combination of a personal journey and a social process and includes a critique of macro level systems that maintain problematic discourses about mental health and wellness (Stylianos & Kehyayan, 2012). In the section about professional competencies, the American Association for Marriage and Family Therapy (AAMFT) code of ethics proposes that marriage and family therapists (MFTs) should be committed to advocacy and also be concerned with public policy and be involved in the discussion about mental healthcare legislation (AAMFT, 2017).

The American Counseling Association's (ACA) Advocacy Competency Model states that mental health counseling should include client-centered advocacy, emphasizing that advocacy should be tailored to meet the specific cultural and contextual needs of each client (Lewis, Ratts, Paladino, & Toporek, 2011).

Client-centered advocacy is defined in the literature as concerted effort to empower clients to achieve a sense of personal autonomy while also helping them to address institutional and social barriers to achieving goals and/or accessing services (Gehart & Lucas, 2007; Lewis et al., 2011). Client-centered advocacy in therapy is influenced by principles of social justice, including a focus on multiculturalism and attention to the impact of systemic racism, sexism, heterosexism, and other facets of oppression and subjugation on the presentation of mental health symptoms (Gehart & Lucas, 2007; Kiselica & Robinson, 2001;

---

N. S. Gutierrez
Alliant International University, San Diego, CA, USA

R. Natrajan-Tyagi (✉)
Alliant International University, Irvine, CA, USA
e-mail: rnatrajan@alliant.edu

Stylianos & Kehyayan, 2012). Adopting an attitude of social justice in therapy includes an integration of feminist and humanistic concepts that purposefully address mechanisms of power, oppression, and discrimination in clinical practice (Gehart & Lucas, 2007). There is a substantial body of research on promoting multiculturalism in the education and training of psychotherapists (Ancis & Marshall, 2010; Burkard, Knox, Clarke, Phelps, & Inman, 2014; Christiansen et al., 2011; Falender, Shafranske, & Falicov, 2014; Soheilian, Inman, Klinger, Isenberg, & Kulp, 2014; Watkins, 2014) and incorporating an attitude of social justice in therapy (Bilynsky & Vernaglia, 1998; Brady-Amoon, 2011; Burnes & Singh, 2010; Greene, 2005; McDowell & Shelton, 2002; Palmer & Parish, 2008; Ratts, 2009). Additionally, there is some research that focuses specifically on incorporating client-centered advocacy in education and training (Durfee & Rosenberg, 2009; Gehart & Lucas, 2007; Grothaus, McAuliffe, & Craigen, 2012; Lewis et al., 2011; McGeorge & Carlson, 2010; Ratts & Hutchins, 2009; Stylianos & Kehyayan, 2012). However, there is limited research on the client's perspective of client-centered advocacy in therapy (Gehart & Lucas, 2007), and virtually no research on the student's/supervisee's experience of client-centered advocacy in supervision and training. Our exploratory qualitative study was specifically aimed to identify aspects of training and supervision that are particularly helpful in terms of educating student trainees and interns about how to carry out client-centered advocacy in clinical practice. Additionally, this research sought to identify ways in which educators and supervisors can better meet the needs of students and supervisees who are engaged in client-centered advocacy throughout the training process.

A key component of qualitative research and the discipline of social justice and client-centered advocacy is addressing the positionality of the researchers, the educators, and/or the supervisors. As such, we believe it is imperative to situate ourselves in the research that we are presenting here. Both authors identify as cis-gendered women in heterosexual marriages and have experienced the privileges of identifying in these dominant groups. Nicole Sabatini Gutierrez identifies as White and is in an interracial relationship with a Mexican-American man. She has experienced significant privilege in regard to her race. She is a first-generation high school graduate and the first in her family to earn any advanced degree. She is a licensed MFT in private practice full-time and primarily works with clients who have experienced sexual trauma and dual diagnosis substance abuse. She has some experience teaching MFT master's level students as an adjunct instructor and has recently begun supervising MFT trainees as part of supervised supervision hours in her doctoral program. She also provides clinical competency trainings for other clinicians who work in residential/inpatient treatment centers. Raji Natrajan-Tyagi identifies as first-generation Asian Indian immigrant and is married to another Asian Indian immigrant and has two second-generation children. She comes from a privileged background in India where higher education was a norm in the family. She is an associate professor in a marriage and family therapy program in a private university in California and is an AAMFT-approved supervisor. She teaches courses at both the master's and the doctoral level and supervises students in their clinical work. She is also a licensed MFT and has a small private practice where she mostly works with first- and second-generation

South Asian couples, families, and individuals dealing with relationship issues, acculturation issues, and bicultural identity issues.

In an effort to be congruent with our belief that acknowledging positionality is essential in education and training of MFTs, it is important that we address the power dynamics at play in our relationship. At the time the study began, we had known each other for about 5 years. Nicole was Raji's student and had served as her teaching and research assistant. Raji taught several of Nicole's master's and doctoral courses. At the time of writing this chapter, Raji was serving as the chair of Nicole's dissertation (a study unrelated to the present topic). So, we acknowledge that there has been an inherent power difference within our relationship. At the same time, in one of our recent discussions regarding power, Nicole acknowledged to Raji that the way she experienced the power difference between us was different than what she experienced with her male professors, especially when they were Caucasians, in that it was easier for her to shift from being in a position of less power to a position of more equal power than it was with these male professors with whom she also co-facilitated courses or co-authored papers. This conversation led to both of us acknowledging how our positionality and ascribed power were an intricate representation of our multiple identities: both of us identifying as female, Raji being a racial minority in the USA and an international faculty with an accent while at the same time coming from a privileged background in her country of origin and having power due to her status as a core faculty in an American university and Nicole being a first-generation college goer and coming from a low socioeconomic background in the USA while at the same time being a racial majority in the USA and speaking English as her first language with an American accent.

While power dynamics are often fixed, as in many employment environments in which someone in a supervisory role maintains the most power in their relationships with subordinates for the duration of their employment, there are many other situations in which power dynamics may be more fluid. An example of this is in the execution of the present study. In writing this chapter, we have tried to have an egalitarian division of power as much as possible. Nicole initially conceptualized the study during her research assistantship under Raji, and as such she was originally determined to be the lead author of this chapter. During the writing process, Nicole opened a discussion about authorship based on the division of labor and invited Raji to take the lead. However, Raji acknowledged that in the big picture of conducting this research, Nicole put in a lot of work and deserved first authorship. As a result of our conversation, we agreed that sharing first authorship was the most representative of the amount of effort put forth and leadership taken by both of us. We tried to collaborate in the writing process by dividing up the chapter into sections, evaluating each other's contributions, and consulting throughout the process to ensure a unified literary voice.

We are familiar with each other's research perspectives because we previously collaborated on other scholarly pursuits that resulted in a publication and conference presentations, so we knew that we share similar interests in terms of research topics. We both align with a more postmodern therapeutic world view and appreciate the fact that our university prides itself on providing an education that is internationally and multiculturally focused. This alignment prompted us to pursue the present study. In our Couple and Family Therapy program, we have continuously tried to deliberately infuse multicultural and social justice consciousness in our training, supervision, and administrative practices. Additionally, being in the State of California, it is inevitable that our clinical practice and research endeavors focus on recovery, wellness, multiculturalism, and client-centered advocacy as these concepts have been progressively adopted by our State Board of Behavioral Sciences to guide the practice of marriage and family therapy.

## Background Information on Social Justice and Client-Centered Advocacy in Psychotherapy

The discussion of social justice advocacy is largely theoretical and seldom includes real-world examples of what advocacy looks like at the client level (Gehart & Lucas, 2007; Grothaus et al., 2012). Advocacy is defined as the act of empowering individuals or groups through actions that increase self-efficacy, remove barriers to needed services, and promote systemic change (Grothaus et al., 2012). Client-centered advocacy in psychotherapy incorporates an attitude of social justice that promotes consideration of contextual factors on the presentation of mental health symptoms and clients' acquisition of resources (Palmer & Parish, 2008). The focus of advocacy in psychotherapy is on issues of power, privilege, discrimination, and violence at three levels: macro, meso, and micro (Goodman et al., 2004; Ratts, 2009). Advocacy at the macro level includes working toward ideological change of social structures, institutions, and public policies or legislation that maintain discrimination and oppression. Meso level advocacy includes working to create programmatic change in local communities and organizations, such as implementing culturally appropriate services and fostering multicultural competency in schools and community programs (Goodman et al., 2004; Lewis et al., 2011). Client-centered advocacy at the micro level is perhaps the most common form that psychotherapists typically engage in, and it includes advocating for clients with individuals (e.g., family members, social workers, probation officers, psychiatrists), with whom the client directly and regularly engages with (Goodman et al., 2004), and fostering individual client autonomy, agency, and empowerment (Lewis et al., 2011; Ratts & Hutchins, 2009). The American Counseling Association further clarifies that these different levels of advocacy occur both *in collaboration with* clients and *on behalf of* clients (Lewis et al., 2011; Ratts & Hutchins, 2009).

The literature on client-centered advocacy in the education and training of psychotherapists often presents a parallel process of empowerment that occurs between educators/supervisors and their students/supervisees, which mirrors the process of therapists fostering empowerment of their clients in therapy (Chang, Hays, & Milliken, 2009; McDowell & Shelton, 2002; Palmer & Parish, 2008; Ratts & Hutchins, 2009). Research suggests that client-centered advocacy should begin in the academic setting by incorporating education on issues of social justice into coursework prior to when psychotherapy students begin seeing clients in practicum in order to acclimate students to the language and various tasks of social justice advocacy (Burnes & Singh, 2010; McDowell & Shelton, 2002; McGeorge & Carlson, 2010; McGeorge, Carlson, Erickson, & Guttormson, 2006). The education system should be evaluated from a social justice lens as well, identifying any systemic issues or biases that might subsist in the existing coursework, and educators should be engaged in a transparent self-reflective process about their own positionality (the intersection of their own diversity factors and their positions of privilege and/or marginalization) with students (Mcdowell & Shelton, 2002). For example, when we recently co-facilitated a lecture on Feminist Family Therapy to MFT master's students, we openly discussed our experiences of power in our own relationship and how the power between us shifts in different contexts. We then engaged the students in a fishbowl activity and facilitated a dialogue about how they experienced our various positions of power and privilege and how these experiences had impacted their level of engagement in classroom discussions, their anxiety about seeing clients in practicum, and other challenges that they faced as master's students. Students should be encouraged to question the status quo of the university when it comes to issues of race, ethnicity, gender, sexual orientation, and any other issues of potential marginalization (Chang et al., 2009; Durfee & Rosenberg, 2009; McDowell & Shelton, 2002). For example, we encourage student participation in the on-campus student organization and invite officers of the student organization to monthly faculty meetings where they can address inequities experienced by students across cohorts. Students are also encouraged to fill out anonymous surveys about their experiences at the end of each course throughout the program. These surveys admittedly could include more specific questions that directly assess students' experiences of racism, sexism, ableism, ageism, heterocentricism, etc. on campus. Students are also encouraged to be actively involved in recruiting faculty members when positions come open and in recruiting and peer mentoring future students. By evaluating these systemic and individual processes, acknowledging the power and privilege associated with higher education, and giving students the chance to dialogue about their experiences of privilege and marginalization within the education system, we are modeling for students the basic tasks of client-centered advocacy. Prior to seeing clients, we encourage students to evaluate how their own acquisition of knowledge has been socially constructed within the context of the systems to which they belong, challenge their own world views in order to increase their own personal agency within these systems, attend to how various social systems support injustice, and recognize how their personal biases and assumptions about the world may impact the way they practice therapy (McDowell & Shelton, 2002).

Once practicum begins, the tasks of client-centered social justice advocacy in both supervision and therapy include ongoing self-examination of the clinician's biases and positionality, sharing power in therapy, giving voice to clients regarding their experiences of oppression, raising consciousness about issues of diversity and/or oppression, building on clients' strengths, and leaving clients with tools for change or tools to better access internal and external resources (Goodman et al., 2004; Ratts & Hutchins, 2009). In order to carry out these tasks of client-centered advocacy, McGeorge and Carlson (2010) proposed that supervision must help student supervisees develop certain skills, including (1) emotional attunement to oppression and suffering; (2) awareness and understanding of the systemic structures that create power imbalances and oppression; (3) the ability to develop and implement interventions to address issues of power, privilege, and oppression; and (4) an awareness of themselves, their own personal values, and their positions of power, privilege, or marginalization in larger social structures.

Our study sought to evaluate the ways in which marriage and family therapy student trainees and post-master's degree interns experienced the incorporation of a social justice framework and client-centered advocacy in their education and supervision and the degree to which their education and training helped them to develop the skills necessary to carry out client-centered advocacy in their clinical practice.

## Giving a Voice to Students and Supervisees

We know that addressing issues of diversity, social justice, and client-centered advocacy in education and supervision of MFTs is considered best-care practice, but we wanted to see how student supervisees are actually experiencing the dissemination of this information and training. In order to get a sense of how therapists in training experience instruction and supervision related to advocacy at their training institutions, a descriptive cross-sectional survey research methodology was chosen. The inclusion criteria for participants was that they needed to be either student trainees in practicum gaining hours toward their degree or registered interns who were gaining hours toward licensure. This study utilized both traditional paper surveys as well as online surveys. The survey included demographic questions (7 questions), Likert scale or questions with response choices (12 questions), and open-ended questions (6 questions).

We gave participants a brief definition of what we meant by social justice and a focus on client advocacy. Social justice in psychotherapy was described as actively attending to issues of institutionally supported discrimination and oppression based upon diversity factors including race, culture, religion, sexual orientation, gender, age, socioeconomic status, and how these issues may impact the client's mental health and emotional well-being. We defined attending to social justice in therapy to include asking questions about clients' experiences of power, privilege, and subjugation in their interactions with various social and institutional systems. The definition also included evaluating the positionality of the client, the therapist, and any others with whom the client interacts. We defined positionality as how one identifies across different intersections of diversity including gender, race, ethnicity, socioeconomic status, sexual orientation, ability, and how they experience power, privilege, and/or oppression across these dimensions. For the purpose of this study, we described client-centered advocacy as any number of things that a therapist may do to assist her or his clients in navigating social or institutional barriers that may impede their ability to access appropriate resources. Client-centered advocacy was defined to include empowering clients and supporting their autonomy. Some examples of client-centered advocacy were given, such as, helping a client who has learning challenges to access supplemental education services or helping a client to understand the expectations and requirements of a social service agency that might be mandating them to treatment. Participants were asked to identify how their coursework and supervision prepared them for addressing issues related to social justice and client-centered advocacy in their clinical work.

We sent out recruitment emails to students who were currently enrolled in an MFT master's or doctoral program through their program directors/faculty members in their program. In order to ensure a better response rate, the recruitment emails were sent to a total of five universities across the nation where we had personal relationships with the program directors or faculty members and to community agencies in Southern California to which we had access. Participants were also recruited by distributing paper surveys to students enrolled in the MFT program to which we belonged. To ensure the anonymity of the participants, the surveys were distributed to the participants and were collected back by one of their course instructors who was not involved in the study. No identifying information were collected either through the online survey or the paper-and-pencil survey.

**Sample** There was a total of 37 respondents. Eighty-seven percent of the respondents were MFT trainees currently in their master's program, and 14% were interns who had finished their master's degree. About 5% of the interns were currently pursuing their doctoral degree. Ninety-four percent of the respondents went to COAMFTE-accredited programs for their master's degree. Twenty-five percent of the participants identified themselves as Asian or Asian American (Indian, Vietnamese, Chinese, and Bengali), 68% identified themselves as White or Caucasian, 14% identified themselves as Hispanic or Latino/Latina (Mexican, Guatemalan, and Ecuadorian), 8% identified themselves as Middle Eastern (Iranian, Egyptian), and 3% identified themselves as biracial or multiracial (Euro-Afghani). The age of the participants ranged from 23 years to 51 years with the mean age being 30 years ($SD = 7.53$). Seventy-three percent of the participants identified themselves as cis-female and 19% identified themselves as cis-male. Eight percent (three participants) chose not to disclose their gender. Participants were from six different states (California, Colorado, Kansas, Texas, Oregon, and Virginia) with the majority (86%) being from California, specifically Southern California.

## *Student/Supervisee Feedback*

The feedback we received from student supervisees is summarized in this section of the chapter. As mentioned previously, we asked student supervisees questions about their experiences in instruction/coursework and in clinical supervision across two domains: addressing issues of social justice and incorporating client-centered advocacy. In this section, we have tried to represent the voices of our participants as much as we can by giving direct quotes.

## Social Justice

We addressed issues of social justice across two different domains: instruction and coursework at educational institutions and clinical supervision at the agency level.

**Instruction and Coursework in Addressing Social Justice Issues** Seventy-three percent of the participants reported that they believed that social justice issues were being "often addressed" or "very frequently addressed" in their coursework. The rest (27%) reported that the topic was "sometimes" or "rarely" addressed. Most of the participants reported that they engaged in issues of social justice in their coursework through assigned readings (89%), self-reflection papers/exercises (76%), lectures/guest lectures (73%), in-class activities (62%), exam questions (54%), and conferences/workshops (51%). One participant also mentioned that they were involved in social justice-related campus clubs/activities. Thirty-nine percent of the participants reported that their instructors "often" (36%) or "very frequently" (3%) addressed their own positionality during coursework, while 62% reported that their instructor either "not at all" (6%), "rarely" (17%), or "sometimes" (39%) addressed issues of their own positionality.

Participants shared several suggestions to improve instruction and coursework regarding issues of social justice. These suggestions included making available more articles related to social justice, more role-plays where students can practice talking about their positionality with clients, workshops and guest lectures by presenters of color, in-class activities that focus on social justice issues, and support from professors to attend more community-based events and activities that promote social justice. One participant commented:

> We took a multicultural course, in which we learned a lot about different races, cultures, gender etc. However, there was not a lot about how to actually address such issues in the therapy room. Still as a white female, it's such a touchy subject. Breaking the barrier is not comfortable or easy to me. I think I still don't know how to navigate those issues. I know, via textbook, lecture and other shared stories about their (minority clients') struggles…but how to talk to them about being in a position of power is a constant inner struggle.

Participants repeatedly suggested that professors and instructors self-disclose about their own positionality, especially when they come from a majority background (such as being White and male), as a way to prepare students to address issues of social justice with their clients. One participant said, "Professors often discussed [their positionality]. However, those who were in power did not discuss it as often or openly. I found [that it would be helpful] to know how they address it in the room." Another participant said, "It would be helpful for professors to disclose how they contribute or have contributed to injustice and what they are doing or have done to stop contributing to injustice." Participants also noted that instructors could improve education about the importance of social justice issues by engaging students in discussions about their own positionality. This would be a helpful isomorphic way to better prepare the class for difficult conversations with clients. Additionally, it can normalize the feeling and expression of strong emotions that arise for students. Instructors, acting as facilitators of these conversations between students, would also be able to model ways of containing strong emotions in the room and ways to create space for opposing views in a constructive but safe manner.

**Clinical Supervision in Addressing Social Justice Issues** About 72% of the participants reported that their clinical supervision "sometimes" (47%), "rarely" (22), or "not at all" (3%) helped them address social justice issues in their clinical work. Only 28% reported that social justice issues were "often" (22%) or "very frequently" (6%) addressed. Seventy-two percent of the participants also believed that their supervisors "sometimes" (28%), "rarely" (36%), or "not at all" (8%) addressed their own positionality in relationship to their supervisees in supervision. Participants reported that the common activities that supervisors used in addressing issues of social justice in supervision were through questioning/activities (89%), self-of-the-therapist work (72%), providing resources (42%), suggesting interventions (42%), and in-house trainings (14%). One participant mentioned that their supervision required mandatory client advocacy excursions to local community places and courthouses. One of the main suggestions given by participants for supervisors to better prepare them (students) in addressing social justice issues was for supervisors to model it for students by addressing issues regarding their "own power and privilege," "self-disclosure," "sharing their clinical and personal experiences," and "getting trained themselves in multicultural issues." Participants also shared that supervisors need to bring up and talk about social justice issues in a more "straightforward way" so that they can convey the importance of this topic in therapy. They wanted supervisors to "identify more often" when issues of social justice presented in cases and challenge supervisees to consider these factors. Other suggestions were to provide supervisees with more workshops, in-service trainings, and community resources. Some also suggested that it would be helpful if agencies organized networking events with local resources and other clinical agencies and planned volunteer activities.

Participants in this study reported that, in general, issues of social justice were addressed more frequently in their coursework and instruction at their various universities than they were in clinical supervision at their practicum/internship sites. Overall, participants also identified (in both education and clinical supervision) a need for increased transparency about issues of instructor and supervisor positionality and intersections of diversity between instructors, supervisors, and peers in the classroom and supervision settings.

## Client-Centered Advocacy

In this section, we summarize the types of advocacy that participants most commonly reported engaging in through their own clinical practice, as well as the challenges they faced in terms of acquiring knowledge about and accessing resources. Additionally, we provide details on participants' responses to survey questions about how well client-centered advocacy was addressed in coursework and instruction and in clinical supervision.

**Types of Advocacy and Challenges Faced** As part of the survey, participants were asked to identify the types of client-centered advocacy that they have engaged in during their prelicensure clinical experience. The two main ways in which participants engaged in client-centered advocacy were:

1. Researching, finding, and connecting clients to resources (such as support/psychoeducational groups in the community, food banks, transportation services, affordable psychiatric services, affordable day care, housing resources, resources for the elderly, resources for those with developmental disabilities, resources for job placement/resume writing workshops)
2. Connecting with people in other systems in the client's lives in order to gain a broader understanding about the client's experiences and to advocate for clients and help them understand how to function within those systems

For example, participants reported engaging with clients' social workers, lawyers, doctors, psychiatrists/psychologists, case managers, teachers, and school administrators in order to coordinate services and advocate for their clients. They also interfaced with various systems in their clients' lives such as the court system, department of children and family services, the social security system, etc. Participants reported that they attended meetings (e.g., Individualized Educational Plan [IEP] meetings) or called and met with persons from these various systems in order to advocate for their clients and to gain an understanding of how these systems affected their clients' lives. In addition to these two primary means of engagement, participants identified other ways in which they practiced client-centered advocacy – by educating oneself in various topics that promoted advocacy (e.g., learning about oppression theory and critical research theory, learning about pathways to naturalization, learning about healthcare options), helping clients within the therapy session to empower themselves (e.g., writing a letter that illuminates client's self-agency, teaching clients about their diagnosis and medication), and doing volunteer work in the community (e.g., volunteering in the courthouse).

Two of the biggest challenges participants faced in accessing culturally appropriate resources and referrals for their clients were "lack of knowledge" and "lack of or limited resources." Participants spoke about not knowing where to find appropriate resources. For example, some participants talked about clients having very specific needs (transgendered clients or clients with psychosis) and not having knowledge about resources that were available in the community to address their needs. Participants used terms such as "lost," "not knowing what is best," and "(not) knowing what to look for" when they spoke about this issue. Several participants also reported that resources were "not available" or "were limited" in their geographical area. For example, participants cited language as an issue when it came to finding appropriate resources. One participant reported, "(there are) limited resources available for clients who don't speak English. (We) never have access to translators." Resources for certain populations, such as the Native American population, were reported to be not readily available. Participants shared that even when they were able to locate resources in their geographical area, they were "overbooked and burnt out."

**Instruction and Coursework in Client-Centered Advocacy** Seventy-seven percent of the participants reported that the topic of client-centered advocacy was "rarely" (26%) or "sometimes" (51%) addressed in their coursework. Only 23% reported that this topic was "often" (20%) or "very frequently" (3%) addressed. Similarly, 77% of the participants described that their coursework "somewhat" (54%) or "minimally" (23%) prepared them to carry out client-centered advocacy in their clinical practice. Three percent reported that coursework "did not prepare them at all," while 20% reported that coursework prepared them "fairly well." Assigned readings and in-class activities such as role-plays, self-reflection papers/exercises, guest lectures, and workshops were identified the primary types of activities that helped them learn and understand the concept of client-centered advocacy. Suggestions shared by participants on how coursework could better prepare them for advocacy work included assignments that focused on gathering local community resources, speakers from various backgrounds, and course resources that address topics on client advocacy. Some topics suggested included identifying when it is appropriate to engage in advocacy, how to look for resources in the community, and understanding government welfare systems and ethical issues in client advocacy. Participants repeatedly brought up the issue of ethical barriers as an area that needed to be addressed in coursework. For example, when participants engaged in client-centered advocacy such as accompanying clients to their doctor's appointments or riding the bus with clients, they reported that there is a need to address how they can at the same time deal with ethical dilemmas involving blurring boundaries, compromising clients' confidentiality, and potentially increasing client dependency on the therapist. Participants shared that it would be helpful if case examples were shared to illustrate these dilemmas and ways to work around them, such as "how to advocate for clients without giving them all the answers," "when is it appropriate to advocate for clients," and "how (advocacy) may have different expressions/components depending on the culture of the client and the trainee." One participant also commented that educators advocating for their students both in school and in their training agencies would be an isomorphic way to role model for the students about client-centered advocacy.

**Clinical supervision in Client-Centered Advocacy** Eighty percent of the participants reported that the topic of client-centered advocacy was "sometimes"

(40%) or "often" (40%) addressed in their supervision. Nine percent felt that the topic was "rarely" addressed while 11% felt that it was "very frequently" addressed in their supervisory context. Most of the participants (83%) also felt that their clinical supervision prepared them "somewhat" (46%) or "fairly well" (37%) to carry out client-centered advocacy in their practice. About 9% of the participants reported that their clinical supervision "minimally prepared them," while another 9% reported that clinical supervision "prepared them very well" to practice client-centered advocacy with their clients. Some of the common types of activities that participants experienced in their supervision related to client-centered advocacy were questions asked by their supervisors around advocacy (82%), suggestions received to carry out advocacy (76%), and provision of resources by the supervisors (65%). Participants also reported that they engaged in self-of-the-therapist work, hands-on activities (e.g., field trips to courthouse and probation office), and in-service trainings in the supervision context that helped promote client-centered advocacy. Participants provided several suggestions for supervisory activities that would help them be better prepared for client-centered advocacy. Besides getting access to more resources and training, participants expressed that they would like to see supervisors guiding and "supporting" students in the process of client-centered advocacy rather than just giving them the answers. One participant reported:

> Oftentimes, there is so much going on in the clinic, that supervisors just give resources out without showing us the process of finding resources or [explaining] why [clients] need [them] or how the 'system' works.

Participants also reported that they would like to hear more "examples" of how supervisors "gained their advocacy skills" and how they have advocated for clients in the past, especially for clients coming from "different cultural backgrounds." Participants also suggested that it would be helpful if supervisors provided them with "working templates" that would help them access resources, such as templates of requisition letters or scripts on how to talk while advocating. Creating space for dialogues, self-of-the-therapist work within group supervision, and possibly adopting a project where the whole team of trainees could advocate for clients/community were suggested as other ways that would be helpful in better preparing trainees for client-centered advocacy.

Participants in this study reported that client-centered advocacy was being addressed in clinical supervision, and it seemed to prepare them for clinical practice. However, participants also reported that supervisors tended to simply provide resources rather than showing them how to locate or access resources on their own.

## *Incorporating What We Learned into Practice*

This study explored the experiences of MFT trainees and interns/associates in terms of learning about and addressing issues of social justice and client-centered advocacy in coursework and instruction and in clinical supervision. Most participants reported that they were currently engaged in or at least wanted to be engaged in various forms of client-centered advocacy throughout the course of their training. This is a very encouraging finding as current literature emphasizes the importance of adopting an attitude of social justice and incorporating client-centered advocacy in clinical work which also indicates the importance of incorporating these topics in the education and training of psychotherapists (Chang et al., 2009; Gehart & Lucas, 2007; Glosoff & Durham, 2010; Palmer & Parish, 2008; Ratts & Hutchins, 2009). Participants reported that issues of social justice were better addressed in coursework and instruction than they were in clinical supervision, whereas issues of client-centered advocacy were better addressed in supervision than in coursework and instruction. We believe this trend may be related to inherent and necessary differences in focus between, as well as the different challenges of education and supervision. For example, addressing issues of social justice may be better suited to the academic environment where there is more time and space to dialogue about such theoretical constructs, whereas in clinical supervision, there are often various pressing issues for supervisors to monitor and address with supervisees, particularly in high-volume agencies like community mental health and nonprofit intensive outpatient and residential treatment centers where clinical training is often conducted. Such issues may include treatment planning and clinical documentation, crisis management, legal and ethical considerations, and gatekeeping issues regarding agency protocol and procedures. Likewise, issues of client-centered advocacy may be better suited to being addressed in clinical supervision simply because this is the environment in which supervisees will actually interact with clients in real-word situations, whereas in the academic setting, issues of client-centered advocacy are most often hypothetical and it would be difficult for instructors to anticipate the types of populations (and all of their various advocacy needs) that students may work with in practicum before they are placed.

There are various templates for incorporating issues of social justice and client-centered advocacy in training (Durfee & Rosenberg, 2009; Glosoff & Durham, 2010; Goodman et al., 2004; Lewis et al., 2011; McDowell & Shelton, 2002; McGeorge & Carlson, 2010; Ratts & Hutchins, 2009). For example, McDowell and Shelton (2002) proposed that MFT educators should emphasize social justice in the classroom in order to create a discourse where students will integrate these concepts into their education and their clinical practice. The authors suggested that this can be done by creating dialogue with students that encourages them to:

1. Reflect on their own experiences to identify ways in which existing social structures support injustice and oppression.
2. Identify ways in which their own world views, beliefs, and foundational assumptions about mental health, how people develop presenting problems, the process of therapy, and the role of the therapist in creating change/healing may affect their relationships with clients and the way that they practice therapy.
3. Continually reflect on and challenge their own world views in order to increase personal agency as therapists who are in a position of power to advocate for their clients (see McDowell and Shelton (2002) for examples of dialogue prompts and reflection questions that can be asked).

All of the social justice models for therapist training and education universally suggest that educators and supervisors address hierarchical issues of power, issues of social oppression, and the impact of institutionalized discrimination and prejudice on the development of clients' presenting problems and symptomology and provide examples of how to advocate for clients and locate appropriate resources and referral training (Durfee & Rosenberg, 2009; Glosoff & Durham, 2010; Goodman et al., 2004; Lewis et al., 2011; McDowell & Shelton, 2002; McGeorge & Carlson, 2010; Ratts & Hutchins, 2009). The participants in our present study reported that educators incorporated in-class activities, assignments, readings, and self-reflection papers that addressed issues of diversity and social justice, congruent with the suggestions in the literature. Participants also reported that clinical supervisors did help them to identify ways of advocating for their clients within various other social systems with which clients were engaged.

The literature suggests that a key component to incorporating social justice and client-centered advocacy into the education and training of psychotherapists includes a significant focus on individual characteristics and experiences of the student supervisees, including their own intersecting diversity factors like gender, cultural background, socioeconomic status, ethnicity, ability, age, and sexual orientation (Durfee & Rosenberg, 2009; Glosoff & Durham, 2010; Goodman et al., 2004; Lewis et al., 2011; McDowell & Shelton, 2002; McGeorge & Carlson, 2010; Ratts & Hutchins, 2009). McDowell and Shelton (2002) suggested that, in addition to evaluating how existing social structures support injustice, students should also be encouraged to challenge their own world views and recognize the role that their views, biases, and assumptions may have on the way that they conceptualize their cases and practice therapy. Participants in our study largely reported that both instructors and supervisors did not adequately attend to issues of positionality or the personal attitudes, beliefs, cultural values, intersecting diversity factors, and power-based interactions between the instructors/students and supervisors/supervisees.

## Implications for Teaching and Supervision

The lack of attention to issues of positionality between instructors/students and supervisors/supervisees found in this study may have several implications for both the academic setting and clinical supervision. A common barrier identified by instructors and supervisors to covering issues of social justice and client-centered advocacy is that they are constantly challenged to find time to fit in all of the educational requirements of institutions and accrediting associations and to address all the gatekeeping issues that they face in the community mental health and agency settings. We believe that instructors and supervisors can integrate issues of social justice, positionality, and client-centered advocacy within the existing structures of instruction and supervision, such as integrating them within in-class presentations, activities, and formal case presentations during supervision (see Appendices A and B for examples). In our own experiences as instructors, we have found it helpful to designate class time specifically for transparent discussions of positionality in addition to providing educational materials about multiculturalism and social justice. Training programs that include courses that focus on self-of-the-therapist development (such as practicum courses and labs) could also more directly address issues of positionality, power, and privilege, in order to model for students how to engage their clients in these often very difficult and emotionally charged dialogues. For example, Raji has adapted the POTT (person-of-the-therapist) model (Aponte & Winter, 2000) to fit within a 16-week practicum course to help supervisees learn about themselves and their positionality. Another option that we have pursued is engaging doctoral students who are licensed and earning hours as AAMFT Approved Supervisor Candidates, in the supervision of second-year master's student trainees. This supervision is more focused on self-of-the-therapist issues, including positionality and intersections of diversity between supervisor/supervisee and therapist/clients. Students in practicum who are at the very beginning of their training have different needs than intermediate or advanced students, and some of these needs (like building basic attending skills and case conceptualization skills) may take precedent and class time away from addressing issues of social justice and positionality. As such, it may be helpful for practicum instructors to separate students based upon developmental levels (i.e., beginning, intermediate, advanced) in order to work in more nuanced ways with students who have moved beyond introductory therapy skills and are at a place where they can better attend to their own positionality with clients. We acknowledge that this could be challenging for smaller programs in which faculty resources may be limited, and it may be more difficult to divide courses based upon clinical experience and students' level of development.

The lack of attention to issues of positionality that student supervisees identified may also have been related to ethical considerations. McGeorge and Carlson (2010) pointed out that instructors/supervisors often fill several roles with their students (e.g., mentor, clinical supervisor, educator, thesis/dissertation advisor, or research supervisor) that may be viewed as dual relationships. We have navigated multiple role changes in our own relationship and in our relationships with other students and supervisees. The uncertainty about maintaining appropriate boundaries in these often very vulnerable contexts might deter some faculty members and supervisors from engaging students in these types of group dialogues. In these situations, we suggest that, in discussions about positionality and intersections of diversity, instructors/supervisors take even more care to directly address the hierarchy that inherently exists between faculty/supervisors and students and avoid a top-down approach to instruction and supervision as much as possible. We have experienced that facilitating these conversations can be draining and can require more from instructors and supervisors emotionally than what is typically expected of a faculty/student or a supervisor/supervisee relationship. Therefore, it is important for instructors and supervisors to be mindful of burnout and to routinely engage in their own self-care (McGeorge & Carlson, 2010; Parra-Cardona, Holtrop, & Cordova, 2005). Throughout this process, we have also found it helpful to consult with one another and other colleagues to process our own emotional experiences of these interactions with supervisees and students and identify any self-of-the-supervisor and self-of-the-educator issues that have come up or have the potential to come up in the future.

## Limitations and Other Considerations

We think that it is important to note a few limitations of the study, including the small sample size (37 respondents to the survey). We think it is important to note that there was an oversight in our demographic questionnaire in that we did not ask for participants to indicate any information about their sexual orientation, which is an important factor of diversity that may impact student supervisees' experiences of addressing positionality and client-centered advocacy in education, supervision, and practice.

Nearly all of the participants in this study (94%) went to COAMFTE-accredited MFT programs, which could have significantly impacted the results and may not be representative of the experiences of students/supervisees who went to nonaccredited programs because of the heavy focus of COAMFTE on community engagement and incorporation of diversity and multiculturalism in coursework and the recruitment of diverse faculty and students (AAMFT, 2017). Similarly, most participants (86%) in this study were seeing clients in California, a state that (at the time of the study) counted client-centered advocacy as applicable hours toward licensure (BBS, 2015), so they may have been particularly motivated to bring up issues of client-centered advocacy in supervision and to request resources from supervisors, which might also not be representative of MFT trainees and interns/associates in other states that do not have this incentive for licensure hours.

Regardless of licensure incentives or program and coursework requirements that may vary state to state, it is important for us as educators and supervisors to understand the impact that we have on our students and supervisees. Who we are, our positions of power, privilege, and even oppression or subjugation affect how our students experience us in relation to their own lived experiences of these constructs and the ways in which they identify themselves. As therapists, we must acknowledge the different dimensions of power that we might hold in relationship to our clients and initiate conversations about intersections of diversity in the therapeutic relationship and elsewhere in our clients' lives. As we are teaching students and supervisees to create these dialogues with their clients, it is imperative to model that by engaging them in similar dialogues about the dynamics that exist in our relationships with them and in their relationships with one another in the classroom and in group supervision.

# Appendix A

## *Case Presentation Outline (Adapted from Natrajan-Tyagi, 2017)*

1. Genogram
2. Presenting problem, date of 1st contact, referral source, and why now?

    (a) In the client's words
    (b) In the words of the referral source
    (c) In your words
    (d) Any co-created words

3. Assessments you will use (have used) consistent with theory
4. DSM/ICD diagnosis: Axis I _____; Axis II _____;
   Axis III _____; Axis IV _____
5. Client's contextual factors

    ___ Class issues? What? _____.
    ___ Cultural/ethnic/immigration issues? _____.
    ___ Money issues (debt, gambling, unemployment) _____.
    ___ Race issues _____.
    ___ Gender/sexual orientation issues _____.
    ___ Religious/spiritual issues _____.
    ___ Physical illness? What? _____.
    ___ Gender/power issues _____

    ___ Medication _____

    ___ Other therapists/professionals involved? _____.
    ___ Other contextual issues _____.

6. Therapist's Contextual Factors as they Relate to or Intersect with the client's (Address most Relevant Factors)

    ___ Class issues? What? _____
    ___ Cultural/ethnic/immigration issues? _____
    ___ Money issues (debt, gambling, unemployment) _____
    ___ Race issues _____
    ___ Gender/sexual orientation issues _____
    ___ Religious/spiritual issues _____
    ___ Physical illness? What? _____
    ___ Gender/power issues _____

    ___ Medication _____

    ___ Other therapists/professionals involved? _____
    ___ Other contextual issues _____

7. Crisis, legal, and ethical issues in the case and steps taken
8. Client-centered advocacy issues addressed/interventions used (see flowchart)
9. Systemic hypothesis for the case (Use language appropriate to your theory of choice. Please indicate your theory)

    (a) Individual
    (b) Relational
    (c) Social

10. Therapy goals (short term, long term, for session)
11. Treatment plan (Based on selected theory, include theoretical terms; early, middle, and late phase treatment goals; and specific interventions for each goal)
12. Reflection of personal challenges, barriers, and conflicts in the therapeutic context (therapists' own issues including positionality, family life cycle, gender, power, FOO, countertransferences)

    *You will reflect on personal challenges, barriers, and conflicts that you may face in the therapeutic context. The goal is to explore these issues within our supervisory group and seek personal clarity.*
13. Course of therapy and outcome
14. Questions for supervision
15. Supervisory feedback

Client-Centered Advocacy: Accessing Resources for Clients

## Client-Centered Advocacy – Accessing Resources for Clients

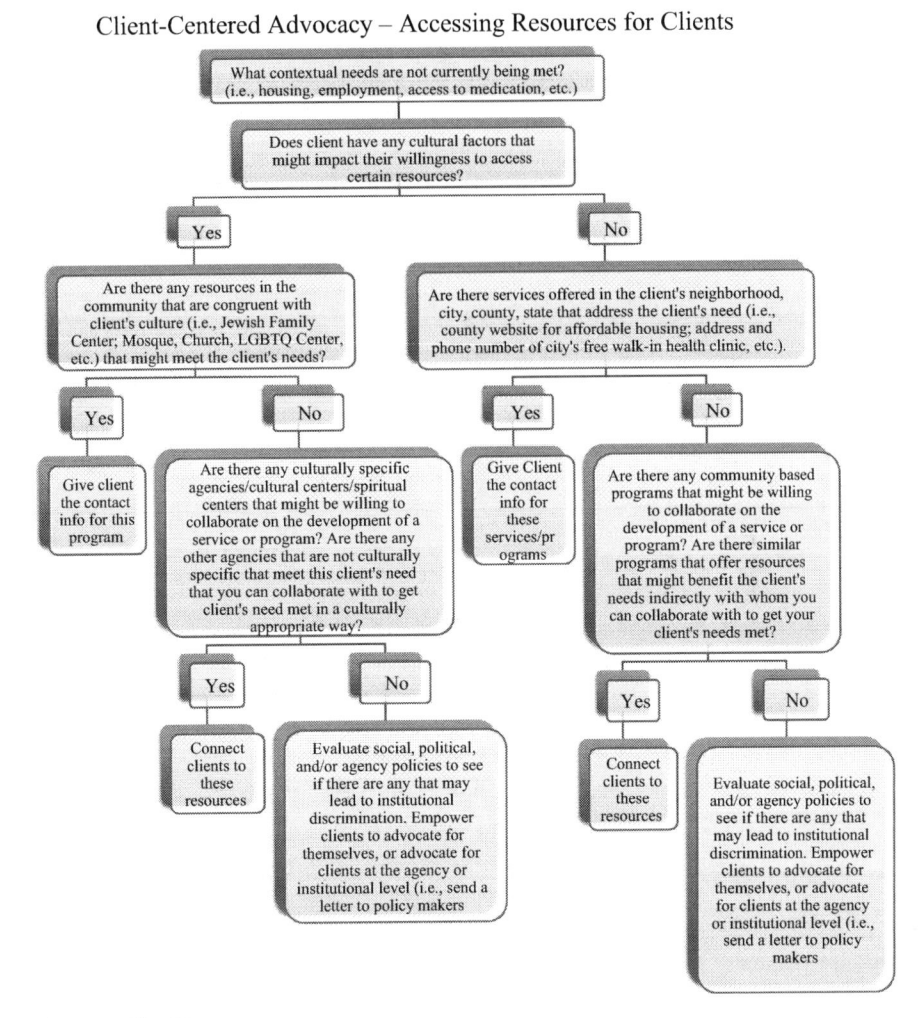

```
What contextual needs are not currently being met?
(i.e., housing, employment, access to medication, etc.)
            │
            ▼
Does client have any cultural factors that
might impact their willingness to access
certain resources?
       ┌────┴────┐
      Yes        No
```

**Yes branch:** Are there any resources in the community that are congruent with client's culture (i.e., Jewish Family Center; Mosque, Church, LGBTQ Center, etc.) that might meet the client's needs?
- **Yes:** Give client the contact info for this program
- **No:** Are there any culturally specific agencies/cultural centers/spiritual centers that might be willing to collaborate on the development of a service or program? Are there any other agencies that are not culturally specific that meet this client's need that you can collaborate with to get client's need met in a culturally appropriate way?
  - **Yes:** Connect clients to these resources
  - **No:** Evaluate social, political, and/or agency policies to see if there are any that may lead to institutional discrimination. Empower clients to advocate for themselves, or advocate for clients at the agency or institutional level (i.e., send a letter to policy makers)

**No branch:** Are there services offered in the client's neighborhood, city, county, state that address the client's need (i.e., county website for affordable housing; address and phone number of city's free walk-in health clinic, etc.).
- **Yes:** Give Client the contact info for these services/programs
- **No:** Are there any community based programs that might be willing to collaborate on the development of a service or program? Are there similar programs that offer resources that might benefit the client's needs indirectly with whom you can collaborate with to get your client's needs met?
  - **Yes:** Connect clients to these resources
  - **No:** Evaluate social, political, and/or agency policies to see if there are any that may lead to institutional discrimination. Empower clients to advocate for themselves, or advocate for clients at the agency or institutional level (i.e., send a letter to policy makers)

# Appendix B

## *Tips for Instructors and Supervisors on Addressing Their Own Positionality and Modeling Client-Centered Advocacy*

### Tips for Addressing One's Own Positionality with Students and Supervisees

When giving examples of cases or discussing multicultural issues in class/supervision:

1. Talk about how you identify yourself (gender, race, nationality, sexual orientation, citizenship, religion, class, etc.). Talk about your multiple identities and

their intersection. What identities of yours are most salient for you or have consequences for you? Then connect this to how it might look in regard to your students'/supervisees' experiences and how they can use this lens to view their clients' positionality and its impact in their lives.
2. Give examples of how both your privilege and lack thereof influence your everyday life. Bring it back to experiences of privilege and lack thereof in your student's/supervisee's everyday life. To make it more experience-near, you can talk about their privilege and lack thereof as students/supervisees in your institution or agency and how it impacts them.
3. When you discuss issues of power, talk about some differences between you and your students/supervisees regarding race, gender, education, experience, status, etc. Discuss how some of these demographic identifiers lend you more/less power compared to your students/supervisees. Then discuss in what ways these differences matter. Then discuss how differences between your students/supervisees and their clients influence power dynamics between them and how that matters in the therapeutic context.

**Tips for Modeling Client-Centered Advocacy**

Besides helping students/supervisees find resources in the community for their clients and sharing examples of how you have done client-centered advocacy, it is important that instructors and supervisors model client-centered advocacy through the process of student–/supervisee-centered advocacy. Given below are some tips for carrying out student–/supervisee-centered advocacy.

1. Have regular check-ins with students/supervisees about barriers they may be facing in completing tasks or fulfilling their responsibilities in the program/agency. Refer them to appropriate resources in the university/agency that will help them overcome their barriers (e.g., counseling services, tutoring, financial aid, mentoring, training, etc.). Make sure you check-in about larger systemic issues that may be impacting their performance and consider advocating for them (e.g., if your student speaks English as a second language, advocate for the student to get more time during examinations).
2. Empower your students/supervisees to advocate for themselves and ask for services (e.g., change of course/supervision schedule, altering course/assignment requirements, seeking additional supervision, etc.). When students bring up these issues in class/supervision, deal with it in a nondefensive and democratic way. Open up the floor for discussion and be transparent about your decision-making process.
3. Encourage students/supervisees to become part of groups that advocate for them (e.g., university student organizations and regional or national units of their professional organization). Encourage them to advocate for themselves and others including influencing policies and procedures that pertain to them.

# References

American Association for Marriage and Family Therapy. (2017, February). *COAMFTE Accreditation Standards*. Retrieved from https://www.aamft.org/imis15/Documents/Accreditation_Standards_Version_11.pdf

Ancis, J. R., & Marshall, D. S. (2010). Using a multicultural framework to assess supervisees' perceptions of culturally competent supervision. *Journal of Counseling & Development, 88*(3), 277–284.

Aponte, H. J., & Winter, J. E. (2000). The person and practice of the therapist: Treatment and training. In M. Baldwin (Ed.), *The use of self in therapy* (2nd ed., pp. 127–166). New York, NY: Haworth.

Bilynsky, N. S., & Vernaglia, E. R. (1998). The ethical practice of psychology in a managed-care framework. *Psychotherapy, 35*(1), 54–68.

Brady-Amoon, P. (2011). Humanism, feminism, and multiculturalism: Essential elements of social justice in counseling, education, and advocacy. *Journal of Humanistic Counseling, 50*(2), 135–148. https://doi.org/10.1002/j.2161-1939.2011.tb00113.x

Burkard, A. W., Knox, S., Clarke, R. D., Phelps, D. L., & Inman, A. G. (2014). Supervisors' experiences of providing difficult feedback in cross-ethnic/racial supervision. *The Counseling Psychologist, 42*(3), 314–344. https://doi.org/10.1177/0011000012461157

Burnes, T. R., & Singh, A. A. (2010). Integrating social justice training into the practicum experience for psychology trainees: Starting earlier. *Training and Education in Professional Psychology, 4*(3), 153–162. https://doi.org/10.1037/a0019385

Chang, C. Y., Hays, D. G., & Milliken, T. F. (2009). Addressing social justice issues in supervision: A call for client and professional advocacy. *The Clinical Supervisor, 28*(1), 20–35. https://doi.org/10.1080/07325220902855144

Christiansen, A. T., Thomas, V., Kafescioglu, N., Karakurt, G., Lowe, W., Smith, W., … Wittenborn, A. (2011). Multicultural supervision: Lessons learned about an ongoing struggle. *Journal of Marital and Family Therapy, 37*(1), 109–119. https://doi.org/10.1111/j.1752-0606.2009.00138.x

Durfee, A., & Rosenberg, K. (2009). Teaching sensitive issues: Feminist pedagogy and the practice of advocacy-based counseling. *Feminist Teacher, 19*(2), 103–121.

Falender, C. A., Shafranske, E. P., & Falicov, C. J. (2014). *Multiculturalism and diversity in clinical supervision: A competency-based approach*. Washington, DC: American Psychological Association.

Gehart, D. R., & Lucas, B. M. (2007). Client advocacy in marriage and family therapy: A qualitative case study. *Journal of Family Psychotherapy, 18*(1), 39–56.

Glosoff, H. L., & Durham, J. C. (2010). Using supervision to prepare social justice counseling advocates. *Counselor Education and Supervision, 50*(2), 116–129. https://doi.org/10.1002/j.1556-6978.2010.tb00113.x

Goodman, L. A., Liang, B., Helms, J. E., Latta, R. E., Sparks, E., & Weintraub, S. R. (2004). Training counseling psychologists as social justice agents: Feminist and multicultural principles in action. *The Counseling Psychologist, 32*(6), 793–836. https://doi.org/10.1177/0011000004268802

Greene, B. (2005). Psychology, diversity and social justice: Beyond heterosexism and across the cultural divide. *Counseling Psychology Quarterly, 18*(4), 295–306. https://doi.org/10.1080/09515070500385770

Grothaus, T., McAuliffe, G., & Craigen, L. (2012). Infusing cultural competence and advocacy into strength-based counseling. *Journal of Humanistic Counseling, 51*(1), 51–65.

Kiselica, M. S., & Robinson, M. (2001). Bringing Advocacy Counseling to Life: The History, Issues, and Human Dramas of Social Justice Work in Counseling. *Journal of Counseling & Development, 79*(4), 387–397.

Lewis, J. A., Ratts, M. J., Paladino, D. A., & Toporek, R. L. (2011). Social justice counseling and advocacy: Developing new leadership roles and competencies. *Journal For Social Action In Counseling & Psychology, 3*(1), 5–16.

McDowell, T., & Shelton, D. (2002). Valuing ideas of social justice in MFT curricula. *Contemporary Family Therapy: An International Journal, 24*(2), 313–331. https://doi.org/10.1023/A:1015351408957

McGeorge, C. R., & Carlson, T. S. (2010). Social justice mentoring: Preparing family therapists for social justice advocacy work. *Michigan Family Review, 14*(1), 42–59.

McGeorge, C., Carlson, T., Erickson, M., & Guttormson, H. (2006). Creating and evaluating a feminist informed social justice couple and family therapy training model. *Journal of Feminist Family Therapy, 18*(3), 1–38. https://doi.org/10.1300/J086v18n03_01

Natrajan-Tyagi, R. (2017). *Practicum* [Syllabus]. Irvine, CA: Couple and Family Therapy Department, Alliant International University.

Palmer, A., & Parish, J. (2008). Social justice and counseling psychology: Situating the role of graduate student research, education, and training. *Canadian Journal of Counseling, 42*(4), 278–292. https://doi.org/10.1037/a0022663

Parra-Cardona, J. R., Holtrop, K., & Cordova, D. (2005). We Are Clinicians Committed to Cultural Diversity and Social Justice: Good intentions that can wane over time. *Guidance & Counselling, 21*(1), 36–46.

Ratts, M. J. (2009). Social justice counseling: Toward the development of a fifth force among counseling paradigms. *Journal of Humanistic Counseling Education and Development, 48*(2), 160–172. https://doi.org/10.1002/j.2161-1939.2009.tb00076.x

Ratts, M. J., & Hutchins, A. M. (2009). ACA advocacy competencies: Social justice advocacy at the client/student level. *Journal of Counseling & Development, 87*(3), 269–275. https://doi.org/10.1080/2326716X.2015.1133334

Soheilian, S. S., Inman, A. G., Klinger, R. S., Isenberg, D. S., & Kulp, L. E. (2014). Multicultural supervision: supervisees' reflections on culturally competent supervision. *Counselling Psychology Quarterly, 27*(4), 379–392. https://doi.org/10.1080/09515070.2014.961408

Stylianos, S., & Kehyayan, V. (2012). Advocacy: Critical component in a comprehensive mental health system. *American Journal of Orthopsychiatry, 82*(1), 115–120. https://doi.org/10.1111/j.1939-0025.2011.01143.x

Watkins, C. J. (2014). Clinical supervision in the 21st century: Revisiting pressing needs and impressing possibilities. *American Journal Of Psychotherapy, 68*(2), 251–272.

# Training and Supervision Across Disciplines to Engage in Cross-Cultural Competence and Responsiveness: Counseling and Family Therapy

Diane Estrada

As the United States population continues to diversify (US Census, 2013), it is imperative that counselors, therapists, and clinical supervisors become culturally and cross-culturally responsive (ACA Code of Ethics, 2014; COAMFTE, 2015). The parallel process between clinical supervision and the delivery of culturally competent counseling and therapeutic services has been well documented (Arczynski & Morrow, 2016; Estrada, Frame, & Williams, 2004; Falender & Shafranske, 2012). Supervisors are charged with supervisees' assessment and development of cultural competency in therapeutic practice. Research studies (Soheilian, Inman, Klinger, Isenberg, & Kulp, 2014; Wong, Ong, & Ishiyama, 2013) explain the process of becoming culturally responsive as including both planned and unplanned cultural experiences. A key factor in this process is the ability of the supervisor to engage in conversations about these experiences with supervisees while demonstrating a reflexive and safe alliance that addresses cultural responsiveness at a supervisory and therapeutic level. In order to be transparent about the cultural factors that influence my perspective of culturally responsive training and supervision, I would like to locate myself in the context of various sociopolitical factors. I would be remiss if I did not mention that the meaning of each of these locations for me is constructed of various experiences in relationship to others that unfortunately cannot be fully addressed in this chapter due to page limitations. Therefore, I request that the reader keep in mind that the discovery process of identity location requires time, face-to-face interactions, and the continuous building of relationship. I identify as a Latina cisgender female, who grew up in a single-parent working-class/lower socioeconomic household and who has now become part of middle class socioeconomically. I partially grew up in Guatemala and the United States. I was born in the United States, affording me citizenship by birth, which, at times, places me in a privileged

---

D. Estrada (✉)
University of Colorado Denver, Denver, CO, USA
e-mail: Diane.estrada@ucdenver.edu

position. Other places of privilege include my identity as heterosexual and well educated. I am mostly able bodied. I also identify as bicultural, valuing aspects of my Guatemalan and US culture. I construct my racial identity as being a human being with a multiracial mix of indigenous, White, and Moroccan ancestry. These sociopolitical identities are the most salient ones at this point in my life. Additional identities include being part of a cross-cultural couple, and I am a proud parent of a multiracial and multiethnic female preteen who visually appears White. In this chapter, I address the notion of professional competencies/responsiveness related to clinical training and supervision of counselors and family therapists. Sociopolitical location awareness and knowledge of privilege and oppression is a primary component of developing professional cultural competencies in the supervisory relationship. Further, this chapter provides a review of the education and supervision literature regarding cross-cultural competency as a launching point into discussions of more process-oriented perspectives in the learning paradigm. The chapter explores the use of active voices in the integration of cultural responsiveness and responsibility in the educator/student and the supervisee/supervisor relationships via literature, case example, and experiential exercises.

## Multicultural Competence Professional Standards

Multicultural counseling has been defined as implementing goals consistent with "the lived experiences and cultural values of clients" (Sue & Torino, 2005, p. 12). This definition acknowledges multiple client identities and uses universal and culture-specific strategies and roles in the healing process while balancing the salience of individualism and collectivism in assessment, diagnosis, and treatment interventions of clients and client systems (Sue & Sue, 2015). The call for practitioners, supervisors, and educators to be culturally responsive can be found in various ethical and accreditation standards in the counseling and family therapy fields. For example, the American Counseling Association endorsed the multicultural and social justice (MSJ) advocacy competency standards (Ratts, Singh, Nassar-McMillan, Butler, & McCullough, 2015) in July 2015. These standards were updated from the original multicultural competency standards endorsed in 1992. The MSJ competencies focus on "intersection of identities and the dynamics of power, privilege, and oppression that influence the counseling relationship." (p. 3). The model highlights the importance of both client and counselor sociopolitical factors in the development of the counseling relationship. It places the responsibility on counselors to develop culturally sensitive and socially just self-awareness of attitudes and beliefs, knowledge, skills, and action as they provide service to all clients. These competency standards call for counselors to be cognizant of systems of privilege and oppression in a client's life context. It also calls for counselors to take their own context into consideration in their provision of counseling services.

Another example of the relevance of cultural competency can be found in the COAMFTE accreditation Standards Version 12, "MFTs are multiculturally-informed and consider a global context" (2016, p. 3). Moreover, the standards go on to state:

> Programs teach ways that MFTs can support marginalized and underserved communities and demonstrate an appreciation for the many ways that discrimination negatively influences the lives of marginalized and underserved people served by MFT professionals, including antiracism and work with sexual and gender minorities and their families. The standards promote inclusion, respect for diversity, non-discrimination, and social responsibility from a perspective that is appreciative of the effects of larger sociocultural factors on experience. (p. 4)

For practicing mental health professionals, ACA and AAMFT ethics codes hold clinical practitioners, supervisors, and educators accountable for not discriminating based on client's sociopolitical identities (e.g., race, ethnicity, gender, sexual orientation, religion/spirituality, etc.). The ethical guideline of practicing within the scope of training emphasizes the importance of multicultural competence and responsiveness in the provision of quality services to diverse clientele. Ethical guidelines that are responsive to our growing multicultural society are imperative in using best practices in clinical, supervisory, and educational settings.

## Conceptual Definitions of Culturally Competent/Responsive Supervision

Cultural-competent and responsive supervision entails engagement in the continuing growth of awareness of supervisor and supervisee as cultural beings, increasing knowledge base of multicultural and advocacy issues and their impact on the therapeutic and supervisory relationship, and applying culturally responsive techniques in assessment, conceptualization, and intervention in client cases (Corey, Hayes, Moulton, & Muratori, 2010). Effective multicultural counseling supervision requires supervisors to holistically address multicultural issues within the supervisor/supervisee/client triad. In order to do so, supervisors must promote multiculturalism within their educational or clinic-based institution, recognize how their own and their supervisees and client's worldviews impact therapy, include cultural issues, and develop specific stage by stage multicultural competency goals for trainees (Leong & Wagner, 1994). The importance of multicultural and cross-cultural supervision is recognized widely and integrated into various clinical supervision frameworks (Falander & Shafranske, 2012). The movement toward outcome-based measures of competency in clinical practice and supervision continues to highlight the importance of vigorous research to guide models of practice for culturally responsive training and supervision. The implications for culturally competent supervision have been described as (1) facilitating and engaging in the transformation to competency-based supervision remaining mindful of power, perspective, the cultural and diversity relativity, and context of competencies; (2) encouraging methodological advances and new constructs in supervision research; (3) attending to multiple identities of client(s), supervisees, and supervisors; (4) translating robust results into frameworks for training supervisors; (5) conducting research on effectiveness of supervision training for supervisors in development and for more experienced supervisors; and (6) increasing attention to cross-national studies of supervision practice, international competency standards, and evolving practices and guidelines in the international arena (Westefeld, 2009).

## The Supervisory Case

The following case is a conglomeration of various clinical and supervisory cases. Identities have been changed in order to protect any potential breach of confidentiality. The case is presented as a tool for further reflection as we explore the concepts, research outcomes, models, and supervisory relationship styles presented in the literature as components of multicultural supervision.

A Latino identified family, the Vegas family, is made up of a biological father, Roberto, and two daughters, Rebeca and Ingrid. The wife/mother, Teresa, had passed away 2 years ago, leaving the father as a single parent. The father identifies as a 50-year-old, cisgender, heterosexual male who grew up in a two-parent household, high SES, and social class. Traditional Latino gender roles were enforced in the family. Catholicism was the identified religion, even though the father stated that he did not have time to go to church and had grown distant from the religious practice. The father's family lived in Chile where he was raised until college when he immigrated to the United States. The father is a surgeon who spends many hours away from the house and has hired a live-in nanny, Sue, to take care of the girls. Rebeca (12 years old) and Ingrid (10 years old) were both born in the United Sates. They currently identify as cisgender females, heterosexual, upper class, able bodied, and non-practicing Catholics. The family presents to therapy after Rebeca's teacher discovers poetry writings referencing thoughts of suicide in Rebeca's notebook.

The therapist/supervisee (Lynn) is a 27-year-old Euro-American, middle-class, able-bodied, cisgender heterosexual female currently completing her doctorate in family therapy. She lived in Costa Rica for a year between her bachelors and master's program. She has an affinity for Latino culture and has focused on exploring multicultural issues as part of her clinical focus. She is supervised by a 43-year-old Latinx (i.e., a term encompassing Latin-American culture and the acceptance of various gender identities) cisgender female (Lorena) who grew up in a working-class single-parent family with external family supports. The supervisor currently holds a PhD and currently identifies as living in a lower middle-class status.

**Culturally Competent Supervision Case Reflection** What are the potential social locations impacting the supervisor-supervisee-client family triad? How do the lived experiences of each person in the triad influence both what we see and what we might be blind to as a result of those experiences? What hypotheses need to be developed about power dynamics based on the intersectionality of social location (e.g., gender and ethnicity, gender and social class, gender and level of education)?

How do these reflections and hypotheses begin to shape the supervisory goals toward increase cultural competency and responsiveness?

## Research and Culturally Competent Supervision

Six domains are suggested for exploration in guiding supervisors' multicultural competence: awareness of personal values, biases, and worldviews, facilitation of supervisees' awareness of personal values and beliefs, facilitating multicultural client conceptualizations, guide supervisees toward utilizing culturally appropriate interventions with clients, attending to multicultural processes in supervision, and effectively evaluating supervisees' multicultural competencies (Ancis & Ladany, 2010). These six domains can be found in most supervision models integrating multiculturalism and have been further supported as crucial ingredients in the development of culturally competent counselors and therapist (Soheilian et al., 2014; Wong et al., 2013).

In a study assessing supervisors' culturally competent responsive supervision, students categorized the following as contributing to effective supervision: (a) competence, (b) competency-facilitation of learning, (c) relationship factors, and (d) effectiveness of evaluation (reference). The categories identified by supervisors for effective supervision include (a) student's development, (b) relationship factors, (c) ethics, and (d) adaptability (reference). Researchers also found positive and negative themes in key areas of supervision. The positive themes included (a) personal attributes of the supervisor, (b) supervision competencies, (c) mentoring, (d) relationship, and (e) multicultural supervision competencies. Negative themes were identified as (a) personal difficulties as a visible minority, (b) negative personal attributes of the supervisor, (c) lack of safe and trusting relationship, (d) lack of multicultural supervision competencies, and (e) lack of supervision competencies (Wong et al., 2013).

In a discovery-oriented qualitative study exploring supervisees' perceived experiences of supervisor multicultural competence in supervision and its impact on supervisees' clinical work, Soheilian et al. (2014) found the most common focus of content in the data was race followed by gender, ethnicity, and religion/spirituality. The researchers examined culturally competent supervisor interventions. The results of this study revealed that supervisors frequently educated about and facilitated exploration of specific cultural issues, discussed culturally appropriate therapeutic interventions and skills, facilitated supervisee self-awareness within the supervision session, and challenged and encouraged cultural openness of supervisee's understanding of client and cultural issues. This intervention in supervision led supervisees to modify their treatment approach, recognize personal limitations, and experience improved self-awareness as a counselor in their work with clients. The supervisees reported developing an enhanced understanding and empathy toward their clients.

**Case Reflection** How do the supervisor and supervisee engage in a mutually reflective assessment of their level of competency, personal attributes, and ethical perspectives as individuals and members of a dyadic and triadic relationship in a clinical and educational context? How does the supervisor begin to gently challenge supervisee's growth in cultural conceptualization and selection of culturally appropriate interventions?

## Relational Factors in Culturally Competent Supervision

Parallel to the therapeutic process, psychosocial or relational functions in supervision impact the supervisory relationship defined as the "supervisee's perceived safety, trust and alliance" (Hernandez, Taylor, & McDowell, 2009, p. 8). A connection between a supervisor and a supervisee, who identifies as a member of a socially marginalized group, needs a culturally responsive relational context for creating a sense of safety, trust, and alliance. An awareness of the supervisor's power in relationship to the supervisee must be mindfully monitored in the creation of a safe alliance. To this end, Bernard (1994) provided an effective summary of standards that many in the field have recommended: (a) supervisors should be at least as multiculturally sensitive as their supervisees; (b) training programs should set multicultural competency standards for allowing a trainee to begin clinical experience and another standard for beginning entry-level practice; (c) supervisors use both developmental supervision models and racial identity development models to gauge supervisee readiness for challenging their multicultural skills and choose appropriate moments to do so; and (d) supervisors themselves should be supervised in enhancing their own multicultural development, in a hope to monitor and manage blind spots.

Attention to supervisory blind spots can also be found in a study of ten AAMFT-approved supervisors (Taylor, Hernandez, Deri, Rankin, & Siegel, 2007). The researchers indicate "all supervisors must be culturally competent or their trainees may continue the cycle of misusing power and privilege that can occur in the therapeutic process" (p. 17). They caution supervisors not to assume that a course on diversity will train students to protect their clients from racial, gender, class, and heterosexist biases. Three themes emerged from study participants describing their experiences as minority supervisors: supervisor's initiative in integrating diversity, the impact of social location on supervision practices, and the need for mentoring the next generation of clinicians and supervisors. The participants in this study highlighted the importance of breaking the silence and addressing cultural issues. In the discussion of social location, participants noted that inability to confront issues from a gender lens analysis affects the interactions in the therapy and supervision room. A reflection of the intersectionality of gender and other sociopolitical factors is an important part of the social location conversation in supervision. Another intersectionality specifically mentioned was religion and sexual orientation. Researchers found this to be one of the strongest issues to address in the supervisor/

supervisee processing and self-examination of differences, identity, and therapeutic role. The third theme, mentoring the next generation, brought to light the importance of identity development, self-care, and advocacy for self and others. Participants also mentioned the need to bridge the experience of supervision with professional development via role modeling and mentoring beyond clinical practice (e.g., presenting at conferences).

Research on feminist multicultural supervision emphasizes the reciprocal and dynamic process of ceaseless reflexive investigation of the impact of sociopolitical identities and contextual factors in the power dynamics within supervisory and therapeutic relationships. This model remains mindful of the realities of power inherent in the supervisory relationship and takes active stance to counterbalance the relentless intrusion of social power dynamics in the supervisory process. Due to the inherent imbalance of power, it is the supervisor's responsibility to initiate the aforementioned reflexive process in the supervisory relationship and to encourage supervisees to engage in a similar process with their clients (Arczynski & Morrow, 2016). Relational factors in clinical supervision stress the importance of developing a safe alliance, assessing developmental level of cultural competency, engagement in a reflexive process, and openness to reciprocal learning. These relational factors and the components of cultural competency and responsiveness in supervision are at the core of multicultural supervision.

**Case Reflection** What is the level of cultural competency of the supervisor and supervisee? How does the supervisor engage the supervisee in a relationship that creates a respectful and safe alliance in supervision? How does the supervisor remain mindful of the inherent imbalance of power? How does the supervisor challenge her own cultural awareness and knowledge-recognizing and role-modeling ways to address one's limitations? What systemic factors are in place that support and hinder the supervisory relationship? How does the supervisor encourage the supervisee to embrace a larger contextual systemic view that promotes advocacy for clients (e.g., restrictions of gender roles within cultural contexts that inhibit potential for emotional intimacy within families), as well as supervisees?

## Learning Paradigms: Models of Multicultural Supervision

In this section I will explore the components of some of the most contemporary models of supervision focusing on the integration of multiculturalism. As with all models of counseling and supervision, the reader is invited to view these models as lenses that influence the conceptualization of supervisory relational dynamics. As such, the models are incomplete by design. The models presented here view the integration of multiculturalism as an ongoing lifelong dynamic process constantly shifting based on the various contexts present in supervision and therapy (Falender & Shafranske, 2012; Hook et al., 2016; Ober, Granello, & Henfield, 2009; Owen, 2013; Porter & Vasquez, 1997).

# Cultural Humility in Clinical Supervision

Cultural humility is identified as a core component and foundational construct in the implementation of a multicultural orientation (Owen, 2013). A multicultural orientation is described as a way of being with clients. Therefore, cultural humility has been defined as "the ability to maintain an interpersonal stance that is other oriented in relation to aspects of cultural identity that are most important to the client [supervisee]" (Hook, Davis, Owen, Worthington, & Utsey, 2013, p. 354). Cultural humility is a lifelong process in which the supervisor continuously reflects on issues of power in the client-therapist-supervisor dynamic (Falender & Shafranske, 2012). A culturally humble counselor/therapist/supervisor is keenly aware of the limitations of one's knowledge and understanding of a client's cultural background. Hook et al. (2016) propose that the same principle of cultural humility can be applied to the supervisory relationship. They accentuate the importance of overcoming one's view that one's cultural worldviews, values, and beliefs are superior to that of others and to embrace and enact the concept of cultural humility in order to develop effective and strong relationships with diverse supervisees. Culturally humble supervisors are aware of cultural differences that may exacerbate the power differential in the supervisory relationship and how those are impacted by social identities. They also regulate their sense of superiority to avoid making assumptions and instead engage in an open and curious stance demonstrating interest in the supervisee's perspective. A culturally humble perspective uses an "initiate-invite-instill approach" (p. 154). The supervisor initiates conversations about diversity and identities in psychotherapy and supervision. The supervisor invites supervisees to engage in and consider the ramifications of ongoing cultural dialogue and instills a value of respectful dialogue about culture in the supervisory context. For example, incorporating reflections of cultural factors that influence one's belief about the change process, case conceptualizations, and treatment planning.

In the Vegas family case, both supervisor and supervisee engaged in a conversation regarding their sociopolitical locations and what each of these meant to them. In the process of this conversation, the supervisee shared her concern regarding "making mistakes" in her cultural approach. Validation of this fear was important at this time in the supervisory relationship as was the supervisor sharing her own "missteps" in her development as a therapist and supervisor. In my experience, an important component of these cultural conversations is the acknowledgement of the lifelong learning process.

The use of outside experiences to increase supervisees' cultural knowledge and humility requires the implementation of an assess-build-connect approach (Hook et al., 2016). In order to help supervisees develop an accurate view of their strengths, weaknesses, and limitations (components of cultural humility), supervisors must first help supervisees assess their strength and weaknesses in providing services to culturally diverse clients. This assessment must include the development of an awareness of limitations, possible biases, or blind spots in working with clients from diverse cultures. The authors of this model suggest the use of cultural genograms and direct observation of supervisees' therapeutic work. Secondly, supervisors are encouraged to work collaboratively with supervisees to build a plan to proactively engage in working toward cultural humility. This might entail recommending coursework or training to strengthen areas of weaknesses. Personal therapy should also be considered. During our assessment of the family in the aforementioned case, we assessed levels of competency related to language proficiency in Spanish, level of acculturation knowledge, and personal and professional cross-cultural experiences. These conversations emphasized the need for acculturation assessment of the supervisor, supervisee, and client family. Additionally, a deeper understanding of the impact of gender from a cultural perspective was imperative, as was the exploration of the impact of intersectionality between gender, education, and social class. These reflections allowed both supervisor and supervisee to construct a set of assessment interventions that would more fully increase our understanding of the client family's multiple identities and how they influenced the relationships and beliefs systems within the family. This in turn provided us with a richer and more dynamic process to develop culturally appropriate interventions.

The third focus of this model is to encourage supervisees to connect with culturally different individuals and groups. Supervisors can encourage supervisees to put themselves in situation where they can have a positive contact with individuals different from them. Enacting cultural humility in the supervisory relationship invites the supervisor to be more attuned to the supervisee's cultural context and in return invites supervisees to become more reflectively curious about their clients' cultural and social context. Many of my supervisees have had cultural immersion experiences via education abroad programs and/or volunteering abroad programs. These experiences have increased their awareness and in some cases, their knowledge base of particular cultures. Both their experiences and my own partially growing up in Guatemala can seduce us into believing we have a more accurate picture of the client family whose country of origin we have had experiences in. It is important during these experiences that we remain vigilant and enact cultural humility as we explore the client's experience of their own culture. Our "visitor" or "temporary citizen status" in their country of origin may cloud our ability to fully listen to the family's own experience in their country or community.

## Synergistic Model of Multicultural Supervision

The Synergistic Model of Multicultural Supervision (SMMS) (Ober et al., 2009) uses Bloom's taxonomy of educational objectives (Bloom, Engelhart, Furst, Hill, & Krathwohl, 1956), the Heuristic Model of Nonoppressive Interpersonal Development (HMNID) (Ancis & Ladany, 2001), and the multicultural counseling competencies (Sue et al., 1992). Bloom's taxonomy offers a model that supports the supervisee's current developmental stage and encourages supervisee growth through intentional cognitive scaffolding, e.g., from rigid thinking to cognitive complexity. The model provides six levels of growth that are cumulative, each level building on the next. Ordered from least to most complex, the levels of the model are knowledge, comprehension, application, analysis, synthesis, and evaluation.

HMNID supports the process of learning and supplies a method for understanding multiculturalism and multicultural counselor competence in personally meaningful ways. This model asserts that every person has components of identity (e.g., race, age, gender, religious affiliation) that identify the person as a member of a group that is either socially oppressed or socially privileged. There can be intersection of identity that belong in socially oppressive and/or socially privileged groups. This idea is acknowledged in the new MSJ competencies model (Ratts et al., 2015). The authors note the critical component of the person's perception of their place in a socially oppressed group or a socially privileged group due to its impact on all interactions with others either within or outside the individual's identified groups. These perceptions and behaviors are terms the means of interpersonal functioning (MIF, Ancis & Ladany, 2001) takes into account as it moves the supervisee through four phases of development that move from complacency and limited awareness about differences, privilege, and oppression to increased awareness about diversity issues and a commitment to multicultural counselor competencies. This model acknowledges that the supervisor and supervisee can be at different phases of development across the various sociopolitical factor/identities. The combination of respective phases can result in four types of supervisory relationships: (1) progressive, where the supervisor has more advanced knowledge of a particular identity; (2) parallel advance or (3) parallel delayed, where the supervisor and supervisee are at similar knowledge bases; and, (4) regressive, the supervisee is more advanced in their knowledge base than the supervisor.

SMMS asks that the supervisor and supervisee determine the specific domain of multicultural competency on which to focus. In order to evaluate the domain to focus on, the supervisees' phase of the MIF is used with the intention of facilitating the supervisee's growth into a higher level of multicultural functioning. Movement through the various phases and domains requires supervisor intervention to aid in the supervisees' movement and growth.

I incorporated the SMMS model in my work with a supervisee who had a broad and deep knowledge of issues of gender identity (i.e., parallel advanced supervisory relationship) but limited knowledge of the intersection of gender, religion, and ethnicity (i.e., progressive supervisory relationship). We targeted the intersectionality of gender, religion, and ethnicity as an area of growth. The incorporation of the SMMS provided the cognitive mapping that would clarify methods of intervention to enhance knowledge of multiple realities within the therapeutic relationship and the relationship between family members. The supervisee explored questions of gender identity, gender socialization, and religious beliefs that increase their ability to hold multiple perspectives and contradictory belief systems within the family. The exploration of belief systems and how they enhanced the family member's survival provided the context necessary for the supervisees to increase their cognitive complexity and learn to respect and respond to the clients' needs from a culturally responsive frame.

## Feminist Multicultural Supervision

Feminist multicultural supervision is defined as collaborative, mutual, and reflective process that attends to contextual and sociocultural processes (FMS) (Porter & Vasquez, 1997). This model integrates a focus on boundaries, hierarchies, gender, race, and diversity of all kinds. FMS encourages supervisor and supervisee reflections on their individual and systemic context as well as the dyad interactional/process and its basis on social identities and issues of privilege, power, and oppression (Arczynski & Morrow, 2016). FMS supervisors help supervisees understand how the work in the counseling room is impacted by the larger sociopolitical context, model advocacy, activism, and social justice qualities as part of the supervisory relationship (Porter & Vasquez, 1997). A qualitative study by Arczynski and Morrow (2016) examined the major dimensions and process of supervision for supervisors whose theoretical orientation integrated feminist and multiculturalism. The major conceptualization and practice component revealed in this study were the anticipation and management of power. There were seven categories associated with this component: (a) complexities of power in supervision (core), (b) bringing history into the supervision room, (c) creating trust through openness and honesty, (d) collaborative process, (e) meeting shifting developmental symmetries, (f) cultivating reflexivity, and (g) looking at and counterbalancing the impact of context. In this context, power was defined as "the ability to influence the lives of others and their own lives" (p. 5). Social locations, evaluation and gatekeeping, and supervisory power encompassed the sources of power that conflicted with supervisors' desires for egalitarian and empowering relationships with their supervisees. Supervisors reported addressing this tension via enlistment of supervisees as partners in co-construction of productive learning experiences and in caring for clients' needs. This process allowed supervisors to share their power with supervisees.

Participants acknowledged bringing history into the room by addressing how their own life experiences dealing with their social identities influenced their supervisory work. Supervisors created trust through openness and honesty by laying things on the table. They acknowledged the influences of "their power, histories and identities early in supervisory relationships in order to subvert traditional power dynamics in supervision" (p. 7). Collaborative processes were enacted by resisting theoretical approaches emphasizing directive, hierarchical supervision interventions and instead focusing on egalitarian-inspired interventions thereby empowering supervisees by facilitating supervisees' sense of competency in their own skills rather than just their limitations. They engaged supervisees in the creation of supervisory goals through dialogue of "supervisees' prior experiences, aptitudes and growth edges, relational preferences, and multicultural competencies..." (p. 7). Supervisors also invited more of their supervisees' perspectives in order to understand their clinical approach. This process allowed supervisors to assess when direct suggestions were needed or when support to help the supervisees find their own direction was more appropriate. Supervisors also discussed the importance of ongoing developmental assessments in order to allow supervisors to respectfully match their supervisory strategies to their supervisees' developmental trajectory. Participants recognized that novice trainees are most dependent on supervisors to provide learning opportunities therefore creating a greater tension among collaboration, transparency, and power at this level of training. However, the focus of supervision continues to be moving the collegial relationships into supervisee-directed unstructured process.

The cultivation of critical reflexivity helps supervisors to limit the cost of using their supervisory power to better implement collaboration and transparency. The growth of critical consciousness to assess the influence of social locations, power, bias, and history is important in decreasing potential for harmful supervision. Indeed, the Arczynski and Morrow study highlights the harmful effects of supervisors "who lack self-awareness of their biases, motives, growth edges, and identity statuses as a strategy to anticipate the influence of their power as supervisors on supervisory processes and relationships" (p. 10). Supervisors counterbalanced the impact of contextual power by engaging in reflexive questioning of the ways internal and external context impacted themselves, their supervisees, and supervisees' clients in the ways they showed up to therapy and supervision. Supervisors also encouraged supervisees to advocate in the community in order to counterbalance the power of different institutions within the community. Additionally, supervisors supported their supervisees' self-advocacy efforts to create healthier environments for themselves and their continuous development.

**Case Reflection** In supervising the Vegas case, the supervisor and supervisee struggled with the "traditional gender roles" to which the father adhered, and that limited his ability to be present and nurturing with his daughters. A discussion ensued about the importance of understanding the family's cultural context within their traditional cultural roles where gender and culture intersected. How did this impact power in the family? How could a female therapist-in-training gently challenge the male doctor regarding the impact of these cultural roles in the family functioning? Was this even appropriate? How did the hierarchical traditions in the family reflect the hierarchical traditions in the supervisory relationship? How were the supervisor and supervisee's gender identifications a strength and limitation in influencing the family? How could we advocate in the client's larger system? Could we invite extended family to communicate a message regarding power and responsibility of fathers in Latino families? How was the Latina supervisor's own ethnic cultural experience influencing her perspective and her knowledge power within the supervisory relationship?

# Multicultural Group Supervision

The interdependent nature of group supervisees' development as counselors requires the vigilant attention of group development dynamics by group supervisors prior to setting individual goals (Hayes, Blackman, & Brennan, 2001). Bernard and

Goodyear (2004) suggest that a supervision group moves through developmental phases similar to a therapy group (i.e., forming, storming, norming, performing, and adjourning). Group supervisees benefit from vicarious learning, peer support and validation, direct feedback from various sources, and exploration of personal dynamics within the group (Bernard & Goodyear, 2004). Group supervision may be useful in addressing multicultural issues because the presence of additional supervisees, who may have received more multicultural training, creates more opportunities for cross-cultural discussions and interactions. Kaduvettoor and co-authors (2009) examined specific multicultural events in face-to-face group supervision. These authors found hindering event (i.e., events that block or limit supervisees' growth in multicultural responsiveness) categories consisting of five items: indirect discussion, peer multicultural conflicts, supervisor multicultural conflicts, misapplication of multicultural theory, and none. They also found helpful event categories including peer vicarious learning, multicultural learning and conceptualization, extra group events, and supervisor direct influence. Suggestions for improvement included no change, more supervisor involvement, more practical application or intervention, more group process, more or better integration of multicultural issues, more personal awareness, and more interpersonal sensitivity.

**Case Reflection** Even though both the client family and the supervisor identify as members of the Latino culture, what are some of the reflections that implement a cultural humility perspective in order to enrich the supervisor and supervisee's understanding of the clients' performance of their own cultural perspective? How does the therapist/supervisee's experience living in a Latin-American country impact her sense of cultural humility when working with this client family? What is the potential power dynamic of intersectionality of cultural age values and gender values in both various subsystems of the triadic relationship? How can a cultural humility stance invite further exploration of these dynamics? How do cultural humility and social advocacy intersect? How are the supervisor and supervisee engaging in a collaborative evaluation process of cognitive growth and cultural understanding? How are identifications with culturally oppressed and privileged groups impacting the various levels of relationships within the triad? How can consultation with a professional group of colleagues influence the conceptualization of the clinical case and the dynamics within the therapeutic and supervisory relationships?

## Cultural Responsiveness Roles and Responsibilities

Supervisors are charged with initiating conversations about the impact of sociopolitical contextual factors on the supervisory and therapeutic relationship (Estrada et al., 2004). Conversations about race and other marginalized identities in supervision need to consider the anxiety and fear that can often accompany a focus on these issues and thereby require the establishing of a context in which relational risks might be taken (Mason, 2005). An example of such is to engage supervisees in the self-reflexive exercise of thinking and talking about their own racial identity and the influence they think it might have upon the supervisory relationship (Pendry, 2012). The supervision literature (Inman & DeBoer Kreider, 2013) calls for examining specific skills and techniques used to integrate cultural diversity issues into supervision. While our education models often center on acquisition of concrete knowledge, cultural responsiveness requires both a planned and unplanned development of knowledge. This point is evidenced in the experience of seven diverse therapists in a supervision course as they struggle with the real-world application of multicultural supervision (Christiansen et al., 2011). In their anecdotal stories of supervisory experiences, the authors found similarities across each of their cases including (a) negative emotional reactions (e.g., anxiety, anger), (b) spontaneous and unplanned instances of multicultural supervision, (c) a need for supervisor's support and validation of their experiences, and (d) a clear need for a safe space to discuss and process their experiences at a supervisory level. The authors emphasize that activities such as cultural genograms (Hardy & Laszloffy, 1995) provide a cognitive awareness of the impact of culture; however the real-world application of multicultural experiences calls for an emotional process in which supervisors and supervisees have the ability to sit with the discomfort of various emotions while simultaneously continue to be open and engaged in the supervisory process by working through the discomfort. The process of cultural sensitivity is an "ongoing experience rather than an endpoint, and it is the affective process that is important" (p. 118).

As a supervisor and educator, I have found the use of cultural genograms to be quite helpful in increasing awareness and knowledge of most supervisees. I would be negligent if I did not mention that there are times when doing a cultural genogram highlights the systems of oppression that have been in place historically and sometimes currently. There are many students of color who have no access to their family histories (e.g., enslavement, lack of records in the country of origin). The emotional processing of these historical facts adds to the responsibility as a supervisor to support and provide resources for supervisees when necessary.

It is also important for supervisors to remember that our own bias and assumptions about particular cultural groups can influence our expectations of what supervisees need to address. In our naivete of multicultural models, well-meaning supervisors can pursue a conversation regarding cultural differences that the supervisee is not ready or willing to have. It is the supervisors' responsibility to assess the supervisee's cultural identity and respect the power dynamic in the supervisory relationship. I have had conversations with supervisees of color who experience the conversation regarding cultural differences as one that is aimed at alleviating white guilt more than enhancing the collaborative process in the supervisory relationship. We are works in progress.

## Conclusion

The major responsibility to provide opportunities and guidance for continued growth and competence in culturally responsive counseling and therapy falls on supervisors and educators as the more experienced members of the profession.

Supervision provides a context for the actualization of the summative experiences of awareness and knowledge from academic coursework (see Appendix A). The reciprocal nature of relationships also means that supervisees have a responsibility to engage in their own learning process and to strive for their continuous growth and development in cultural sensitivity and responsiveness in clinical practice. This chapter investigated the definitions of cultural competency and responsiveness, the research facilitating our understanding of supervisees and supervisors' perspectives on cultural competency and responsiveness, the models integrating multicultural supervision, and the roles and responsibilities of enacting such concepts in the process of culturally responsive supervision. It is a shared belief that cultural competency and responsiveness are lifelong processes that entail a constant reflection of social identities, power dynamics, and internal and external contextual factors. As a supervisor and clinician, I find myself often reflecting on what I know and what I do not know. Part of this process requires me to confront my own biases and complacency in looking at the world through my lenses and having to make myself uncomfortable by embracing the limitations of my own lack of knowledge. The supervisory alliance is a key factor in the continuous growth of future generations of culturally responsive counselors and therapists.

## Assessment of Oppression Sensitive Process by the Gainesville Family Institute

Race, gender, class/SES, ethnicity, culture, age, sexual orientation, religion/spirituality, health/ability, and environment/ecology are sociopolitical organizing principles of existential meaning that must be considered in our lives and our work as therapists and supervisors. They provide basic constructs or meanings that influence our perceptions, attitudes, and behaviors. Take some time to consider:

1. Have you looked at yourself and your work in relation to any of the sociopolitical organizing principles of existential meaning? Which ones have you considered? Which ones haven't you considered?
2. If you have, what encouraged you to take these steps?
3. Has this been a painful or comfortable process? Why?
4. What have you found out?
5. If you haven't considered any of these organizing principles in your work, what has kept you from doing so?
6. How do these organizing principles influence your interaction with your clients?
7. How do they influence your expectations of relationships with clients?
8. What experiences have you had in the past that have encouraged or restricted you from considering these organizing principles in your personal and professional life?
9. What might be the cost or danger if you continue to explore these areas?

10. What is your next step?
11. How do you think exploring these areas will influence your appreciation of yourself as a person?
12. What are your reactions to these questions?
13. How do these issues most commonly present themselves in your work?
14. What do you find most challenging in your work in regard to these organizing principles?

# References

American Counseling Association. (2014). *ACA code of ethics*. Alexandria, VA: American Counseling Association.

Ancis, J. R., & Ladany, N. (2001). A multicultural framework for counseling supervision. In L. J. Bradley & N. Ladany (Eds.), *Counselor supervision: Principles, process, and practice* (pp. 63–90). Philadelphia, PA: Brunner-Routledge.

Ancis, J. R., & Ladany, N. (2010). A multicultural framework for counseling supervision. In L. J. Bradley & N. Ladany (Eds.), *Counselor supervision* (4th ed., pp. 53–96). New York, NY: Routlege.

Arczynski, A. V., & Morrow, S. L. (2016). The complexities of power in feminist multicultural psychotherapy supervision. *Journal of Counseling Psychology, 64*(2), 192–205. https://doi.org/10.1037/cou0000179

Bernard, J. M. (1994). Multicultural supervision: A reaction to Leong and Wagner, Cook, Priest, and Fukuyama. *Counselor Education & Supervision, 34*(2), 159–171.

Bernard, J. M., & Goodyear, R. K. (2004). Fundamentals of clinical supervision (3rd ed). Upper Saddle River, NJ: Pearson.

Bloom, B. S., Engelhart, M. D., Furst, E. J., Hill, W. H., & Krathwohl, D. R. (1956). Taxonomy of educational objectives: the classification of educational goals. New York: D. McKay

Christiansen, A. T., Thomas, V., Kafescioglu, N., Karakurt, G., Lowe, W., Smith, W., & Wittenborn, A. (2011). Multicultural supervision: Lessons learned about an ongoing struggle. *Journal of Marital and Family Therapy, 37*(1), 109–119. https://doi.org/10.1111/j.1752-0606.2009.00138.x

Commission on Accreditation for Marriage and Family Therapy Education (COAMFTE). (2015). *Accreditation Standards: Graduate and post graduate Marriage and Family Therapy Training Programs* (version 12.0). Retrieved from http://dx5br1z4f6n0k.cloudfront.net/imis15/Documents/COAMFTE/COAMFTE_Accreditation_Standards_Version_12.pdf

Corey, G., Haynes, R., Moulton, P., & Muratori, M. (2010). *Clinical supervision in the helping professions* (2nd ed.). Alexandria, VA: American Counseling Association.

Estrada, D., Frame, M. W., & Williams, C. B. (2004). Cross-cultural supervision: Guiding the conversation towards race and ethnicity. *Journal of Multicultural Counseling and Development, 32*, 307–319.

Falender, C. A., & Shafranske, E. P. (2012). The importance of competency-based clinical supervision and training the twenty-first century: Why bother? *Journal of Contemporary Psychotherapy, 42*(3), 129–137. https://doi.org/10.1007/s10879-011-9189-9

Hardy, K. V., & Laszloffy, T. A. (1995). The cultural genogram: Key to training culturally competent family therapists. *Journal of Marital and Family Therapy, 21*, 227–237.

Hayes, R. L., Blackman, L. S., & Brennan, C. (2001). Group supervision. In L. J. Bradley & N. Ladany (Eds.), *Counselor supervision: Principles, process, and practice* (pp. 183–206). Philadelphia, PA: Brunner-Routledge.

Hernández, P., Taylor, B. A., & McDowell, T. (2009). Listening to ethnic minority AAMFT approved supervisors: Reflections on their experiences as supervisees. *Journal of Systemic Therapies, 28*(1), 88–100.

Hook, J. N., Davis, D. E., Owen, J., Worthington, E. L., Jr., & Utsey, S. O. (2013). Cultural humility: Measuring openness to culturally diverse clients. *Journal of Counseling Psychology, 60*, 353–366.

Hook, J. N., Watkins, C. E., Davis, D. E., Owen, J., Van Tongeren, D. R., & Ramos, M. J. (2016). Cultural humility in psychotherapy supervision. *American Journal of Psychotherapy, 70*(2), 149–166.

Inman, A. G., & DeBoer Kreider, E. (2013). Multicultural competence: Psychotherapy, practice and supervision. *Psychotherapy, 50*(3), 346–350. https://doi.org/10.1037/a0032029

Kaduvettoor, A., O'Shainghenessy, T., Mori, Y., Beverly, C., Weatherford, R. D., & Ladany, N. (2009). Helpful & hindering multicultural events in group supervision: Climate and multicultural competence. *The Counseling Psychologist, 37*(6), 786–820.

Leong, F. T. L., & Wagner, N. S. (1994). Cross-cultural supervision: What do we know? what do we need to know? *Counselor Education & Supervision, 34*, 117–131.

Mason, B. (2005). Relational risk-taking and the training of supervisors. *Journal of Family Therapy, 27*, 298–301.

Ober, A. M., Granello, D. H., & Henfield, M. S. (2009). A synergistic model to enhance multicultural competence in supervision. *Counselor Education & Supervision, 48*, 204–221.

Owen, J. (2013). Early career perspectives on psychotherapy research and practice: Psychotherapist effects, multicultural orientation, and couple interventions. *Psychotherapy, 50*, 496–502.

Pendry, N. (2012). Race, racism and systemic supervision. *Journal of Family Therapy, 34*, 403–418. https://doi.org/10.1111/j.1467-6427.2011.00576.x

Porter, N., & Vasquez, M. (1997). Covision: Feminist supervision, process, and collaboration. In J. Worell & N. G. Johnson (Eds.), *Shaping the future of feminist psychology: Education, research, & practice* (pp. 155–171). Washington, DC: American Psychological Association. https://doi.org/10.1037/10245-007

Ratts, M. J., Singh, A. A., Nassar-McMillan, S., Butler, S. K., & McCullough, J. R. (2015). *Multicultural and social justice counseling competencies*. Retrieved from http://www.multiculturalcounseling.org/amcd-endorses-multicultural-and-social-justice-counseling-competencies.

Soheilian, S. S., Inman, A. G., Klinger, R. S., Isenberg, D. S., & Kulp, L. E. (2014). Multicultural supervision: Supervisees' reflections on culturally competent supervision. *Counselling Psychology Quarterly, 27*(4), 379–392. https://doi.org/10.1080/09515070.2014.961408

Sue, D. W., Arredondo, P., & McDavis, R. J., (1992) Multicultural Counseling Competencies and Standards: A Call to the Profession. *Journal of Counseling & Development, 70*(4), 477–486.

Sue, D. W., & Sue, D. (2015). *Counseling the culturally diverse: Theory and practice* (7th ed.). Hoboken, NJ: Wiley and Sons.

Sue, D. W., & Torino, G. C. (2005). Racial-cultural competence: Awareness, knowledge, and skills. In R. T. Carter (Ed.), *Handbook of racial-cultural psychology and counseling: Training and practice* (pp. 3–18). Hoboken, NJ: John Wiley & Sons.

Taylor, B. A., Hernández, P., Deri, A., Rankin, P. R., & Siegel, A. (2007). Integrating diversity dimensions in supervision. *The Clinical Supervisor, 25*(1–2), 3–21. https://doi.org/10.1300/J001v25n01_02

U.S. Census Bureau. (2013). *State and county quick facts*. Retrieved from http://quickfacts.census.gov/qfd/states/00000.html

Westefeld, J. S. (2009). Supervision of psychotherapy: Models, issues, and recommendations. *The Counseling Psychologist, 37*, 296–316. https://doi.org/10.1177/0011000012453945

Wong, L. C. J., Ong, P. T. P., & Ishiyama, F. I. (2013). What helps and what hinders in cross-cultural clinical supervision: A critical incident study. *The Counseling Psychologist, 41*(1), 66–85. https://doi.org/10.1177/0011000012442652

# Cross-Cultural Relevance of Systemic Family Therapy and Globally Responsive Cross-Cultural Training: An Indian Case Study

Rajeswari Natrajan-Tyagi

The practice of Western-originated psychotherapy in other cultures has been in vogue since the early 1900s (Lim, Lim, Michael, Cai, & Schock, 2010). Family therapy as a field has its origins in mainly a Euro-American cultural context beginning around 1956 (Nichlols & Schwartz, 1998). There has been a lot of momentum since the 1950s in Western literature to document and propagate various models of family therapy, especially from a Western Eurocentric perspective. As a family therapy practitioner and educator of international origin, this propagation and export of knowledge to non-Western cultural contexts are of great concern to me.

The exportation of family therapy to non-Western nations can be viewed within the framework of globalization. The concept of globalization has been defined in various ways. For the purposes of this chapter, globalization will be defined as the flow of people, information, and culture across border (Dodds, 2008). The term globalization comes with both positive and negative connotations. The pessimistic view of globalization tends to look at this phenomenon as something that erodes the indigenous culture and infuses it with Anglo-American cultural symbols and artifacts (Hill, 1995). It is seen as a new form of colonization (Hill, 1995; Mittal & Hardy, 2005; Nwoye, 2004). Some theorists suggest that globalization has skewed higher education toward the Western model (Dodds, 2008), with English being considered the legitimate and credible language in the global flow of knowledge (Pennycook, 1994). It is argued that the flow of information is more or less one directional, from the West to the East, rendering indigenous know-how and expertise to marginalization and exclusion. This exclusion and marginalization, according to Hancile, is a dynamic associated with the process of globalization (as cited in Nwoye, 2004).

R. Natrajan-Tyagi (✉)
Alliant International University, Irvine, CA, USA
e-mail: rnatrajan@alliant.edu

I was trained as a social worker in India and later moved to the United States to continue my higher education in the field of marriage and family therapy. As a student of family therapy, it was clear that the concepts that I learned were very relevant to families that I worked with back home, but the expression of certain dysfunctions, the very understanding of what is culturally functional and dysfunctional, and the process of therapy did not seem like they would seamlessly transfer over. I believe in the incredible power that nationality, geographical location, and language have in determining which knowledge is considered credible and which ones are not. I believe that the unquestioned, unidirectional export of knowledge is an important social justice issue that needs to be attended to in all cross-cultural training contexts. The propagation and export of family therapy from the West to the East have highlighted the need for creating and practicing culturally relevant family therapy that fits cultures outside of the United States and Europe (Nwoye, 2006).

## Impact of Colonialism on Systems of Education and Medicine

Any discussion of export and import of knowledge between Western and non-Western countries is not complete without a discussion of colonialism and its impact on education and medicine. Colonization of particularly the Eastern, African, and Latin American countries brought with it not only a new political system but also a profound transformation of its educational and medical systems. Education has long been used as a tool to promote the values, beliefs, language, religion, and customs of the colonizers (Viswanathan, 1988). The encounter between the knowledge and education systems of the native cultures and the Western colonizers has resulted in the former being labeled as inferior and weak. Similarly, the native cultures' systems of medicine and healing have also suffered. Besides being looked at as inferior, weak, and lacking in scientific rigor, practitioners of indigenous systems of healing were looked upon as B-class practitioners (Supe, 2016). This attitude has been passed down over the generations, and in the postcolonial era, the validity of the indigenous methods of healing is questioned by the native people themselves who find Western medicine more credible than their ancient systems. As a result, in many Asian and African countries, it is very common to see Western education being taught and Western medicine being practiced without being questioned or being challenged as legitimate. My own educational experience is an example; I was educated in an English-medium, convent, K-12 institution in India followed by an undergraduate education in another English-medium, Christian college. My family believed in the superiority of the British educational system, and a convent, English education was believed to propagate that system of education. This was at the expense of me not having any formal education in my native language, Tamil. When I went on to graduate education in social work, I experienced a lot of challenges, especially in my field placements, in being able to connect and work with primarily Tamil-speaking populations and being able to advocate for them. Similarly, despite my interest in Hindu spirituality and in the Ayurvedic system of healing, I personally chose to pursue higher education in the United States in marriage and family therapy as I considered this education to carry more weight and credibility than a postgraduate training in spirituality or in the ancient systems of healing in India. The unquestioned superiority of Western education, medicine, and ways of healing is an important consideration to have when trying to study the issue of cultural relevance and cross-cultural training in non-Western nations. In the following paragraphs, I discuss the cultural relevance of family therapy models in non-Western cultures.

## Cultural Relevance of Family Therapy in Non-Western Cultures

There have been emerging conversations about the applicability of the systemic theory and models in several non-Western countries such as China (Lim et al., 2010; Sim & Hu, 2009), Malaysia (Ng, 1998), India (Carson & Chowdhury, 2000; Mittal & Hardy, 2005; Nath & Craig, 1999; Rastogi, Natrajan, & Thomas, 2005), Kenya (Nwoye, 2004, 2006), and Singapore (Tan, 2003). In this chapter, I will use the words "non-Western," "native," "indigenous," and "local" interchangeably to talk about non-Western/non-European cultures and more specifically cultures that have Asian (e.g., China and India), African (e.g., Kenya), and Latin American (e.g., Argentina) roots. Though there is a lot of theoretical speculation of what aspects of Western family therapy models fit with non-Western cultures and what aspects are cultural misfits, there has been no systematic empirical research study done on the issue. Only a few practitioners from non-Western cultures have reported on their use of family therapy models within their cultural context and addressed issues of fit. The reasons for this may be because of the following:

1. The use of family therapy models as articulated in the Western countries is not yet widespread in non-Western cultures.
2. Mental health practitioners in non-Western cultures may not be comfortable with the English language (which is the dominant medium of scholarly dissemination) and may be experiencing difficulties translating information from English to their local languages and back. This may deny them access to information and prevent them from contributing their local know-how to the literature on how to work with families in their cultural groups.
3. Mental health practitioners do not see themselves as researchers and important players in the process of using and indigenizing Western models and possibly even coming up with their own culturally relevant models. Thus, there is a gap in our understanding of how non-Western practitioners view the theory and practice of family therapy and the cultural relevance of these models to the local cultures.

It is useful to first talk about the general fit of family therapy in non-Western countries. Family therapy concepts are based on the broad platform of systemic thinking that fits very well with the general worldview of several non-Western cultures (Sim & Hu, 2009). The ecosystemic view of family therapy in most cases fits very well with these cultures. The focus on family, hierarchies, circularity, relationships, strength-based approaches, use of stories and metaphors, and holistic perspective makes the field of family therapy attractive to the local cultures (Qian, Smith, Chen, & Xia, 2002; Sim & Hu, 2009). However, the cultural fit of the systemic theories and models may end there.

Even though some of the theoretical concepts of family therapy fit well with the non-Western cultural zeitgeist, the models in practice are very Western and individualistic. For example, the nondirective/collaborative approach (Standke-Erdmann, 2005; Wu, 1982), emphasis on insight development (Wu, 1982), focus on individual rights, empowerment, and expression of emotions (Gao, Ting-Toomey, & Gudykunst, 1996; Sim & Hu, 2009), focus on gender equality (Sim & Hu, 2009), ideas about therapeutic boundaries and personal space (Kakar, 1997; Standke-Erdmann, 2005), simplistic ideas about the structure of the family system and dynamics (Carson & Chowdhury, 2000; Standke-Erdmann, 2005), and lack of integration of traditional religious/spiritual/medical healing methods often single out family therapy models as being non-viable for practice with the local population. Even though, theoretically, family therapy is conceptualized to include various systems, in actual practice in the West, only immediate family systems are generally taken into consideration. Other ecological systems, such as systems of economics and politics, rarely enter the therapy room, and this makes the practice of family therapy elitist and bourgeois and thus marginalizes much of the population in non-Western countries (Nwoye, 2006). The therapeutic role of the mental health practitioner may need to extend beyond the therapy room to encompass various issues of advocacy and social justice which has traditionally not been the purview of family therapy. Therefore, there is a need to expand the nature and practice of family therapy to fit the cultural contexts of non-Western societies. In this chapter, I will use the practice of family therapy in India as a case study to illustrate how Western-originated concepts of family therapy miss the cultural mark when trying to address familial and systemic problems around the world.

## *An Indian Case Study*

As an Asian Indian family therapy educator, one of my passions is to share what I have learned in the United States with counselors and social workers in India. Before I embarked on this endeavor, I wanted to figure out what was the most culturally sensitive and relevant way to introduce the concepts. In my review of existing literature on how Western family therapy models have shown to be a cultural misfit in the context of the Indian culture, I came across both theoretical speculations (Carson, Jain, & Ramirez, 2009; Mittal & Hardy, 2005; Natrajan & Thomas, 2002) and clinical observations made by practitioners in India and those working with the Indian Diaspora outside of India (Baptiste, 2005; Carson &

Chowdhury, 2000; Hutnik, 2005; Nath & Craig, 1999; Sonpar, 2005). The crux of the discrepancies seems to lie in the fundamental differences in the worldviews regarding the nature of self, locus of control, definition of marriage, family organization and kinship patterns, nature of relationships, gender relations, and intergenerational linkages (Carson & Chowdhury, 2000; Hutnik, 2005; Juvva & Bhatti, 2006; Karuppaswamy & Natrajan, 2003; Nath & Craig, 1999; Sonpar, 2005). My review of the literature revealed that some of the cultural barriers faced by therapists trained in or using the Western systemic family therapy models while working with Indian families included (1) attributing the presenting problem to poor marital quality, lack of marital intimacy or porous marital boundaries (Nath & Craig, 1999), and intervening at the marital level; (2) focusing on strengthening the marital dyad and placing it in opposition to other more culturally significant familial relationships such as parent-adult son relationship, daughter-in-law-parents-in-law relationship, the parental subsystem, and the mother-child relationship (Nath & Craig, 1999; Sonpar, 2005); (3) encouraging a Western concept of an egalitarian marital relationship with symmetrical equality (Sonpar, 2005); (4) directly challenging gender roles, hierarchies, and abuse of power within the marital pair and the family system (Hutnik, 2005); (5) assuming that intergenerational patterns of triangulation are necessarily dysfunctional (Nath & Craig, 1999; Sonpar, 2005); and (6) not understanding the expectations of clients regarding therapist's role as that of expert who is directive yet willing to share a reciprocal relationship, being more emotionally close and sharing personal spaces (Mittal & Hardy, 2005; Hutnik, 2005; Standke-Erdmann, 2005). Though it is important to not evaluate all cultural traits as necessarily culturally appropriate or functional behaviors (Montalvo & Gutierrez, 1983), it is also important to understand that what is considered functional and dysfunctional is strongly dictated by one's cultural worldviews (Nath & Craig, 1999). As D'Ardenne (1994) states, family therapy, as it is widely practiced now, represents the values and worldviews of the white, middle-class, nuclear families.

These theoretical speculations and clinical observations have not been systematically studied. I decided to undertake a study in India to explore the perceptions of local mental health practitioners regarding the theory and practice of family therapy and its cultural relevance to their local cultural context. First, I conducted six workshops in my native city of Chennai for students of social work and for mental health professionals in the community. The participants were first introduced to general systems theory. Some of the main concepts that I discussed were subsystems, importance of context, recursive causality, homeostasis, communication and information processing, meta-communication, feedback loops, and content versus process. I then introduced the participants to structural therapy, strategic therapy, and postmodern ideas in family therapy. I introduced the main concepts of the models and approaches, followed by common therapeutic techniques and the various phases in therapy in each model/approach. I used the Becvar and Becvar (1996) text, "Family Therapy: A Systemic Integration," as a resource for teaching the content of the workshop. I showed movie clips from Indian movies to help students understand the patterns and dynamics in families and to understand the main concepts of systems theory and the models/approaches. Participants practiced creating structural maps, conceptualizing cases using the models and coming up with treatment plans that fit the respective models. Finally, the participants participated in role-plays and later discussed the role-plays. Then using focus groups, I gathered the perspectives and assessment of the mental health professionals and trainees on how the theories and the techniques fit with their clients and cultural context.

I conducted a total of seven focus group interviews lasting for about a half hour to one hour. The participants for the focus group were from the six workshops. There was a total of 56 focus group participants with an average of 8 participants per group. The ages of the 33 participants who were social work trainees ranged from 20 to 37 years with a mean of 23.55 (SD 3.39). Fifty-two percent of the participants were male and 48% were female. Fifty-eight percent of the participants were in the first year of their social work program and 42% were in the second year. Out of the total participants, only 5% had their undergraduate degree from social work programs. Sixteen percent of the participants had a sociology/family science background. Eighty percent had other undergraduate degrees such as science, liberal arts, or business. Eighty percent of the participants reported that they had never had any training in systems theory or concepts. The rest reported that they had previously had some kind of training in systems theory. Out of the total participants who had prior training in systems theory, about 92% reported that they learned systems theory as part of a course, while the rest reported that they learned systems theory as part of a workshop. More than half of the participants (56.3%) had less than 1 year of clinical experience. Thirty-six percent had 1–4 years of clinical experience, while 6% of the participants reported that they had 5–9 years of clinical experience.

There were 23 participants who were mental health professionals in the field. The age of these participants ranged from 23 to 54 years with the mean age of 34.3 (SD 9.76). Thirteen percent were male and 87% were female. Thirty-nine percent of the participants were single, while the rest were married. All the participants except one had graduate-level education. More than half of the participants (52%) had a graduate degree in social work. Thirty-five percent had a graduate degree in psychology, 4% in medicine, and 4% in sociology. Only 2 out of the 23 participants reported that they had some kind of prior exposure to systems theory. They explained that they had learned systems theory as a topic in one of their courses in graduate school. There was great variability in the participants' level of clinical experience. The mean years of clinical experience fell within the range of 1–4 years (SD 1.05).

I used the following questions to guide the focus group interviews: (1) How was the workshop useful? (2) What techniques and concepts will fit your work with clients? (3) How culturally relevant are the theories and techniques? (4) What might be some barriers in using some of the concepts or techniques?

My analysis of the focus-group interviews revealed that participants had expressed both views; that is, (1) systemic theories and techniques are culturally relevant, and (2) there are cultural and therapeutic barriers in applying systemic theories and techniques. In the following paragraphs, I have shared the main findings of the study using as much as I can the voices of the participants through relevant quotes.

## *Systemic Theories and Techniques Are Culturally Relevant in the Indian Context*

It appeared that the participants of the workshops were actively engaged in making sense of whether the family systems theory and techniques fit with their cultural context. Most (over 80%) of the participants felt that the systemic theories and techniques were culturally relevant to the Indian context. Participants seemed to believe that they would be able to adapt systemic theories and techniques to suit the Indian context, especially since they had done role-plays in the training session and also since other theories and techniques from psychoanalytical models had been adapted before. One participant expressed:

> You cannot say that the Indian culture is traditional and so these techniques are not applicable. It is applicable to all. Family plays a role in the whole world. The therapy situation reminds me of the usual village headman or "panchayat" who deals with family problems.

Yet another participant reported:

> The symbols (in the structural map) used in the technique we learnt can be used with anyone...anywhere...whether they are illiterate or they are educated. They will all definitely understand symbols. I think the techniques are very relevant.

This finding fits with the literature that the focus of systems theory on family interactions patterns and the broader systems makes it attractive to indigenous cultures (Sim & Hu, 2009). Even though families may be diverse in some ways, all families are societal systems interacting with each other for a common purpose and are organized to serve a specific function everywhere (Lee, 2002; Sue & Sue, 2003), making the basic tenets of family therapy theories highly relevant irrespective of cultural differences.

## *Cultural and Therapeutic Barriers in Applying Systemic Theories in the Indian Context*

Participants also identified several cultural barriers in practicing family therapy and applying systemic theories and techniques in the Indian therapeutic context.

**Concept of Family Therapy Is Alien** Participants mentioned that the lack of awareness of services such as family therapy may be a barrier to accessing family therapy services. They also mentioned that families may feel inhibited talking about their personal problems to an outside person. Participants expressed that counseling and family therapy services were not considered mainstream healthcare services that people readily accessed or were even aware of. While some participants were optimistic that the concept of family therapy may catch on, others were quite pessimistic. One participant expressed that "most families prefer to solve problems within themselves or else they prefer that their relatives solve them. They do not go to therapy. Lack of awareness is also a major barrier."

Participants mentioned that families may feel inhibited about sharing personal information with an outsider and may not be willing to divulge family issues even if they come to therapy on their own volition. They reported that families in general do not want a "third-party person" to interfere in their family matters. One participant reported:

> When families come for therapy it is not easy for therapists to bring out the truth. They might speak of a lot of issues but not about the real issue that they are facing. Sometimes they want to conceal it.

Another participant observed that "people may not come out with their problems because they may feel very shy. If they do come for therapy, they may base the problems on some other problems rather than the real issue."

These findings support the findings of an earlier study that I conducted with middle-class families in India (Natrajan & Thomas, 2002). In that study, participants had shared that some of their barriers in seeking therapy is their fear of "losing face," distrustfulness of outside members, women's socialization within the patriarchal system, and their fatalistic view of life which made them accept and tolerate their situation rather than attempt to change it.

**Language Barrier** Language barrier was mentioned as one of the issues that might hinder the process of family therapy. Some participants were concerned that equivalent terms have not yet been coined in the colloquial language, for some of the family therapy concepts. Therefore, they feared that this might pose a barrier to practicing family therapy. One participant expressed:

> The biggest barrier here is language. The case worker or the counselor has to work with families from different backgrounds, different sectors and parts of the country. So they have to deal with the problem of language…applying these techniques in a language that may be alien to them. That seems to be the biggest barrier.

The participants' apprehension is understandable, especially since there may not be an equivalent term in Indian languages that are commonly used for terms such as "structure," "boundaries," or "triangulation." India, having been a colonial country, uses English as one of its official languages. English is also the medium of instruction in several of its schools and colleges. However, in many of the educational institutions outside of the major metropolitan areas, the applied skill of listening to and speaking in English is seldom taught (Kaushik, 2011), rendering most of the non-urban college-educated Indian citizens not fluent in the language. This also means that a majority of the Indian population who have little or no formal school education are also not socialized to speak or understand the English language. This has a direct impact on the accessibility of family therapy. Family Therapy, which is mainly a form of talk therapy that has been conceptualized and formalized in the English language, is automatically rendered inaccessible to majority of practitioners and clients in India. At a secondary level, even practitioners who are well versed in the English language find a cultural barrier in using the vocabulary found in the practice of family therapy because of the following reasons: (1) lack of equivalent terms in the colloquial language, sometimes even when the language of choice is English (Bhui, Mohamud, Warfa, Craig, & Stansfeld, 2003; Natrajan, Karrupaswamy, Ramadoss, & Thomas, 2005); (2) differences in understanding role expectations of family members and consequently the differences in the understanding of what behaviors are functional/dysfunctional (Nath & Craig, 1999); and (3) cultural awkwardness in using certain words, even if equivalent terms in the local languages are found, because of the cultural taboos that may exist in verbalizing certain aspects of one's relationships (Natrajan et al., 2005). This points to a real need that exists for creation of family therapy texts in India by Indian authors who can not only translate the existing family therapy texts to the local language of choice but can also critically analyze the models, adapt them to suit the cultural context, and provide case examples that adequately represent the current cultural zeitgeist.

**Age of Therapist**  Another theme that came up was concerns about the age of the therapist. A few participants (social work students) were concerned about their age and whether family therapy would be a good fit for them. It appeared that they were not conscious of their age when they took on the identity of "social workers." However, in order to take on the identity as a "family therapist," they felt they did not have enough life experiences. One participant expressed:

> I think a major barrier would be my age because I do not think that people will accept it when I use these concepts to solve their problems. They will think that I am too young to do family therapy.

This finding also supported the findings in my earlier study. Both service providers and families in India seem to consider the role of a therapist to be that of a "guru" or a benefactor which presupposes that the therapist is a wise and old person (Jayakar, 1994; Natrajan & Thomas, 2002). This explains the concern that both service providers and families have about the age of the therapist and the level of competency that it suggests. Marital counseling, since the beginning of the professionalization of the field, has been seen as something to be practiced by highly trained and mature practitioners and not something to be engaged in by the youthful and inexperienced. Nichols (1979) states that the maturity and personal-professional integration required in the adequate practitioner are partly a function of age and experience, in addition to education and training. It may be assumed that beginning clinicians who proceed directly from bachelor's degrees into masters and/or doctoral studies (a common occurrence in the Indian educational setting) may not be perceived to possess the high degree of skill and maturity needed for entering the field of family therapy.

**Presenting Problem Not Being Dealt with**  Yet another theme that came up was that participants felt that family therapy focused on broader systemic issues and was losing focus of the presenting problem. Participants expressed concern that they might lose their clients if they fail to pay attention to the issues their clients posed as the presenting problem. In some cases, the participants felt that it would only be ethical to focus on the immediate presenting problems as it might need urgent care, for example, an active psychosis. One participant reported:

> We may face problems when patients come into the psychiatric ward for psychiatric problems and they have to be medicated first and dealt individually, and then after that we may bring in the whole family. So, family therapy as the starting point for people with psychosis may be difficult.

Some participants acknowledged that they found the techniques of family therapy to be very useful. However, they reported that they might use family therapy as a secondary phase in treatment, especially in cases where they feel they have to focus first on the presenting issue:

> There is a definite shift in my perspective (after attending the workshop), but in my clinical setting I think I should deal with the content. I cannot negate the content in my setting and work with process alone. I will definitely incorporate working with the process.

At the same time, participants recognized some situations where they might use family therapy in the initial stages, for example, for clients facing marital issues. This was summarized by one participant as follows: "Mostly it (family therapy) can go as a secondary process. In some areas like family conflict, adjustment problem, this process can be used…at the initial stages itself it (family therapy) can be used. But this technique is useful in other stages too."

The hesitation among clinicians to use systemic family therapy as the only therapeutic modality seemed to come from their sense of urgency in wanting to meet the clients where they were at. They wanted to work with the presenting problem in order to first build rapport and then, once the trust was built, to move into more systemic and relational work.

**Importance of Individual Therapy in the Indian Context** Participants expressed concern that family therapy techniques discouraged therapy with individuals. They expressed that they found individual therapy very useful in the Indian context, especially when certain members of the family felt inhibited to talk in front of other family members. One participant expressed that "talking to an individual is useless according to family therapy. However, we find individual counseling more useful. I find that maybe this is one of the barriers to using this concept here.".

Another participant reported:

> It was actually very useful and apt, but the only thing is that in a therapy session the wife might feel very comfortable to talk to the counselor individually rather than in front of the patient (alcoholic husband). So, certain issues when the lady of the family talks, she might be very comfortable talking individually to the counselor. So, except for that, family therapy is useful.

Clinicians in the study stressed the importance of individual therapy, especially for women, who may not want to disclose certain issues in front of their husbands. This finding highlights the fact that it is important to assess whether the couple coming into therapy has an "old Indian marriage" (that is mainly arranged and focuses on procreation, duty, low expression of emotions with opaque to translucent communication style) or a "new Indian marriage" (that has greater individual participation in mate selection with focus on intimacy and companionship, more transparent and direct communication style) (Nagaswami, 2011) before deciding on the format of therapy. An implication for future family therapy training in India may also be the importance of clarifying the systemic framework from the unit of treatment. That is, clinicians can use the systemic family therapy perspective even while working with an individual family member, the latter being an important cultural necessity due to power differential in families and family hierarchies.

**Difficulty in Involving All the Family Members** Some participants observed that a barrier to conducting family therapy would be the challenge in involving all the family members in the process. Two reasons that were given for the inability to involve family members were (1) physically having all the family members in the room may be difficult, and (2) family members may not agree that they contribute to the problem. As one participant reported "it will be difficult to use family therapy in our context because the presence of all the family members (in the therapy room at the same time) is difficult." While another participant expressed that "it will be a great barrier to make people understand that they are also part of the problem. I don't think people in India will accept that." However, some participants expressed that the first barrier (inability to physically have family members in the therapy room) can be overcome as clinicians who are social workers regularly make home visits to their clients' homes.

Some participants expressed that it may be difficult for counselors to practice family therapy in situations where they have to work in collaboration with other service providers who may be rigid in their thinking about issues such as "who the identified patient was." One participant expressed:

> Here (in the Indian context) people will only concentrate on the real client or on the potential client. They think that only the problematic (symptomatic) clients should be dealt with. For example, when I was in the police station setting, they had lots of myths about who the client is. So such settings should be taken into consideration.

An important finding in this study was the considerable anxiety among the clinicians to redefine the problem in interactional terms and work with the relational processes in the family as opposed to working with the identified patient individually. Participants seemed concerned about involving other members of the family in therapy because family members may not buy into the idea that they may be contributing to the presenting problem. This may tie into the idea of "saving face" where parents, adults, and more powerful members of the family system may find it difficult to own up to their issues in front of less powerful members of the family. This brings to the forefront that the hierarchical nature of familial relationships is an important consideration when planning interventions (Sim & Hu, 2009).

**Time Frame Involved in This Kind of Therapy** Participants were concerned that the process of family therapy may take a long time to help clients reach resolution. They expressed that, as most of the clients they saw in therapy were in a hurry to solve their issues, the therapists may lose out on their clients if they used a long-term therapeutic technique. One participant stated it as follows:

> A barrier would be the time frame involved throughout the process of this intervention. The clients who come to the counseling center want instant solutions. So, because of this mindset, they may not come to the next session. It will take a long time to sit with the clients and go through this (family therapy) process.

Another participant expressed:

> When people come to us for guidance, they want immediate solution. So when we try to apply the concepts that we learnt in the past two days, we will miss on the immediate problems. So, we may miss out on our clients. So, that is what is worrying me when I think of applying it.

Literature review supports the fact that there is a lot of expectation from Asian clients for short-term, action-oriented therapy (Lim et al., 2010). A take-home point from the results of my study is that in order to engage Indian clients or the Indian family system in therapy, it is important to initially focus on individual symptom reduction before launching into more systemic second-order change. Short-term systemic therapies such as solution-focused therapy and brief-strategic therapy modalities that have been found to be effective with populations having Asian origins (Berg & Miller, 1992; Steenbarger, 1983). These modalities could be the preferred treatment of choice although it is too premature to rule out other emotion-based or classical modalities such as Bowenian/contextual therapy as effective modalities with the Indian population.

**Subjective Methods of Assessments in Family Therapy** Some participants expressed concern over the lack of objective methods (paper and pencil methods) of assessments in family therapy. They expressed concern over the "great responsibility" that therapists have to shoulder in order to make "such subjective" assessments. One participant expressed:

> Another thing in the systems theory is that we cannot vouch for the authenticity and scientific evidence. It is subjective. It is based on subjective observation rather than on some well standardized test. So the therapists' sensitivity and capability to assess is very, very important. So, it (the therapists' assessments) may be questioned sometimes. When you are doing psychotherapy (other well established methods of psychotherapy) it is not on the basis of our own evaluation. It is rather on the basis of your assessment with the help of well standardized psycho-diagnostic tests. So here (in family therapy) some tools are not there to assess. It is your own observations and assessments. I do not say that it is wrong…rather the authenticity…sometimes the therapist may go wrong and the responsibility will finally come to you. So if the therapist is not capable or trained well enough to accurately assess the problem, we may miss. That is my concern.

Another participant expressed:

> We (the family therapist) should have a balanced kind of mind so that we can decide what to analyze and what not to. We have to take (responsibility for) all the analysis in our hands and come to a conclusion. That will be one of the barriers.

The practice of Western medicine with its emphasis on using standardized assessment tools has strong roots in a colonized nation like India, and hence, the importance of establishing the scientific credibility of systemic therapy is crucial before there is large-scale acceptance of systemic models as a legitimate framework for treatment. MFT as a field has made significant strides in becoming an evidenced-based discipline (Sprenkle, 2003), with a significant body of literature on the efficacy and effectiveness of MFT in the areas of conduct disorder and delinquency (Henggeler & Sheidow, 2003), substance and alcohol abuse (O'Farrell & Fals-Stewart, 2003; Rowe & Liddle, 2003), childhood behavior disorders (Northey, Wells, Silverman, & Bailey, 2003), marital problems (Johnson, 2003), and domestic violence (Stith, Rosen, & McCollum, 2003) to name a few. Several key members in the field have also over the years been engaged in the process of integrating issues of diversity and culture (McGoldrick, Giordano, & Garcia-Preto, 2005; Hardy & McGoldrick, 2008) into its purview. It is important to contextualize this information while presenting to and training clinicians in India in order to establish the credibility of the field and its relevance to their context.

**Not Enough Training** Another concern that participants expressed was that they did not feel prepared to apply the family therapy ideologies and techniques. Some mentioned that they need to specialize further in order to put these techniques to practice and seemed open to the idea of further training. One participant expressed:

> In general, this was a good introduction to a new method but we need to continue working on it and see how applicable it is to our setting. I am not sure if methodologically...how well we are trained and how much we are capable of dealing with such systems. To deal with such a method within a short period...within a short training...is difficult, but we can train into this further and equip ourselves better. That may be possible.

Overall, the concerns about the cultural relevance and fit of systemic family therapy models in India were varied. The findings added to the existing body of literature that reported on areas where the Western-generated theories and models were culturally amiss. As an educator and trainer who is interested in teaching and training family therapists in India, it is extremely important for me to attend to the concerns expressed by the Indian counselors and be deliberate about addressing the concerns. It would be faulty to assume that just because I am of Indian origin, I would automatically be culturally knowledgeable and have the ability to calibrate the existing models to Indian cultural conditions. If family therapy is to succeed in India, it would be critical to address the concerns surrounding the idiosyncratic, and culture-specific aspects of the Indian families and the mental health delivery system (Lee, 2002; Sue & Sue, 2003) in a systematic and disciplined way. In order for globalization, in this case, the flow of knowledge and information across cultural borders, to be more globally responsive, the phenomenon has to be something that increases personal freedom, promotes cultural exchange, and revitalizes both the native culture and the exporting culture (Legraine, 2003). At this juncture, I want to introduce the concept of *glocalization* (Nwoye, 2004; Robertson, 1992). Glocalization is a highly relevant framework, where the global and the local cultures are engaged in a reciprocal relationship which would be experienced as empowering rather than disempowering by the local culture (Hill, 1995). The idea of "knowledge flow," where knowledge is reciprocally exchanged between global cultures and digested by local cultures through active engagement with the new knowledge, is important. It is different than the idea of "knowledge transfer," where one culture (typically Euro-American cultures) are the givers of knowledge and the others (typically the Eastern, African, or Latin American cultures) are the consumers of knowledge and the knowledge is simply transplanted into the receiving culture at the cost of local know-hows (Hill, 1995; Nwoye, 2004). It is my bias that with globalization, the Western-created knowledge of family therapy is inevitably entering into the mental health systems of non-Western cultures. However, for effective and culturally responsive utility of its theory and practice, it is important to have an active engagement between the existing knowledge and the knowledge generated from localized realities and sociocultural structures of the indigenous societies. There is a need for more indigenous trainers who can translate the material to culturally suit the native context. There is a greater need to write and publish family therapy textbooks where the theories and the techniques are culturally adapted with plenty of case examples that integrate the cultural nuances of native families. In order for reciprocal knowledge flow to happen, it would be ideal if there is an exchange of students and scholars between family therapy/mental health programs in the Western and non-Western countries and collaboration between them to understand and appreciate their respective cultures and traditions and to establish *glocalized* bodies of knowledge in the field of family therapy.

## References

Baptiste, D. A. (2005). Family therapy with East Indian immigrant parents rearing children in the United States: Parental concerns, therapeutic issues, and recommendations. *Contemporary Family Therapy, 27*(3), 345–366. https://doi.org/10.1007/s10591-005-6214-9

Becvar, D. S., & Becvar, R. J. (1996). *Family therapy: A systemic integration.* Boston, MA: Allyn and Bacon.

Berg, I. K., & Miller, S. D. (1992). Working with Asian American clients: One person at a time. *Journal of Contemporary Human Services, 73*, 356–363.

Bhui, K., Mohamud, S., Warfa, N., Craig, T. J., & Stansfeld, S. A. (2003). Cultural adaptation of mental health measures: Improving the quality of clinical practice and research. *The British Journal of Psychiatry, 183*, 184–186. https://doi.org/10.1192/bjp.183.3.184

Carson, D., & Chowdhury, A. (2000). Family therapy in India: A new profession in an ancient land. *Contemporary Family Therapy, 22*, 387–406. https://doi.org/10.1023/A:1007892716661

Carson, D. K., Jain, S., & Ramirez, S. (2009). Counseling and family therapy in India: Evolving professions in a rapidly developing nation. *International Journal of Advanced Counselling, 31*, 45–56. https://doi.org/10.1007/s10447-008-9067-8

Dodds, A. (2008). How does globalization interact with higher education? The continuing lack of consensus. *Comparative Education, 44*(4), 505–517. https://doi.org/10.1080/03050060802481538

Gao, G., Ting-Toomey, S., & Gudykunst, W. B. (1996). Chinese communication process. In M. H. Bond (Ed.), *The handbook of Chinese psychology* (pp. 280–293). New York, NY: Oxford University Press.

Hardy, K. V., & McGoldrick, M. (2008). Re-visioning training. In M. McGoldrick & K. V. Hardy (Eds.), *Family therapy: Race, culture, and gender in clinical practice* (pp. 442–460). New York, NY: Guilford Press.

Henggeler, S. W., & Sheidow, A. (2003). Conduct disorder and delinquency. *Journal of Marital and Family Therapy*, 29(4), 505–522. https://doi.org/10.1111/j.1752-0606.2003.tb01692.x

Hill, S. (1995). Globalization or indigenization: New alignments between knowledge and culture. *Knowledge and Policy*, 8(2), 88–112. https://doi.org/10.1007/BF02825970

Hutnik, N. (2005). Towards holistic, compassionate, professional care: Using a cultural lens to examine the practice of contemporary psychotherapy in the west. *Contemporary Family Therapy*, 27(3), 383–402. https://doi.org/10.1007/s10591-005-6216-7

Jayakar, K. (1994). Women of the Indian subcontinent. In L. Comas-Diaz & B. Greene (Eds.), *Women of color: Integrating ethnic and gender identities in psychotherapy* (pp. 161–184). New York, NY: Guilford Press.

Johnson, S. M. (2003). The revolution in couple therapy: A practitioner-scientist perspective. *Journal of Marital and Family Therapy*, 29(3), 365–384. https://doi.org/10.1111/j.1752-0606.2003.tb01213.x

Juvva, S., & Bhatti, R. S. (2006). Epigenetic model of marital expectations. *Contemporary Family Therapy*, 28(1), 61–72. https://doi.org/10.1007/s10591-006-9696-2

Kakar, S. (1997). *Psychoanalysis and non-western cultures: Culture and psyche.* New Delhi, India: Oxford University Press.

Karuppaswamy, N., & Natrajan, R. (2003). Family therapy from a Hindu Indian worldview. In M. Rastogi & E. Wieling (Eds.), *Voices of color: First person accounts of ethnic minority therapists* (pp. 297–312). Thousand Oaks, CA: Sage Publications.

Kaushik, S. (2011). Teaching English in Indian contexts: Towards a pedagogic model. *World Englishes*, 30(1), 141–150. https://doi.org/10.1111/j.1467-971X.2010.01693.x

Lee, W. (2002). One therapist, four cultures: Working with families in Greater China. *Journal of Family Therapy*, 24, 258–275. https://doi.org/10.1111/1467-6427.00215

Legraine, P. (2003). Cultural globalization is not Americanization. *The Chronicle of Higher Education*, 49(35), B7.

Lim, S., Lim, B. K. H., Michael, R., Cai, R., & Schock, C. K. (2010). The trajectory of counseling in China: Past, present and future trends. *Journal of Counseling and Development*, 88, 4–8. https://doi.org/10.1002/j.1556-6678.2010.tb00141.x

McGoldrick, M., Giordano, J., & Garcia-Preto, N. (Eds.). (2005). *Ethnicity and family therapy.* New York, NY: Guilford.

Mittal, M., & Hardy, K. V. (2005). A re-examination of the current status and future of family therapy in India. *Contemporary Family Therapy*, 27(3), 285–299. https://doi.org/10.1007/s10591-005-6210-0

Montalvo, B., & Gutierrez, M. (1983). A perspective for the use of the cultural dimension in family therapy. In C. J. Falicov (Ed.), *Cultural perspectives in family therapy* (pp. 15–32). Rockville, MD: Aspen Publications.

Nagaswami, V. (2011). Presentation at the 2nd India immersion program: *Couple Intervention in 21st Century India.* Chennai, India.

Nath, R., & Craig, J. (1999). Practicing family therapy in India: How many people are there in a marital subsystem? *The Journal of Family Therapy*, 21, 390–406. https://doi.org/10.1111/1467-6427.00127

Natrajan, R., Karrupaswamy, N., Ramadoss, K., & Thomas, V. (2005). Adaptation of two family therapy training instruments to culturally suit the Indian context. *Journal of Contemporary Family Therapy*, 27, 415–434. https://doi.org/10.1007/s10591-005-6218-5

Natrajan, R., & Thomas, V. (2002). Need for family therapy services for middle-class families in India. *Contemporary Family Therapy*, 24, 483–503. https://doi.org/10.1023/A:1019819401113

Ng, K. S. (1998). Family therapy in Malaysia: An update. *Contemporary Family Therapy*, 20(1), 37–45. https://doi.org/10.1023/A:1025036600703

Nichlols, M., & Schwartz, R. (1998). *Family therapy: Concept and methods.* Boston, MA: Allyn & Bacon.

Nichols, W. (1979). Education of marriage and family therapists: Some trends and implications. *Journal of Marital and Family Therapy, 5*, 19–28. https://doi.org/10.1111/j.1752-0606.1979.tb00550.x

Northey, W. F., Wells, K. C., Silverman, W. K., & Bailey, C. E. (2003). Childhood behavioral and emotional disorders. *Journal of Marital and Family Therapy, 29*(4), 523–545. https://doi.org/10.1111/j.1752-0606.2003.tb01693.x

Nwoye, A. (2004). The shattered microcosm: Imperatives for improved family therapy in Africa in the 21st century. *Contemporary Family Therapy, 26*(2), 143–164. https://doi.org/10.1023/B:COFT.0000031240.00980.88

Nwoye, A. (2006). A narrative approach to child and family therapy in Africa. *Contemporary Family Therapy, 28*(1), 1–23. https://doi.org/10.1007/s10591-006-9691-6

O'Farrell, T., & Fals-Stewart, W. (2003). Alcohol abuse. *Journal of Marital and Family Therapy, 29*(1), 121–146. https://doi.org/10.1111/j.1752-0606.2003.tb00387.x

Pennycook, A. (1994). *The cultural politics of English as an international language*. New York, NY: Longman.

Qian, M. Y., Smith, C. W., Chen, Z. G., & Xia, G. H. (2002). Psychotherapy in China: A review of its history and contemporary directions. *International Journal of Mental Health, 30*(4), 49–68. https://doi.org/10.1080/00207411.2001.11449532

Rastogi, M., Natrajan, R., & Thomas, V. (2005). On becoming a profession: The growth of Marriage and Family Therapy in India. *Journal of Contemporary Family Therapy., 27*, 453–471. https://doi.org/10.1007/s10591-005-8233-y

Robertson, R. (1992). *Globalization: Social theory and global culture*. London, UK: Sage Publications.

Rowe, C. L., & Liddle, H. A. (2003). Substance abuse. *Journal of Marital and Family Therapy, 29*(1), 97–120. https://doi.org/10.1111/j.1752-0606.2003.tb00386.x

Sim, T., & Hu, C. (2009). Family therapy in the forbidden city: A review of Chinese journals from 1978–2006. *Family Process, 38*(4), 559–583. https://doi.org/10.1111/j.1545-5300.2009.01302.x

Sonpar, S. (2005). Marriage in India: Clinical issues. *Contemporary Family Therapy, 27*(3), 301–313. https://doi.org/10.1007/s10591-005-6211-z

Sprenkle, D. H. (2003). Effectiveness research in Marriage and Family Therapy: Introduction. *Journal of Marital and Family Therapy, 29*(1), 85–96. https://doi.org/10.1111/j.1752-0606.2003.tb00385.x

Standke-Erdmann, B. (2005). Working with families from the Indian sub-continent: An Indo-German experience. *Contemporary Family Therapy, 27*(3), 315–327. https://doi.org/10.1007/s10591-005-6212-y

Steenbarger, B. N. (1983). Multicontextual model of counseling: Bridging brevity and diversity. *Journal of Counseling and Development, 72*, 8–15. https://doi.org/10.1002/j.1556-6676.1993.tb02269.x

Stith, S., Rosen, K. H., & McCollum, E. E. (2003). Effectiveness of couples treatment for spouse abuse. *Journal of Marital and Family Therapy, 29*(3), 407–426. https://doi.org/10.1111/j.1752-0606.2003.tb01215.x

Sue, D. W., & Sue, D. (2003). *Counseling the culturally different: Theory and practice* (4th ed.). New York, NY: John Wiley.

Supe, A. (2016). Evolution of medical education in India: The impact of colonialism. *Journal of Postgraduate Medicine, 62*, 255–259. https://doi.org/10.4103/0022-3859.191011

Tan, N. (2003). Family and family therapy in a fast changing metropolis. *Australian and New Zealand Journal of Family Therapy, 24*(4), 224–224. https://doi.org/10.1002/j.1467-8438.2003.tb00566.x

Viswanathan, G. (1988). Currying favor: The politics of British educational and cultural policy in India. *Social Text, 19*(20), 85–104.

Wu, D. Y. H. (1982). Psychotherapy and emotion in traditional Chinese medicine. In A. J. Marsella & G. M. White (Eds.), *Cultural conceptions of mental health and therapy* (pp. 285–301). Dordrecht, NL: D. Reidel.

# Couple and Family Therapy Training in the Context of Turkey

**Nilufer Kafescioglu and Yudum Akyıl**

In the last 10 years, due to several developments in Turkey such as the establishment of a new family and social policies ministry, new policies relevant to the couple and family therapists, increasing number of couple and family therapy (CFT) training programs, and the burgeoning of CFT professional organizations, CFT has attracted a great deal of attention from policymakers, educators, students, and the public alike. More specifically, a new policy regarding family counseling centers came into effect in 2012 with implications for CFT training and practice that the authors will further discuss in this chapter. This new policy included the professional standards and qualifications for family counselors, the requirements to establish family counseling centers, and the services that can be provided at these centers. Further, increasing numbers of CFT training programs, whether it be certificate programs or master's level programs in universities, have emerged over the last 10 years. Thus, we are at the beginning of a period in which the identity of the CFT profession in Turkey is taking shape, and there is an increasing need for a structure to define and regulate the training and practice standards in order to ensure the well-being of clients, therapists, students, and the public.

As the authors of this chapter, we (NK and YA) are two couple and family therapists who were born and raised in Turkey, and we both received our doctoral degrees in CFT from universities in the United States. Upon our return to Turkey, we each found ourselves taking part in establishing professional organizations, starting CFT certificate and master's level programs, teaching at existing certificate programs, attending policy-making meetings, and collaborating with couple and family therapists nationally and internationally to support the development of the field in our country. Thus, in this chapter we are interested in documenting the

---

N. Kafescioglu
Ozyegin University, İstanbul, Turkey

Y. Akyıl (✉)
Istanbul Bilgi University, İstanbul, Turkey

© Springer International Publishing AG, part of Springer Nature 2018
S. Singh Poulsen, R. Allan (eds.), *Cross-Cultural Responsiveness & Systemic Therapy*, Focused Issues in Family Therapy, https://doi.org/10.1007/978-3-319-71395-3_9

history of the field in Turkey to date, as we have experienced it and learned about it from other couple and family therapists in Turkey. There is an oral history about the emergence of the field in Turkey, but there is little formal documentation in scholarly work, of this history. Therefore, this chapter is an attempt to collect together what we have learned and experienced about the history of the field, its current developments, and the challenges and future of the field in our country.

After summarizing the brief history of the field in Turkey, we will discuss the formation of two major professional CFT organizations in the country and their influence on professional identity development, policy-making initiatives, and attempts to standardize CFT training programs. We will summarize the current, somewhat worrisome, state of the CFT training programs in the country as well as the establishment of some programs that are more in line with the international standards for CFT training. In addition, since we are both practitioners and educators, we experience, on a daily basis, the consequences of the policies that are being issued as well as the lack of legal regulations in Turkey. We will also summarize the historical account of the policies that are having an impact on the further development of the field, its practice, and training programs in Turkey. Finally, we will share our recommendations on the future directions of CFT in Turkey based on the issues we examine in this chapter.

## History of CFT in Turkey

The roots of the CFT profession in Turkey go back to the 1980s when the concepts of systemic thinking were being addressed in clinical psychology or counseling programs in large cities such as Istanbul, Ankara, and İzmir. Family systems were a subject of interest for academicians of psychology, as one of the major influences on the personality and psychopathology of the individuals. Kağıtçıbaşı (1982, 1996), Fişek (1991), and Sunar (2002) are pioneer Turkish academicians who have written on the topic of family dynamics. Their ideas regarding the inevitability of attending to the whole family system and its impact on child development were later implemented in various outreach programs such as AÇEV (Mother-Child Education Foundation, founded in 1993, targeting early childhood education and parent training for underprivileged families).

The family system as theoretically significant in the understanding of personality development and psychopathology, and later in parenting programs, was not initially integrated into psychotherapy trainings. Initially, schools of psychotherapy were mostly psychodynamically oriented, while later cognitive behavior therapy gained recognition in the mental health community in Turkey. Some counseling programs initially focused on teaching skills for working with groups including families. Systemic theory and CFT sparked an interest in some of the graduates of psychology, counseling, and psychiatry programs, who wanted to learn how to work with the couples and/or the family as a whole in their clinical practice. These graduates subsequently went to US-based CFT programs such as the Mental Research Institute (MRI) and the Ackerman Institute and after a few years of training came back to Turkey to start their own training programs utilizing the knowledge and experience obtained in their US-based training. One of the Turkish MRI graduates founded the first professional CFT association (Aile ve Evlilik Terapileri Derneği, AETD; Association of Family and Marriage Therapies) in 1997 and hosted the 2004 International Family Therapy Association (IFTA) and 2013 European Family Therapy Association (EFTA) conferences in Istanbul.

Of historical consequence, the 1999 earthquake was a significant turning point for family therapy in Turkey (Arduman, 2013) and was similar in impact to the transformations that WWII brought to the development of family therapy in the United States. (Nichols, 2013). The earthquake, a traumatic event where almost 50,000 people died, pulled different mental health professionals together to share and apply their knowledge and expertise. Psychologists, psychological counselors, and psychiatrists, with different theoretical orientations, united under nongovernmental organizations (NGOs) and traveled to the earthquake zones where the affected families were living in prefabricated houses in great panic and devastation. Clinicians, coming out of their sheltered private practices, faced the immediate needs of traumatized families. Therapy had to be flexible, inclusive, collaborative, and short term. Many Israeli family therapists, who were experienced in working with trauma, moved to Turkey at that time to provide clinical support to local clinicians. This experience underlined the importance of working systemically which set groundwork for the development of systemic models and systemic training in Turkey in the years following the devastating impact of the 1999 earthquake.

In 2009, the IFTA conference at Portoroz, Slovenia, initiated and facilitated the collaborations between IFTA and Turkish family therapists. After the IFTA conference in 2011 in the Netherlands, IFTA initiated an active collaboration with a group of Turkish couple and family therapists with the aim of setting standards for trainings and initiated approved supervisor trainings in Turkey. Coming back from the conference, the group of couple and family therapists from Turkey, who initiated the collaboration with IFTA and the authors of this chapter, founded the CFT Task Force (Çift ve Aile Terapisi Komitesi, CATKOM) in 2009 as a group that worked together to build the foundations of CFT as a distinct profession in Turkey with its own standards and guidelines. CATKOM has collaborated with the Social Services and Child Protection Institution (which has now been transferred to the Ministry of Family and Social Policies) in forming the standards regulating the family counseling centers; this collaboration created a necessity for the CFT Task Force to become a formal association in order to expand and have more recognition by governmental and professional agencies.

In June 2012, the Association of Couple and Family Therapies (Çift ve Aile Terapileri Derneği, ÇATED) was founded, and in 2017 it reached over 300 members in Turkey. Currently, the association is in the process of starting a clinical membership to recognize clinicians who graduated from programs with the necessary CFT theoretical knowledge and clinical and supervision experience. In an effort to define good quality CFT programs in Turkey, we have adapted IFTA and EFTA standards to the conditions of the country and created ÇATED standards. We also have formed a Clinical Membership Committee who will evaluate and approve/disapprove applications.

The association, at this time, has five other committees, namely, Public Relations, Training, Family and Alternative Family, Research and Professional Development, and, as of March 2017, Medical Family Therapy. ÇATED runs a yearly symposium, monthly family therapy seminars, supervision groups, community and research projects, and a quarterly systemic bulletin. A couple therapy casebook was edited from the chapters that were written by some of the association's experienced members (Akyıl & Güven, 2016). The most significant role of the association is to increase the quality, recognition, and reputation of the profession and to provide couple and family therapists a professional "home" where they can obtain trainings, conduct research, and be a part of a professional CFT community. In collaboration with its sibling association (AETD) and other mental health associations, ÇATED puts much of its effort and support into standardization of CFT education and training in Turkey. In 2014, with my (NK) and my co-author's (YA) initiative, CFT became a branch in the Turkish Psychological Association with aims to work collaboratively with other branches of the association such as trauma, women and gender studies, and clinical psychology.

## Training Programs

In order to better understand the current picture of the CFT profession in Turkey, a descriptive study was conducted by the members of the ÇATED Research Committee (Akyıl, Üstünel, Alkan, & Aydın, 2015) in which demographic characteristics, educational background, and clinical practices of professionals, who work with couples and families in Turkey, were investigated. Results revealed that, like their American counterparts, most of the clinicians working with couples and families (87%) were women (Beaton, Dienhart, Schmidt, & Turner, 2009). However, compared to the United States, the Turkish clinicians were younger (25–30 years old vs. 47–52 years old) and less experienced (5 years vs. 13–15 years).

In the same study (Akyıl et al., 2015), it was reported that 53% of the clinicians, working in Turkey with couples and families, had an undergraduate education in psychology, 17% in counseling, 7% in social work, and 9% had a medical degree. Only 57% of the sample had a graduate degree (US: 64–75%, Morris, 2007; Northey, 2002), out of which only 15% had a graduate degree in CFT. These results showed that compared to 2012 demographics, clinicians using family therapy currently are coming from more diverse clinical training backgrounds. In fact, in 2012, 13% of the 321 professionals practicing couple and family therapy in Turkey were psychiatrists, and 77% were psychologists (Eraslan, Camoglu, Harunzade, Ergun, & Dokur, 2012). This shift may be due to the recognition of the CFT as a distinct discipline by a larger group of clinicians and the acceptance of CFT as a uniting and standardized framework for working clinically with systems.

In this study (Akyıl et al., 2015) when participants were asked whether they had any training in CFT, 80% responded yes with half of them reporting having received their training from a "private clinic." This means that 20% of the participants worked with couples and families without any specialized training in CFT, and this we found to be worrisome. Those who had some CFT training differed widely in their training experience, clinical hours and the content of coursework, and supervision. Thirty-four percent of the participants worked without any supervision especially if they were in cities other than Istanbul (Akyıl et al., 2015). This problem underlines the need for qualified, accessible, and economically viable supervision and training options and solutions. Based on this information, we concluded that options such as online supervision, group supervision, and well-structured peer supervision could be offered as alternatives toward efforts in improving CFT training in Turkey.

Another significant finding in this study was that the participants felt competent in working with child-parent and couple relational issues and anxiety and depression; however, they did not report feeling competent in working on issues such as domestic violence, sexual problems, and addictions (Akyıl et al., 2015). This finding reveals that there is a need for standardized, systemically oriented programs, that also include some of these clinical issues of concern in their curriculum. Unfortunately, many of the certificate programs in CFT mainly focus on specific techniques (e.g., Satir-focused experiential therapy) but lack components that give an overall systemic perspective to address a variety of individual, couple, and family issues.

The study (Akyıl et al., 2015) also underlined that compared to the clinical focus and climate in 2001 (Korkut, 2001), a systemic approach has become more prominent for clinicians working with couples and families, and solution-focused and emotionally focused therapies have gained interest and momentum in Turkey. This finding points to the belief that family therapy and systemic models are becoming much better recognized and valued in Turkey over the last 15 years. Additionally, there is a postmodern trend in clinical, mental health work in Turkey that is congruent with the trends in other parts of the world (Beaton et al., 2009) which makes it possible for absolute truths to be challenged and multiple realities and ideas to be explored and validated.

Most clinicians in Turkey working with couples and families identify themselves as psychologists or psychological counselors rather than as couple and family therapists (Akyıl et al., 2015). This could be related to the insufficient number of structured and standardized CFT training opportunities in Turkey and also to the lack of recognition of the CFT profession within the mental health field and to the public. Clinicians working with couples and families stated that what they need from professional organizations are well-structured standards and guidelines for practicing family therapy and efforts in making the profession acknowledged and recognized within the mental health community as well as in the public arena. For this purpose, CFT professional organizations in Turkey need to focus on collaborating and strengthening their efforts to make an impact on regulations and act as a consulting institution for lawmakers. Additionally, we need to inform the public and other professionals about CFT and its effectiveness by using media, social media, trainings and symposiums. This active involvement by the professional organizations has the potential to bring a sense of containment and belonging on behalf of couple and family clinicians who may feel ostracized within the mental health community in Turkey.

As mentioned earlier in this chapter, systemic ideas were first addressed in psychology and counseling programs by professors who were personally and professionally interested in the CFT field and who had systemic training from abroad. Later, a few of these clinicians started training programs in their private practice clinics. In the early 2000s, most of the clinicians who worked with families and couples gained their family therapy and systemic knowledge from individual courses in universities or seminars in private clinics (Korkut, 2001).

One of the turning points that influenced the development of family therapy training in Turkey was initiated by the Social Services and Child Protection Institution, a government institution. In 2009, with the aim of protecting the family institution and to intervene in the rising divorce rates, the ministry initiated "private family counseling centers" and published regulations for their establishment and functioning. We will review these regulations in more detail later in this chapter. In 2012, the regulations were revised and published under the new name of the ministry, the Ministry of Family and Social Policies. The opening of public and private family counseling centers and the increasing demand from the public led the emergence of many certificate programs (Konuk, Akyıl, Arduman, Erenel, & Sarımurat Baydemir, 2011). As early as 2012, the total number of CFT training hours was increased from 100 to 450; however, there continued to be some insufficiencies in terms of the theoretical content, qualifications of the trainers, and clinical and supervision hours' requirements. This development of certification programs was well-intended as a response to the increased need for trained CFT professionals, but too fast. Family counseling certificate programs opened without the necessary educational foundation, and over 25,000 people were able to claim to have "graduated" as family counselors. Although some certificate programs have been accredited by the Ministry of Education since 2014, there is a lack of consensus among the educators and the lawmakers on the criteria for quality CFT training which we will discuss further in this chapter.

On the positive side, among these certificate programs, there are some university-based or private programs that follow EFTA or IFTA standards and provide a well-rounded family therapy and systemic education with theoretical, ethical, and research training and clinical and supervisory hours. However, many programs tried to fit their curriculum to the existing expertise of their available trainers, rather than a well-rounded understanding of systemic and family therapy theories and clinical work. This created programs that teach family law and trauma work with limited information regarding systemic principles and CFT conceptualization and interventions. There are also programs that teach only one approach (e.g., strategic therapy, solution-focused therapy) without providing a strong systemic foundation.

In 2010, the first CFT master's program was established at Doğuş University in Istanbul by me (NK) and my co-author (YA) in collaboration with a US licensed couple and family therapist, Sibel Erenel, and a faculty member with a PhD in Family Studies, Aslı Çarkoğlu. This program had to close after 3 years due to some problems with the university administration; the faculty members subsequently moved to other universities and established CFT programs at their new institutions. In 2013, one of the university-based certificate programs, the Istanbul Bilgi University certificate program, became a part of the Clinical Psychology Master's program as a CFT track after adult and child/adolescent tracks were established. This CFT track is co-founded and is being coordinated by one of the authors (YA) of this chapter. As a growing community, most of the master's students are also involved in different committees under ÇATED, work in community projects, and work toward increasing awareness and recognition of family and systemic therapy in Turkey. The graduates work in public or private mental health centers and hospitals or pursue a PhD (usually in the United States).

In 2016, as the former founder of the Doğuş University CFT program, I (NK) and my CFT colleagues at Ozyegin University in Istanbul started a master's program in CFT. I (NK) am currently the director of the Ozyegin University Couple and Family Therapy Program. Both Bilgi and Ozyegin University programs have a well-equipped clinic with one-way mirrors and state-of-the-art recording equipment and technology. These clinics serve the university and surrounding communities, charging only minimal fees for therapy services. As a pioneering academic foundation of CFT in Turkey, these programs support and encourage family and systemic therapy research to generate knowledge within the country, and train family therapy researchers as well as competent therapists for the future.

At the onset of the development of these international CFT training and education endeavors such as those in Turkey, international CFT associations, such as IFTA, did not want to be accrediting bodies. However, due to the increased interest in family therapy internationally, the need for standards and training models from various countries, and a specific request from Turkey, IFTA decided to set up a semiautonomous entity to be an independent accrediting body and founded the International Accreditation Commission for Systemic Therapy Education (IACSTE). The goal of the commission is to accredit programs that have no independent accreditation sources as well as programs that had achieved accreditation from another source (e.g., the Commission on Accreditation for Marriage and Family Therapy Education [COAMFTE]) (Becvar, personal communication). In 2015, Istanbul Bilgi University's CFT program was the first to receive the IACSTE accreditation in Turkey and the second around the world. The CFT master's program at Ozyegin University is currently in the process of applying for IACSTE accreditation, having recently admitted its second cohort of CFT master's students.

## Regulations

The previous section of this chapter provides an overview of the state of CFT clinical work and CFT training and education, to date, in Turkey. In the next section, we will first discuss the absence of a mental health law in Turkey and its impact on couple and family therapists and CFT training. Then, we will describe the regulations on "family counseling" in Turkey issued by two government institutions in their chronological order: the Social Services and Child Protection Institution and the Ministry of Family and Social Policies of Turkey. We will examine these policies using a systemic perspective and discuss the implications for couple and family therapists and CFT training in Turkey.

## *Lack of Mental Health Laws*

One of the greatest challenges for mental health professionals in Turkey is the lack of mental health legislation. The field of mental health has been regulated by a law that was first issued in 1928, law number 1219, namely, the Law on the Practice of Medicine and Its Branches/Related Fields (Tababet ve Şuabatı San'atlarının Tarzı İcrasına Dair Kanun, 1928). This law defines the standards related to the competencies and practice of medicine and related fields in Turkey. According to this law, any kind of treatment, including mental health treatment, can only be practiced by professionals with a medical degree. Since the Ministry of Health in Turkey conceptualizes "therapy" as medical treatment, mental health professionals who do not hold a medical degree, even if they have the adequate training and competencies in psychotherapy, can only practice under the supervision and oversight of a specialist in medicine (Türk Psikologlar Derneği, 2008). This means that couple and family therapists, or any other mental health professionals in Turkey, cannot call themselves therapists or practice or conduct psychotherapy independent of a specialist in medicine, such as a psychiatrist.

Recently in 2011, an additional law was issued (number 6225) that included the definition of a "clinical psychologist" for the first time in Turkish mental health history (Bazı Kanun ve Kanun Hükmünde Kararnamelerde Değişiklik Yapılmasına Dair Kanun, 2011). In Article 13 of this law, clinical psychologists are defined as healthcare professionals with a psychology or counseling and guidance degree who should also hold a master's degree in clinical psychology. Since requiring those coming from psychology or counseling majors to complete a master's degree yields to at least 6 years of graduate education, individuals who majored in other fields were required to complete a doctoral degree in addition to a master's degree in clinical psychology to yield 6 years of education as well. Neither couple and family therapists nor any other mental health professionals were included in this law under the definition of healthcare professionals. At the same time, Article 13 of this law has also limit the practice of clinical psychologists to psychological assessment and the provision of psychotherapy with the exclusion of disorders listed in the international diagnostic and classification systems. In the case of such disorders, clinical psychologists are allowed to practice psychotherapy only after a medical specialist (e.g., a psychiatrist) issues the diagnosis and provides a referral for therapy treatment.

The most recent development on the proposal of a mental health law in Turkey is the establishment of the Mental Health Platform-Turkey (MHPT) in 2006. Fifteen mental health organizations in the country formed the MHPT as a task force to improve the mental health services in Turkey (Turkish Neuropsychiatric Society, 2017). One of the major actions the task force agreed to take on was the issuance of the mental health law in Turkey (Türkiye Psikiyatri Derneği, 2006). Currently, the MHPT continues to work on the draft proposal of the law (Türkiye Psikiyatri Derneği, 2017), which proposes to concentrate on issues such as the definition of psychotherapy and psychotherapist, the rights of individuals with mental health disorders, and preventive measures and deals with issues such as the protection of client confidentiality (Türk Psikolojik Danışma ve Rehberlik Derneği, 2017).

## *Emergence of "Family Counseling" and Its Regulations*

Thus far the regulation of the CFT field and its practice has not been considered for the mental health law oversight in Turkey. Our view is that one reason for this lack of attention might be that CFT is viewed as a subspecialty of clinical psychology even though, with the exception of one graduate program in clinical psychology with a CFT track, none of the current master's clinical psychology programs offer comprehensive and systematic CFT training. At most, what these graduate programs in clinical psychology might offer is an elective course in family therapy with an emphasis on foundational couple and family theories and systemic perspective but no applied supervision in the practice of CFT. Another reason might be that the couple and family therapy professional organizations, with the exception of the relatively new ÇATED, have not, to date, concentrated on legislation issues relevant to CFT practice and training.

Furthermore, the two government organizations that issued regulations about the provision of support to families, first the Social Services and Child Protection Institution and then the Ministry of Family and Social Policies, have refrained from the use of the term "family therapy" but rather use the term "family counseling." The restrictions to the use of the term "therapy" brought by the aforementioned health law in Turkey due to its reference to treatment, which can only be provided by medical specialists, are considered as one of the reasons for these government institutions' preference for the term "counseling" rather than "therapy" (Roberts et al., 2014). The wording of what CFTs do described as "counseling" versus "therapy" has been viewed as problematic for several reasons. First of all, majority of the couple and family therapists who received a certificate or master's degree (mostly abroad) in CFT have developed their professional identities as couple and family therapists, not counselors. There is the need to be recognized as a separate profession and distinct discipline by itself, separate from counseling and other mental health professionals and fields including clinical psychology in Turkey. Secondly, the CFT practice and education, while having some commonalities with the professions of counseling and clinical psychology, also do require knowledge of theories and skills unique to the CFT field because of its systemic view and the number of individuals that can be included in the therapy process.

In 2007, the regulation on family counseling centers was first issued by the Social Services and Child Protection Institution of Turkey (Sosyal Hizmetler ve Esirgeme Kurumu Genel Müdürlüğü Aile Danışma Merkezleri Yönetmeliği, 2007). The regulation was revised in 2009 (Gerçek Kişiler ve Özel Hukuk Tüzel Kişileri ile Kamu Kurum ve Kuruluşlarınca Açılacak Aile Danışma Merkezleri Hakkında Yönetmelik, 2009). This regulation aimed to describe how family counseling centers could be established, the requirements for the physical conditions of such centers, the services that could be provided in these centers, and the job descriptions, competency requirements, and responsibilities of professionals practicing at the centers. In this regulation, the term "family counselor" was defined by a regulation in Article 4. Family counselors were described as the social workers, psychologists, child development professionals, physicians, psychological counselors, and nurses with a training of at least 100 h in family counseling theories. The training in family counseling could be provided by either universities or professional organizations. Family counseling was defined in this same Article, as the treatment process by which the family counselors aim to resolve the disordered relationships among family members through the acquisition of new communication and interaction patterns. Interestingly, the makers of this regulation did not refrain from using the term treatment even though they did prefer the term counseling over therapy. The definition of family counseling in this regulation can be considered to resemble a somewhat systemic approach due to its focus on change through new communication and interaction patterns. However, we also cannot help but notice the use of the term "disordered" relationships that makes us think about a psychopathological perspective on the family issues that clients bring to therapy which is contrary to the nonpathological and systemic view of problem development and maintenance in CFT. In sum, the most problematic issue with this older regulation was that 100 h of training in theories were seen sufficient for someone with an undergraduate degree to counsel couples and families. In addition, the contradictions mentioned in the language of the regulation were problematic. Refraining from using the word "therapy" but using the word "treatment" and also using a pathological language and systemic understanding of problems simultaneously might be considered as a reflection of the identity crises and confusion of the field that has been going on since its very beginning. The identity of the CFT field in Turkey is being shaped ever since then, by the agenda of the policy makers, non-CFT-trained professionals who identify themselves as couple and family therapists, couple and family therapists with training in CFT, and all the other professionals who attend any policy-making meetings.

As the next development in 2011, the Ministry of Family and Social Policies was established as a new ministry in Turkey concentrating on family affairs and the provision of social services to all citizens. In 2012, the ministry issued regulations for the establishment of family counseling centers (Gerçek Kişiler ve Özel Hukuk Tüzel Kişileri ile Kamu Kurum ve Kuruluşlarınca Açılacak Aile Danışma Merkezleri Yönetmeliği, 2012). The aim of this regulation was described as the regulation of the standards for the professionals who work and provide services at family counseling centers, the ethics code, fee policies, establishment and termination of the counseling centers, activities held at these centers, and the information on the inspection of the centers. Family counseling was defined as "the services that included special techniques and strategies, provided to individuals, couples, and families to change and improve the resolution of their problems based on the assessment of their family system and their interactions with the social environment." Clearly, the framers of this regulation intentionally refrained from using the term therapy or treatment. The practice that family counseling involves is described as "special techniques and strategies." We believe the definition of "family counseling" to include individuals as well as couples and families to be an improvement compared to the previous regulation, as it signifies that family counseling is not just defined by the number of individuals that are involved in the therapy process. We also consider the inclusion of the term "family system" and the focus on the sociocultural context in this definition as the root of problems faced by individuals, couples, and families, as a positive step toward a more systemic thinking in the framing and articulation of this regulation.

The definition of family counselor has been somewhat modified or revised through the 2011 regulation by the Ministry of Family and Social Policies as well. In Article 14, the training and qualifications of family counselors have been redefined. Graduates of 4-year undergraduate degree programs in social work, sociology, psychology, psychological counseling and guidance, medicine, nursing, and child development were allowed to receive the title of family counselor. The family counseling training they had to obtain included a minimum of 300 h of theoretical knowledge and 150 h of supervised applied hours. The supervision hours had to be at least 30 h. To become a family counselor, one had to either complete a certificate program or a graduate degree in family counseling. The graduate programs are regulated by the Higher Education Council in Turkey. The certificate programs had to be approved by the Ministry of Education or continuing education departments of universities in Turkey. This regulation has also delineated that the trainers, who were not employed in universities, must hold certification in family counseling at the national or international standards with a minumum of 5 years of experience in family counseling or must have taught in graduate programs in family counseling without a specification to, for example, minimum number of years of teaching that might be required of them.

The abovementioned Article 14 of the regulation includes some improvements as well as some problems. One improvement is the increase of training hours from 100, in the previous regulation, to a total of 450 in this revised regulation which ensures a greater number of training hours. However, what is problematic is that the quantity of training hours does not ensure the quality of training because no specific control mechanisms, such as accreditation standards and procedures, are in place. Another improvement of this regulation is the mention of supervision. Even though, supervision is not described as "clinical supervision," the regulation still highlights the need for at least 30 h of supervision for every 150 h of applied clinical work, which is a 1:5 ratio. However, the definition of supervision or criteria for becoming a supervisor are not included in the regulation. In addition, what is meant by applied work is very vague and could be misinterpreted to include nonclinical hours rather than as direct client hours as is typical in quality CFT training programs. In this regulation, some standards have been imposed upon the trainers of CFT certificate programs, which is an improvement. However, the specific qualifications of trainers in both the graduate programs and certificate programs, offered by the continuing education departments at universities, are left out and subject to misinterpretation. This development has led to an explosion of family counseling certificate programs offered at universities in Turkey without any established criteria for trainers. Since the regulation did not include any standards and guidelines for the content of family counseling training nor appointed an entity to determine such content, there has been a wide range in variability in the quality of training programs at every level, certificate or graduate. For example, while some programs focused on child development more in depth, others included topics such as the family court systems that were not included in other programs, while others primarily focused on the mainstream CFT models and their applications in therapy.

## Future Directions

The developments in the CFT field in Turkey are promising; however, as Roberts and colleagues (2014, p. 561) stated "family therapy in Turkey is in its infancy." The biggest challenge for the profession is the lack of standards for family therapy trainings (Akyıl et al., 2015; Korkut, 2001, 2007). This is not a new problem when we look at the history of the development of the profession in the United States and is parallel to the search for and development of core competencies in CFT (Kaslow, Celano, & Stanton, 2005; Miller, Todahl, & Platt, 2010; Nelson et al., 2007). The adoption of core competencies into the system in Turkey will be helpful for the future of CFT in the Turkish mental health professional context.

Moreover, professional organizations and the government need to come to a consensus in terms of mental health laws in general and family therapy regulations in particular so that the standards can be formed and enforced in family therapy training settings. Instead of increasing the number of programs to meet the increasing demand for CFT training, the quality of the programs needs to be the focus. Even though there are newly emerging master's programs in CFT that are aligned with international standards, there are no PhD programs in CFT in Turkey at this time. Currently, there are only seven trainers in Turkey with doctoral degrees in CFT (six PhDs and one PsyD). We, as the authors of this chapter, are two of them. We collaborate with each other and other CFTs in Turkey a great deal. However, there is a need for more professionals with doctoral degrees who can teach at master's or doctoral level CFT programs in Turkey. Doctoral programs would contribute to the development of the field as a separate discipline (separate from clinical psychology or counseling) as well as to research in the field and training of future trainers and supervisors. In addition, having doctoral programs in CFT offered at universities in Turkey would eliminate the need to live abroad to get doctoral degrees in CFT and would allow us to have academics in our discipline who obtained their education and clinical training in our own culture.

Improving the quality of the training programs will also require an accrediting and supervising body such as COAMFTE. Currently, the number of CFT supervisors is very low and concentrated in bigger cities in Turkey and mainly in Istanbul. We need to develop ways to require and provide training for supervisors and create ways to spread supervision to the rest of the country.

Currently, there is no licensing process in place for any of the mental health fields in Turkey including CFT. When assessment of trainees' competencies is considered, the master's programs apply their regular testing and assessment methods in their courses; however, certificate programs do not offer any sort of evaluation to the trainees as far as we know. Eventually, there needs to be a licensing process in place both for the CFT field and other mental health fields in the country. There are challenges and potential obstacles to the future of CFT training, education, and practice in Turkey; however, as we have outlined in this chapter, there are also great opportunity and interest in the field and its application in the mental health service context in Turkey.

## References

Akyıl, Y., & Güven, N. (2016). *Yüzyüze: Türkiye'den çift ve aile terapisi öyküleri*. İstanbul, Trukey: Pegasus Yayınları.

Akyıl, Y., Üstünel, A. Ö., Alkan, S., & Aydın, H. (2015). Türkiye'de çift ve ailelerle çalışan uzmanlar: Demografik özellikler, eğitim ve klinik uygulamalar. *Psikoloji Çalışmaları Dergisi, 35*, 57–84.

Arduman, E. (2013). A perspective on evolving family therapy in Turkey. *Journal of Contemporary Family Therapy, 35*, 364–375. https://doi.org/10.1007/s10591-013-9268-0

Bazı Kanun ve Kanun Hükmünde Kararnamelerde Değişiklik Yapılmasına Dair Kanun. (2011). Resmi Gazete (Sayı: 27916). Retrieved from http://www.resmigazete.gov.tr/eskiler/2011/04/20110426-1.htm

Beaton, J., Dienhart, A., Schmidt, J., & Turner, J. (2009). Clinical practice patterns of Canadian couple/marital/family therapists. *Journal of Marital and Family Therapy, 35*, 193–203. https://doi.org/10.1111/j.1752-0606.2009.00116.x

Eraslan, D., Camoglu, D., Harunzade, Y., Ergun, B., & Dokur, M. (2012). Interpersonal communication in and through family: Structure and therapy in Turkey. *International Review of Psychiatry, 24*, 128–133. https://doi.org/10.3109/09540261.2012.657162

Fişek, G. O. (1991). A cross-cultural examination of proximity and hierarch as dimensions of family structure. *Family Process, 30*, 121–133. https://doi.org/10.1111/j.1545-5300.1991.00121.x

Gerçek Kişiler ve Özel Hukuk Tüzel Kişileri ile Kamu Kurum ve Kuruluşlarınca Açılacak Aile Danışma Merkezleri Hakkında Yönetmelik. (2009). Resmi Gazete (Sayı: 27152). Retrieved from http://www.resmigazete.gov.tr/eskiler/2009/02/20090225-4.htm

Gerçek Kişiler ve Özel Hukuk Tüzel Kişileri ile Kamu Kurum ve Kuruluşlarınca Açılacak Aile Danışma Merkezleri Yönetmeliği. (2012). Resmi Gazete (Sayı: 28401). Retrieved from http://www.mevzuat.gov.tr/Metin.Aspx?MevzuatKod=7.5.16567& MevzuatIliski=0&sourceXmlSearch=

Kağıtçıbaşı, Ç. (1982). *The changing value of children in Turkey*. Honolulu, HI: East-West Center.

Kağıtçıbaşı, Ç. (1996). *Family and human development across cultures*. Mathway, NJ: Lawrence Erlbaum Publisher.

Kaslow, N. J., Celano, M. P., & Stanton, M. (2005). Training in family psychology: A competencies-based approach. *Family Process, 44*, 337–353. https://doi.org/10.1111/j.1545-5300.2005.00063.x

Konuk, E., Akyıl, Y., Arduman, E., Erenel, S., & Sarımurat Baydemir, N. (2011). *CFT in Turkey: Legal regulations and standards for education*. İstanbul, TR: VI. National Family and Marriage Therapy Congress.

Korkut, Y. (2001). Aile danışmanlığı ve aile terapisi hizmetleri. *Psikoloji Çalışmaları Dergisi, 22*, 111–133. https://doi.org/9411/117823

Korkut, Y. (2007). Türkiye'de aile terapisi ve terapistlerinin durumu: eğitim standartları, terapi yönelimleri, çalışma biçimleri ve eğitim ihtiyaçları üzerine bir çalışma. *Psikoloji Çalışmaları Dergisi, 27*, 13–30.

Miller, J. K., Todahl, J. L., & Platt, J. J. (2010). The core competency movement in marriage and family therapy: Key considerations from other disciplines. *Journal of Marital and Family Therapy, 36*, 59–70. https://doi.org/10.1111/j.1752-0606.2009.00183.x

Morris, J. (2007). Characteristics and clinical practices of rural marriage and family therapists. *Journal of Marital and Family Therapy, 33*, 439–442. https://doi.org/ 10.1111/j.1752-0606.2007.00043.x

Nelson, T. S., Chenail, R. J., Alexander, J. F., Crane, D. R., Johnson, S. M., & Schwallie, L. (2007). The development of core competencies for the practice of marriage and family therapy. *Journal of Marital and Family Therapy, 33*, 417–438. https://doi.org/. https://doi.org/10.1111/j.1752-0606.2007.00042.x

Nichols, W. (2013). *Family therapy: Concepts and methods*. Boston, MA: Pearson.

Northey, W. F. (2002). Characteristics and clinical practices of marriage and family therapists: A national survey. *Journal of Marital and Family Therapy, 28*, 487–494. https://doi.org/10.1111/j.1752-0606.2009.00147.x

Roberts, J., Abu-Baker, K., Fernandez, C. D., Garcia, N. C., Fredman, G., Kamya, H., … Vega, R. Z. (2014). Up close: Family therapy challenges and innovations around the world. *Family Process, 53*, 544–576. https://doi.org/10.1111/famp.12093

Sosyal Hizmetler ve Çocuk Esirgeme Kurumu Genel Müdürlüğü Aile Danışma Merkezleri Yönetmeliği. (2007). Resmi Gazete (Sayı: 26666). Retrieved from http://www.resmigazete.gov.tr/eskiler/2007/10/20071007-1.htm

Sunar, D. (2002). Change and continuity in the Turkish middle class family. In F. Özdalga & R. Liljestrom (Eds.), *Autonomy and dependence in family: Turkey and Sweden in critical perspective* (pp. 217–238). Istanbul, Trukey: Swedish Research Institute.

Tababet ve Şuabatı San'atlarının Tarzı İcrasına Dair Kanun. (1928). Retrieved from http://www.mevzuat.gov.tr/MevzuatMetin/1.3.1219.pdf

Türk Psikologlar Derneği. (2008). Meslek yasası çalışmaları. Retrieved from https://www.psikolog.org.tr/ozluk-haklari/Meslek-Yasasi-Calismalari-1975-2008.pdf

Türk Psikolojik Danışma ve Rehberlik Derneği. (2017). Ruh sağlığı yasa tasarısı toplantısı 24 Mart 2017. Retrieved from http://www.turkpdristanbul.com/ruh-sagligi-yasa-tasarisi-toplantisi-24-mart-2017/

Turkish Neuropsychiatric Society. (2017). Retrieved from http://wpanet.org/detail.php?section_id=7&content_id=1964

Türkiye Psikiyatri Derneği. (2006). Ruh sağlığı platform: Basın duyurusu "ruh sağlığı yasası hemen şimdi". Retrieved from http://www.psikiyatri.org.tr/121/ruh-sagligi-platformu-basin-duyurusu-ruh-sagligi-yasasi-hemen-simdi

Türkiye Psikiyatri Derneği. (2017). Ruh sağlığı yasası çalışmaları sürüyor. Retrieved from http://www.psikiyatri.org.tr/1729/ruh-sagligi-yasasi-calismalari-suruyor

# The Future of MFT: Clinical Implications of Cross-Cultural Responsiveness and Social Justice Lens to the Field

Shruti Singh Poulsen and Robert Allan

In our final chapter of this volume, we summarize the information from our contributors' chapters and provide an overview of the future of the field of marriage and family therapy (MFT) and the continued need for attention to cross-cultural responsiveness and social justice. We bring together the overall themes of the book and how each of the authors has contributed to these themes as well as to the larger implications and conclusions we can draw regarding the future of systemic therapies and multiculturalism.

As we stated at the beginning of this volume, cross-cultural competence and sensitivity have been acknowledged as critical in the mental health professions for many decades as there has been continuing recognition of the rapidly changing demographics in the USA. In this volume, we the co-editors and the authors have attempted to address and challenge the notion that cultural competence and sensitivity are adequate in addressing the complex and unique needs of increasingly diverse client populations. We have tried to address these complex issues and concerns by bringing forth ideas and recommendations that are not "passive" but that require the active and persistent critique and analysis of ourselves as people, scholars, and clinicians, of the systemic models and theories that most of us "grew up with" professionally, and of the complex contexts and needs of our increasingly diverse client populations. Additionally, this volume goes beyond a focus on cross-cultural responsiveness and systems that work only in the USA; it includes attention to a diversity of systems: the microsystem of the individual and individual identity issues, to the much larger global and international macrosystemic context and the future of systemic therapies. In short, we have attempted to exemplify in our contributions exactly the kind of cultural responsiveness, attention to diversity, and social

---

S. Singh Poulsen (✉) · R. Allan
University of Colorado Denver, Denver, CO, USA
e-mail: Shruti.Poulsen@ucdenver.edu

justice concerns that we believe is also needed in the field of couple and family therapy and to the work of systemic therapists everywhere.

As indicated earlier in this volume in our introduction, the contributors to this book themselves represent a wide range of diversity: in racial and ethnic identity, gender identity and sexual orientation, professional work settings and areas of expertise, years of experience as scholars and clinicians, and professional and clinical experiences past and present, in the USA as well as beyond in the global and international settings. This volume, we believe, gives voice to the diverse systemic clinicians and scholars in the field of systemic work and, through that expression, also gives voice in culturally responsive ways, to the diverse and cross-cultural client populations we all are committed to and whom we serve.

As we finalized the contributions and organized the volume, we became aware of several themes that had evolved almost organically over the course of this project; most important of these themes that emerged was a critical examination of therapist identity, privilege, power, social justice, and, in particular, white identity and privilege. Other important themes that emerged as we organized the volume included the cross-cultural responsiveness and implications of utilizing and training therapists in empirically based systemic models, the cross-cultural responsiveness and adaptation of more traditional and foundational systemic models, the cross-cultural responsiveness in systemic supervision and training, and the experiences, challenges, and implications for training therapists in systemic therapies and models in global and international contexts. As we conclude this project, we reflect on these overarching themes that emerged through the authors' contributions and provide our (the co-editors as well as the authors) thoughts on the implications for the future of systemic therapies and the culturally responsive work of systemic therapist.

## Therapist Identity, Privilege, Power, and Social Justice

A challenge right at the beginning of this volume was presented by co-authors Iman and Manijeh. In their chapter, the authors enjoin the reader to consider that the only way to move forward in our field to fully embrace social justice and advocacy work is for systemic therapists to start with their own understanding of their own societal positions and unearned privileges. The authors caution that if systemic therapists, in their efforts to be socially just and to advocate for their diverse clients, only focus on exploring clients' marginalized experiences, therapists verge on perpetuating what the authors refer to as "systemic coercion and subjugation of clients." According to the authors, "preparing the next generation of conscious therapist" who must be involved in social justice and advocacy work must include therapists' own work on becoming more aware of their sociopolitical positions within their larger contexts and macrosystems and attend to issues of power and privilege within these structures. Therefore, as the authors so convincingly express, before we can understand another's pain, we must face our own privilege and power and the impact, both good and bad, that this can have on the clients we are attempting to serve and advocate for. Thus, neutrality on our part as systemic therapists and in our understanding and application of our models, theories, and interventions is not an option if we are to be socially just and socially conscious in our work.

Carrying forward Iman and Manijeh's focus on social location and unearned privilege, Cheryl closes her chapter on white identity and white privilege with a poignant statement, ostensibly from our clients' desperate need to be heard, to be understood: *Being that you've finally heard me, may I reschedule for another session? I think I can trust you now.* As Cheryl highlights in her chapter, counselors and therapists (and developers of counseling and therapy theories and models) have historically been, and are currently still, predominantly white. However, the field of counseling and therapy has continued to operate more or less on the assumption that this is not of great concern to the delivery of mental health services to an increasingly diverse and often marginalized client population. Ignoring whiteness and the emotionalities of whiteness in our field is a "dangerous game" as Cheryl exhorts and one that buries "more deeply a chance for freedom in developing humanizing relationships." Therapists and the field of counseling and therapy that ignore these realities risk undermining the very conditions needed to develop trust, understanding, and emotional investment in our diverse clients. Becoming a culturally responsive and culturally competent therapist involves first examining and courageously facing the emotionally difficult: the whiteness of the field and the white privilege that comes with it. As Cheryl points out, deep introspection, examination, and courage are required by counselors and therapists, to unmask our own emotional racial biases. Safety, trust, connection, and ultimately serving our clients and especially our clients of color, in socially just ways, will only come when therapists invest themselves fully in the painful process of investigating their own racial trauma and their unearned privilege and the impact to others around them.

## Cross-Cultural Responsiveness: Implications for Utilizing and Training in EBPs

A second theme of our volume focuses on the implications for utilizing and training in evidence-based practices (EBPs). Robert's chapter provides a comprehensive exploration of the field of couple and family research and its conceptualization of EBPs in how they take into consideration the issue of context and effectiveness. Robert's chapter highlights the need for research on EBPs that focuses on first-person accounts of culturally adapted EBPs and that investigates which aspects are most meaningful and useful for clients who receive those treatments. Thus, while Robert makes a compelling case for the use of EBPs in our systemic work, he also highlights that those (our clients) on the receiving end of that work need to have a voice regarding the impact on them, their contexts, and their lives. The chapter points out that there is growing research evidence that culture and context influence almost every area of our clinical work. Thus, a critical element of our systemic work must be continuing to attend to cultural factors in our work, in our clients' lives, and in the clinical practices we choose to employ. Employing EBPs effectively and in culturally responsive ways requires attention to contextual aspects of our clients' experiences.

Practitioners, researchers, and trainers/educators will need to give continual attention to their evidence-based work, its impact on culturally diverse clients, and how it needs to be culturally adapted.

Given Robert's attention to the cultural adaptation of EBPs so that they can be applied in culturally responsive ways, Senem's chapter, focusing on her experiences bringing an EBP, emotionally focused couple therapy (EFT) training, and practice to her home country, Turkey, is a useful follow-up to Robert's chapter. Senem's chapter outlines her experiences collaborating with US-based and Turkey-based EFT trainers and clinicians to bring EFT training and practice to systemic therapists in Turkey. In her chapter, she describes the trainings she and colleagues have provided to date, their experiences related to the pragmatics of such a venture, ways in which they had to adapt the model, and the training aspects of teaching the model. Poignant descriptions of events such as the recent terrorist attacks in Istanbul and Turkey and how these events have had very real-life impact on where trainings are held, how they are provided, and the safety of trainees and trainers are reminders that when we think of "adaptations," we must at times "think outside of the box" depending on the particular cultural, political, geographical context in our field. Certainly, issues such as language, translation, cultural considerations in obtaining permission and participation in live sessions in training sessions, and other cultural considerations and experiences in a context outside of the USA are also important. Senem's description of providing EFT trainings in the Turkish context highlights in a very relevant way the important considerations Robert's chapter provided – that continual attention must be given to clinicians and trainers' evidence-based work and how it needs to be culturally adapted to needs of clients and therapists' contexts. Thus, Senem's experiences in providing EFT training and practice in Turkey move her and others like her to develop their clinical work further, increasing the number of EFT-certified supervisors and therapists and conducting extensive clinical research in working with Turkish couples using EBPs such as EFT and developing culturally responsive guidelines for working through challenges of strict gender norms, refraining from expressing negative feelings and talking about conflict. Implications for those of us not directly working and training in these cultural contexts include supporting in whatever way we can our colleagues who are committed to the dissemination of not only systemic therapies but in particular EBPs such as EFT in culturally, socially, and politically diverse global contexts such as Turkey. We believe this type of support and collaboration can only lead to further improvement and application of systemic therapies in culturally responsive ways here in the USA as well as globally.

## Cross-Cultural Responsiveness and the Use of Foundational Systemic Models

While EBPs and the cultural adaption of EBPs such as EFT here in the USA as well as abroad are cutting-edge endeavors, my (Shruti) interest in and love of foundational models and techniques and cross-cultural responsiveness and competence are often the foci of my work. However, given that I am also a systemic therapist that "grew up" professionally with postmodern sensibilities, much of my philosophical and intellectual lens has been on how to adapt and utilize foundational models and techniques such as the genogram, in ways that are congruent with my commitment to cultural responsiveness and working with diverse clients. The crux of my chapter is on using the genogram and cultural genogram from a common factor lens/perspective in my systemic practice. When I was in my doctoral program, Dr. Douglas Sprenkle, one of my professors, would often exhort us students to "not throw the baby out with the bath water" when it came to sorting through all the theories and models, foundational and postmodern, that we were learning and practicing. While the metaphor certainly brought to mind all sorts of vivid imagery, it has remained in my consciousness as a reminder that there are ways in which we can more effectively use many of the models and systemic therapies in ways that are integrative and much more culturally responsive than what the originators of the models may have intended or even bothered with given their own historical and cultural contexts. I have found it helpful to use the common factor lens particularly when using foundational systemic therapies as it allows me to adapt and use these models flexibly as I navigate as a clinician in an increasingly diverse and complex clinical world. While it can be challenging to use a lens such as common factors because there is no step-by-step template for applying it, I believe using such postmodern lenses is critical to our ability as systemic therapists to respond in culturally responsive and responsible ways to our diverse clients. Our field's historical and foundational models have much to offer in our increasingly diverse world; but we also have to ensure that our use of these models that were not originally created with consideration to cultural and racial diversity does not contribute to the further marginalization and oppression of our most vulnerable clients.

## Cross-Cultural Responsiveness in Systemic Supervision and Training

Nicole and Raji's and Diane's chapters focus on cultural responsiveness of our systemic supervision and training models. Committed as we all are to our own culturally responsive, socially just, and ethical systemic practice, we are also aware of our roles and responsibilities as educators, as supervisors, and as "gatekeepers" in our profession. Nicole and Raji, in their chapter, highlight the importance of understanding the impact we have on our students and supervisees given who we are and our positions of power and privilege. They also remind us of the possibility that in our roles as educators and supervisors, there is the potential for oppression or subjugation which also affects how our students experience us in relation to their own lived experiences and their identities. Implications for training and supervision include overtly acknowledging the power differentials of the relationships between therapist and supervisor and therapist and client and initiating and facilitating dialogue on all our intersectionalities and identities within these relationships.

Diane's chapter reminds us of the critical role supervisors and educators have for providing students and trainees opportunities, guidance, and support in their growth and development toward cultural competence and cultural responsiveness. While supervisors and educators, often with their vast years and range of experience and expertise, bear the burden of providing appropriate opportunities to their supervisees, Diane also reminds us of the reciprocal nature of these relationships and that the responsibility to engage in their learning and growth also lies upon supervisees as well. This chapter is a useful reminder that as supervisors and supervisees, we have a shared belief and commitment that cultural competency and responsiveness are lifelong professional and personal processes that require a constant reflection of social identities, power dynamics, and internal and external contextual factors. Diane also shares in this chapter that her process as a supervisor and clinician is one of the constant reflections on what she knows and does not know; and she encourages us to engage in our own processes similarly in an effort to serve our supervisees, their clients, and our clients in culturally responsive ways. Confronting our biases, our assumptions, and our deficiencies in our knowledge and experience base is part of the "discomfort" in recognizing our limitations but also finding the courage to fully engage in our own and our supervisees' learning processes.

## Experiences, Challenges, and Implications: Systemic Training in International Contexts

The final two chapters of this volume focus on systemic therapy training in international contexts, specifically in India and in Turkey. Raji outlines in her chapter the need for globally and culturally responsive flow of knowledge and information across cultural and geographical borders in ways that have the potential to "increase personal freedom, promote cultural exchange, and revitalize both the native culture and the exporting culture." She introduces the concept of "glocalization," a framework for conceptualizing how global and local cultures interact reciprocally so that the experience is empowering for local cultures. Raji's research in India provides insight on effective and culturally responsive application and training of systemic theory and practice, with attention to the active engagement needed between existing knowledge coming from the outside and the knowledge relevant to and originating from local entities and sociocultural structures of the indigenous societies. Recommendations for future engagement globally in systemic training include meeting the need for more indigenous trainers who can be a bridge between the outside source of knowledge and the native context. Educational materials focusing on systemic therapies and models need to include cultural adaptations and culturally relevant case examples that honor the nuances and needs of globally and culturally diverse client and systemic trainees' contexts. Most importantly, the flow of knowledge should not be considered only unidirectionally; ideally, an exchange of students and scholars between family therapy/mental health programs globally would necessarily increase collaboration, understanding, and appreciation of different cultures and traditions and the mental health needs and practices in these different cultural contexts.

This volume ends with Nilufer and Yudum's chapter on the developments and their professional experiences in the MFT field in Turkey. Their experiences are reminiscent of the early days of systemic therapies in the USA and Europe, when regulations, rules, ethics, and structure for the field, and its application and training, were rare or nonexistent. These were exciting and innovative times for the field of couple and family and systemic therapies in the West. In reading Nilufer and Yudum's chapter, we are reminded of the promise and the potential our field brought to the mental health arena. We are also reminded that for the survival of our field, we must also look further and outside of our comfort zones, especially in the West where much of the field is regulated, structured, organized, and almost lost in the ever-increasing numbers of new treatment modalities popping up every day. Systemic therapies have a rare potential and gift to offer to the larger context of mental health services: the focus on context, ecology, environment, macrosystems, and culture. This lens is at the heart of systemic therapies, and we must have a continued commitment to promote the inherent cultural responsiveness systemic therapies have to offer. As with the experiences in Turkey, the field of course should continue to focus on critical core competencies; however, systemic therapies and those who utilize them, train and supervise in them, and promote them must do so with the guiding principles of cultural responsiveness and social justice. Just as systemic therapy trainers, clinicians, and educators in Turkey are at the forefront of ensuring the survival and future of MFT as a culturally responsive mental health practice, we in the USA must also commit to this in our own cultural context. Collaborations such as this volume, with the inclusion of multiple and diverse voices and insight, are just the beginning of an exciting and promising future for culturally responsive and socially just systemic therapies in the USA and globally.

# Index

**A**
Ackerman Institute, 137
American Association for Marriage and Family Therapy (AAMFT), 11, 79
American Counseling Association (ACA), 79, 82
American Psychology Association (APA), 41
Association of CFT, 137
Association of Family and Marriage Therapies, 137
Ayurveda system, 121

**B**
Blackness, 24
British educational system, 120

**C**
Case presentation outline, 95–97
Cartesian dualism, 7
ÇATED, 137, 138
Catholicism, 104
CATKOM, 137
CFT in Turkey
    certificate and master's level programs, 135
    COAMFTE, 147
    developments, 135, 146
    doctoral degrees, 135
    doctoral programs, 146
    history, 136–138
    licensing process, 147
    organizations, 136
    professional organizations, 135, 146
    regulations
        and emergence of family counseling, 143–146
    family counseling, 141
    lack of mental health laws, 142–143
    social policies ministry, 135
    trainers, 146
    training programs
        academic foundation, 141
        certification programs, 140
        clinical focus and climate, 139
        clinical issues, 139
        descriptive study, 138
        development, 140
        graduate degree, 138
        IACSTE, 141
        international CFT training and education endeavors, 141
        Istanbul Bilgi University's, 141
        master's program, 140, 141
        participants felt competent, 139
        private clinic, 139
        private family counseling centers, 140
        psychology and counseling programs, 140
        public family counseling centers, 140
        structured and standardized, 139
        and supervision, 139
        undergraduate education, 138
        uniting and standardized framework, 138
        university-based certificate programs, 141
Chronic stress, 2

Classism, 4
Client-centered advocacy
    clinical supervision, 89
    COAMFTE, 94
    definition, 79
    limitations, 94
    literature, 82, 92
    local community resources, 89
    MFT trainees, 80, 90
    positionality and modeling, 97–98
    power dynamics, 81
    qualitative research, 80
    social justice, 91, 92
    students and supervisees, 84–86
    teaching and supervision, 92–94
    therapy, 79
Clinical psychologist, 142
Clinical psychology, 136
Clinical supervision, 103, 107–109
Clinical training, 102
Cognitive interventions, 57
Collaborative approach, 64
Colonialism
    family therapy, 120–121
Commission on Accreditation for Marriage
        and Family Therapy Education
        (COAMFTE), 141
Counseling, 21–23, 27, 28
    and family therapy
        ACA and AAMFT ethics, 103
        cultural humility, 109
        cultural-competent and responsive
            supervision, 103
        emotional processing, 114
        feminist multicultural supervision,
            107, 111
        HMNID, 110
        MSJ competencies, 102
        multicultural group supervision, 112–113
        parallel process, 101
        potential social locations, 104
        reflective assessment, 106
        six domains, 105
        SMMS, 110
        sociopolitical identities, 102
        therapeutic process, 106
        United States population, 101
        Vegas family, 104
    programs, 136
    training institutions, 74
Couple and family therapy (CFT), 44–47
    APA guidelines, 43, 47
    cultural responsiveness, 48
    EBPs guidelines, 43
    efficacy research, 42
    intentional practice, 47
    practical application
        decision making, 46
        efficacy studies, 44
        empiricism, 45
        quality of service, 45
        RCT, 44, 47
        social justice, 45, 46
    program, 82
Critical race theory (CRT), 23, 30
Critical whiteness studies (CWS), 22, 23
Cross-cultural relevance, 119
    family therapy (see Family therapy)
Cross-cultural responsiveness, 59, 72
Cultural competence, 27, 33
Cultural humility, 108
Cultural responsiveness
    CFT, 48, 49
    EBPs, 49
    ethnic and sexual minority, 48
    mental health services, 48

**D**

Discovery-oriented qualitative study, 105
Disordered relationships, 144
Diversity, 5, 10, 11
Doctoral programs, 146

**E**

Earthquake, 137
Emotionalities of whiteness, 23, 24, 34, 35
Emotionally focused couple therapy (EFT), 152
    arranged marriage, 55
    clinical populations, 54
    culturally responsive training, 59
    effectiveness, 54
    emotions and attachment, 53
    ICEEFT, 58, 59, 66
    learning, 54
    literature, 54
    marital relationships in Turkey, 56
    Middle-Eastern couples, 55
    negative interactional cycle, 53
    Philadelphia Center, 57
    psychology programs, 59
    RISSC, 63, 65
    skills, 65
    socioeconomic class, 56
    structured approach, 53
    trainings, 60, 65
    treatment, 54
    Turkish terminology, 60
Emotions

whiteness, 26
Empathy, 35, 36
Empiricism, 45
Epistemological fallacies, 12
European Family Therapy Association (EFTA), 137
Evidence-based practices (EBPs), 41
  APA, 41
  benefits, 47
  CFT (see Couple and family therapy (CFT))
  cultural responsiveness, 48, 49
  funding agencies, 44
  treatment criteria, 42, 43
  utilizing and training, 151–152

**F**
Family counseling, 143–146
  CFT in Turkey
    certificate/master's degree, 143
    certificate programs, 145
    child development, 146
    clinical psychology, 143
    definition, 144, 145
    disordered relationships, 144
    government organizations, 143
    graduate programs, 145
    lack of attention, 143
    Ministry of Family and Social Policies, 143, 144
    practice and education, 143
    refraining, 144
    regulation, 144
    Social Services and Child Protection Institution, 143
    special techniques and strategies, 145
    supervision, 145
    training, 144, 145
Family counselor, 145
Family system, 145
Family therapy
  colonialism, 120–121
  colonization, 119
  education and medicine, 120–121
  in Euro-American cultural context, 119
  exclusion and marginalization, 119
  globalization (see Globalization)
  Indian case study (see Indian context)
  in non-Western cultures, 121–122
  to non-Western nations, 119
  practitioner and educator, 119
  propagation and export, 120
  social worker in India, 120
Family therapy praxis, 9
  classism, 4, 5
  cross-cultural responsiveness, 8, 9
  poor clients, 4
  social class, 3
  social justice paradigm (see Social justice)
  socioeconomic status, 3
Feminist multicultural supervision, 111
Fertility center in Tehran, 54

**G**
Gay, 33
Genogram, 72, 74
Genogram technique, 75
Genograms, 71, 72, 75
Globalization
  concept, 119
  definition, 119
  flow of knowledge and information, 131
  positive and negative connotations, 119
Glocalization, 131

**H**
Heterosexual marriage, 69
Heuristic Model of Nonoppressive Interpersonal Development (HMNID), 109
Hindu spirituality, 121

**I**
IFTA conference, 137
Immigrants, 2
Indian context, 125–131
  clinical observations, 122, 123
  cultural and therapeutic barriers
    age of therapist, 127
    concept of family therapy, 125
    inability to involve family members, 129
    individual therapy, 128
    language barrier, 126
    not enough training, 131
    presenting problem, 127
    subjective assessments, 130
    time frame, 129
  cultural barriers, 123
  families, 123
  Family Therapy: A Systemic Integration, 123
  focus group interviews, 124
  mental health professionals, 124
  models/approaches, 123
  systemic theories and techniques, 125
  systems theory, 123
  theoretical speculations, 122, 123

Individual therapy, 128
Individualized Educational Plan [IEP]
    meetings, 88
Integrative and common factors
    conceptualization, 72
    culturally responsive and respectful, 70
    education and training, 69
    expectation and hope, 76
    genogram, 71
    integrative and holistic approach, 71
    literature, 71
    physical and mental health, 73
    systemic models, 70, 71
    systemic training process, 73
    therapeutic relationship, 74
    therapy and counseling training
        institutions, 74
International Accreditation Commission for
    Systemic Therapy Education
    (IACSTE), 141
International Center for Excellence in
    Emotionally Focused Therapy
    (ICEEFT) guidelines, 58
International Family Therapy Association
    (IFTA), 137
Israeli family therapists, 137
Istanbul Bilgi University, 141

**K**
K-12 institution in India, 120

**L**
Language barrier, 126
Lesbian, gay, bisexual and transgender
    (LBGT), 2

**M**
Marriage and divorce, 55
Marriage and family therapy (MFT)
    contributions and organized, 150
    cross-cultural competence and
        sensitivity, 149
    cross-cultural responsiveness, 149
        EBPs, 151–152
        foundational systemic models, 152–153
        systemic supervision and training,
            153–154
        systemic training in international
            contexts, 154–155
    fields, 149
    microsystem, 149

    power, 150–151
    privilege, 150–151
    range of diversity, 150
    social justice, 149–151
    therapist identity, 150–151
Means of interpersonal functioning (MIF), 110
Mental health laws, 142–143
Mental Health Platform-Turkey (MHPT),
    142, 143
Mental health practitioners in non-Western
    cultures, 121
Mental Research Institute (MRI), 137
Meso level advocacy, 82
Ministry of Family and Social Policy, 55, 56,
    143, 144
Models and therapy techniques, 76
Multicultural and social justice (MSJ), 102
Multicultural clients, see Multiculturalism
Multicultural competency, 82
Multicultural counseling, 102
Multicultural group supervision, 112–113
Multiculturalism, 57, 80, 107
    Cartesian dualism, 7
    colonial gaze, 8
    minority clients, 7
    multicultural society, 5
    psychotherapy, 6, 7
    racism, 6
    trainings and workshops, 6
    white hegemony, 7

**N**
Native American population, 89
Nondirective/non-collaborative
    approach, 122
Nongovernmental organizations (NGOs), 137
Non-Western cultures
    cultural relevance of family therapy
        and addressed issues, 121
    applicability, 121
    ecological systems, 122
    ecosystemic view, 122
    mental health practitioner, 122
    nondirective/non-collaborative
        approach, 122
    and non-European cultures, 121
    practitioners, 121
    theoretical concepts, 122

**P**
People of Color (PoC), 23, 28
Personal therapy, 109

Personality development, 136
Practicum, 83, 84, 87, 91
Psychopathology, 136
Psychotherapy, 82, 136

**R**
Race
  blackness and whiteness, 24
  emotional abuse, 31
  gay, 33
  PoC, 24
  psychoanalysis, 22
  self-awareness, 22
  trust, 31
  whites, 24, 25
Randomized controlled trial (RCT), 44, 45, 47

**S**
Self-of-the-therapist, 12
Social justice, 86–87
  AAMFT, 11
  advocacy, 82
  CFT, 46
  chronic stress, 2
  de-ideologization, 9
  discrimination and racism, 2
  and diversity, 10
  family therapy, 10
  minority clients, 10
  oppressed groups, 9
  social disparities, 1
  social inequalities, 9
  sociopolitical factors, 2
Social oppression, 12–14
Social policies ministry, 135
Social Services and Child Protection Institution, 143
Social work program, 124
Socioeconomic status, 3, 4
Student/supervisee feedback, 85–86
Supervisory relationship, 102–104, 106–114
Synergistic Model of Multicultural Supervision (SMMS), 109

Systemic theory, 69, 136
Systemic thinking, 136

**T**
Tamil-speaking populations, 120
Theoretically sound and integrative approach, 70
Traditional gender roles, 112
Transportability research, 43
Traumatic event, 137
Traumatization, 29
Turkey, 135
  CFT (*see* Couple and family therapy (CFT) in Turkey)
  cultural context, 61
  population, 55
Turkish culture, 55, 59, 62

**U**
US-based CFT programs, 137
US-based EFT trainer, 60

**V**
Vegas family case, 108

**W**
Western-originated psychotherapy, 119
White privilege, 27
White supremacy, 24, 25, 28
Whiteness
  cultural competence, 37
  emotionalities, 30–32
  emotions, 26
  psychoanalytic analysis, 29
  racial traumas, 29
  and therapy
    cultural competence, 27
    emotionalities, 28
    multiculturalism, 27
    PoC, 27, 28
Whites, 25